KV-577-766

95p

DESIGN YOUR OWN
DRESS PATTERNS

Also by Adele P. Margolis

HOW TO DESIGN YOUR OWN DRESS PATTERNS

PATTERN WISE

THE COMPLETE BOOK OF TAILORING

THE DRESSMAKING BOOK

HOW TO MAKE CLOTHES THAT FIT AND FLATTER

DESIGN YOUR OWN
DRESS PATTERNS

A Primer in Pattern Making
for Women Who Like to Sew

Adele P. Margolis

Illustrated by Judy Skoogfors

Doubleday & Company, Inc.

Garden City, New York

Mills & Boon Limited, London

Library of Congress Catalog Card Number 78–139046
Copyright © 1971 by Adele P. Margolis
All Rights Reserved
Printed in the United States of America
Published in Great Britain, 1971
by Mills & Boon Limited, 17–19 Foley Street
London W1A 1 R
ISBN 0 .263 . 516.74.1

To my editor and very good friend
HAROLD KUEBLER
who has borne up nobly through a decade of darts

INTRODUCTION

The making of beautiful clothes is an art. Its joys are those of any other art—the soaring of the imagination, the excitement at the birth of a new idea, the sensual pleasure of handling the material, the satisfaction of watching a thing of beauty emerge.

Whether she regards herself so or not, every sewer is large-part artist. She may think of herself as a frugal soul but from the moment her selectivity begins (style, fabrics, buttons, trimmings) the home economist departs and the artist in her takes over. Of course sewers save money but anyone who has spent hours of just plain drudgery can tell you there are many easier ways to save than by sewing. It is the experience of creating that is the compensation for endless hours of work.

For most sewers, creativity is often blocked by dependence on ready-made patterns. The artist-sewer has visualized something which cannot be found for all the looking in pattern books. What she is really searching for is her own design, which, of course, is not there. Some sewers give up. Many begin apprehensively to take liberties with existing patterns. Timidly, they attempt to combine one pattern with another but are too fearful to make much progress. How they wish they knew more about patterns! How they wish they could make their own!

If you are one who has been scared to death to move a dart (you think it was put there by an act of Congress) or one who is awed by the seeming complexity of a pattern (the professionals in the field like to keep you that way), or one who doubts her ability to create ("I'm really not an artist")—relax! The basic principles of pattern construction are really neither too mysterious, too numerous, nor too difficult for the home sewer. Any woman who can work her way through the labyrinthian directions for sewing which accompany the commercial pattern can surely learn the comparatively simple and clear rules for pattern making. For the "I-can't-draw-a-straight-line-myself" crowd, there are plenty of helpful drafting tools.

Even for the home sewer who prefers the timesaving use of commercial patterns to developing her own, a knowledge of pattern making is essential. Without it, she is a slave to the pattern she has bought. With it, she is free to make such changes as she desires. Most important of all, understanding what she is working with will give her an independence in design, construction, and yes, even in fitting.

It is my hope that the simple non-technical instructions for pattern making contained in this book will open the door to a new world in which sewers may find creative excitement in executing their own dress designs.

Philadelphia, Pennsylvania   ADELE POLLOCK MARGOLIS

CONTENTS

Flat pattern and not-so-flat you – dart control, the key to shaping – dart control represents a relationship – dart control divided: front, back, and side – design by darts – tools you'll need for pattern making – slopers, the basis of new designs – standard slopers for standard patterns – personalized slopers for individual patterns – how to shift the sloper dart control to new positions: the French underarm dart, a neckline dart, a dart that originates at center front – a bulging block – swing-around-the-sloper – how to shift the skirt dart – how to shift a sleeve dart – simple curved darts – compound curved darts – asymmetric designs – how to make a pattern for an asymmetric design – structural design vs. added decoration – shaping should suit the fabric, too – "Look, Ma, no darts," – how to use the dart control as gathers or smocking at the waistline, at the neckline – how to shift the dart control for a gored skirt – how to convert the elbow dart to gathers – a dart-free sloper for youthful figures and décolleté designs – an "easy" way to eliminate a dart

From exercise to pattern – refining the pattern: how to correct a line distorted by pattern changes, designer's darts vs. dressmaker's darts, how to shorten a dart, how to lengthen a dart, how much to shorten a dart, a pair of shapely dart legs – signs and symbols – to be noted on the pattern: the name of the pattern piece – to fold or not to fold – the grain line (straight of goods), how to establish the lengthwise grain – how to establish the crosswise grain – how to establish the bias grain – stitching lines; seams, darts, decorative topstitching – seam allowance – the cutting line – notches – guidelines – shoulder and underarm markings – placement marks: for a zippered closing, for a buttoned closing, pockets and welts, applied decorative details – spot markings – fold lines – hems: straight skirt, blouse, dress or blouse sleeve, jacket hem, jacket-sleeve hem, coat hem, coat-sleeve hem – any markings that will help

One dart good, two darts better, more darts better yet – from the standpoint of fit, from the standpoint of fabric design, from the standpoint of grain – divide and conquer – Method I for divided control: waistline-underarm combination, waistline-shoulder combination – fitted or full – Method II for multiple darts or dart tucks: how to make multiple French darts, multiple skirt darts, multiple waistline darts, multiple sleeve darts – dart tucks (part of a dart) – how to make multiple dart tucks at the shoulder, at the neckline, at the shoulder and neck, at center front – suggestions for new pattern makers

A dart, an incomplete line to a designer – design by style lines – shaping by seams – how to make the pattern for a control seam: shoulder to waistline – a control seam for the back bodice: from the shoulder, from the armhole – the control seam moved off the dart point: toward the center front, toward the side seam – non-vertical control seams: a pattern for diagonal control seaming, a pattern with horizontal control seaming – fabric—a consideration – some suggestions for designing yokes – for design purposes only – gathers below a yoke – multiple darts below a yoke—when dart control is concealed in a yoke seam: the skirt yoke, a midriff yoke—call attention to a beautiful midriff—a yoke that doesn't quite make it—the contour belt, a yoke—the double-contour belt, two yokes—stitch and rejoin, design possibilities—repeat performance: similar seams—control seams in bodice back, skirt, sleeve—the bodice back yoke, control seam in a two-piece sleeve, the six-gored skirt, the eight-gored skirt —hip-length slopers—full-length slopers—new slopers, same principles of dart control—fashion-in-the-round: unlimited number of divisions of dart control—pattern-wise: you're on your own!

Chapter V   Slash, Spread, and Swirl   **124**

Flare or flounce: it's feminine!—two types of additional fullness: circular and balanced—slash and spread for circular fullness— slash and spread for balanced fullness—a curve that comes to you straight: slash and overlap—another way to get a curve: by darts—the way to add circular fullness at a bodice waistline and the waistline of a skirt—circular fullness at the hem of a skirt— how to make a dartless skirt sloper, the basis for flare—add fullness to the dartless sloper—an easy way to make a circular skirt—how to make the pattern for a semi-circle skirt, a circle skirt, a double-circle skirt, for a gathered circle or semi-circle skirt—piecing the fabric—skirt waistbands—corrected waistline measurement and waistband for circular skirt—non-vertical, non-axial fullness: horizontal, diagonal, asymmetrical—how to add circular fullness at a neckline, in a side-front skirt, at the cap of a sleeve, at a sleeve band, below a bodice yoke, below a hip yoke, above a midriff, to a dart that enters a dart—the way to add balanced fullness for a gathered or smocked bodice, for a gathered skirt, for a short puffed sleeve, for gathers below a bodice yoke, for gathers below a hip yoke, for a skirt flounce, for a draped bodice, for drapery at the center of a skirt, for diagonal drapery—stay the fullness—pleats for additional fullness—meet the pleat—things to consider about pleats—how deep a pleat?—how to make a knife-pleated or box-pleated skirt without a pattern – pleat meets – pretty pleats: how to make a pattern for a pleated bodice front, a pleated sleeve, a bodice with an inverted pleat below a shaped yoke, a knife-pleated skirt with a yoke panel, a skirt with an inverted pleat, a side-pleated dress – ways of eliminating bulk in a pleated garment – a kick pleat – a flared box-pleated skirt: with a single pleat, a double or triple pleat – a many-gored skirt – how to make a gored skirt of a circular one – add flare to a gore – fullness upon fullness: pleats or godets added to seam or slash – research and development department: an aid to your own artistry and skill

PART II   STYLING

Chapter VI   High—Low Neckline 181

The neckline, important part of the picture – scooped-out neck-lines – how to make the pattern for a dropped neckline – the V neckline, what to do about the back-shoulder dart, the square neckline, an oval neckline, variations of classic types, coming-and-going necklines, novelty necklines, dropped necklines with additional fullness – the asymmetric neckline – finish with a fac-ing – how to make a pattern for a facing and an interfacing – facing to the fore – first aid for gapping necklines: why the neck-line gaps – correction of sloper for a narrow chest – correction of sloper for narrow shoulders – correction of sloper for smaller-than-average bust – the bare-and-beautiful department – a basic halter design – one-shoulder designs – strapless dresses – the more the exposure, the greater the engineering required – from a low low to a high high: basic raised neckline, a raised neckline with style details – the bateau neckline, raised standing neckline – drapery softens the neckline: the cowl, a high cowl with a single drape, a cowl on a dropped neckline, a deep cowl neckline, a cowl yoke, for deeper, fuller folds – other cowls: the skirt with deep cowl drapes at the sides, the cowl on the sleeve

What, no exit?—decision, decision: the pattern depends on the kind of closing you choose—the zippered closing: invisible zipper, regulation closing, slot-seam closing—the buttoned closing: extensions, placement of buttons, button sizes, buttonhole markings—how to make the single-breasted closing—how to make the facing for the single-breasted closing: a separate facing, a facing all-in-one with the extension—buttoned on a band—how to make the double-breasted closing—the surplice closing—the asymmetric closing—asymmetric designs with deep laps—a right side that doesn't know what the left side is doing—the wrap-around skirt—the fly front—the two-piece fly front—the tailored neck-opening placket—without benefit of extension—right or left? —tabs are not trifles—buttons, bows, buckles, and bands—the pocket picture—for-real pockets—fake pockets—pattern procedure for pockets—a pocket applied to the right side of the garment: the patch pocket—the pocket set in a construction seam —a pocket set in a style line—the pocket in a slash: the bound pocket (classic variety), the bound pocket (contemporary variety)—the welt pocket: part applied, part set in a slash or seam —the flap pocket—fake flaps and fake welts

The collarless neckline for the young and beautiful—for the rest of us, a flattering collar—a word for it: terms used in collar construction—collars, curves, and stands—before you begin your collar designing—you can't beat a band collar—a bias fold becomes a collar—standing collars: the Chinese collar—the fichu —fan-shaped frame—flat collars: the plastron, temporary attachment—cape collars: a circular cape collar, a fitted cape collar— a cape foundation pattern—collars with a soft roll: the Peter Pan collar, the sailor collar—collars with a deeper roll: how to make a flat collar have a deeper all-around roll—collars with a very deep roll—collars with a deeper roll at back only: the roll-fitted

der styles – cuffs: a band for a separate turnback cuff, the turnback cuff all in one with the sleeve, a fitted cuff on a fitted sleeve, a flared turnback cuff, a flared turndown cuff, a fitted cuff with a closing extension, the French cuff – the sleeveless dress

The timeless appeal of the all-in-one sleeve – the kimono sleeve: problems of bulk and movement – a pattern for a fitted kimono sleeve and its gusset – the drama of deep kimono sleeves – new sloper placement results in new designs – the short, wide kimono sleeve – a flared kimono sleeve – a kimono sleeve that fits close to the body – the burnoose sleeve – the dropped-shoulder design – what to do with the lower sleeve of a dropped-shoulder design – juggle the pieces – the cap sleeve – a modified cap sleeve – a cap sleeve with a shaped style line – part of the bodice joined with the sleeve: the dolman sleeve, the strap-shoulder sleeve, the raglan sleeve – dart control variations in a raglan sleeve – raglan round-up – more of sleeve and yoke in one piece – sleeves in one with a yoke panel – the dropped or extended shoulder on a yoke – add a part

Sew it seems – patterns with a purpose: sloper staples, slopers for jackets and coats, sleeve slopers for jackets and coats – shoulder-pad allowance for tailored garments – tailored collars: the shawl collar, the notched collar, other tailored collars – pants pattern – making patterns for children's clothes, children's slopers – draping: what you'll need for draping, let the fabric tell you what it wants to do, have the courage to cut, learn to use your hands, half a design is often better than the whole design, suggested procedure for draping – grading: where pattern changes are made for size, how much change, how to make a pattern larger by a size—or smaller, the slash-and-spread method, the split-or-tuck method, the shifting method – let's make the pattern! – where do design ideas come from? – a working sketch – information, please – select the appropriate slopers – trial run: the muslin model – it's a pattern – jigsaw puzzle – possible pattern layouts – how much yardage – they've got to fit – changes if the pattern doesn't fit the material – "I made the pattern for this myself" – bargain patterns – freedom of choice – you'll never be the same!

DESIGN YOUR OWN
DRESS PATTERNS

PART I

PATTERN WHYS
Principles of Pattern Construction

Chapter I

THERE'S AN ART TO A DART

There is a folklore that tells of someone's mother or great aunt or clever little dressmaker who could cut out any garment without a pattern. Like many a myth there is an element of truth in the story. Anyone—amateur or professional—who sews a great deal can be so familiar with the shape of a sleeve or a collar or a neckline that she can cut from memory. Some day you, too, may be able to do this. In the meantime, there's safety in sticking with patterns.

PATTERN WHYS

A pattern is flat while you are not. And thereby hangs a tale.

The body has height, width, and depth. Within this roughly cylindrical framework there are a series of secondary curves and bulges. In a woman's body there are eight such bulges (each with its high point) which concern the pattern maker (Fig. 1).

(1) bust, (2) abdomen, (3) side hip, (4) buttocks, (5) upper shoulder blades, (6) lower shoulder blades, (7) elbow, (8) dowager's hump (back of neck).

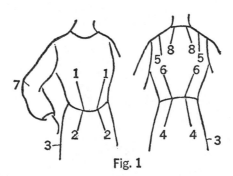

Fig. 1

No matter how much or how little you have of any of the above, the problem remains the same. The pattern must provide enough length and width of fabric to cover the high points (where the body is fullest, the measurement is largest, the fabric requirements are greatest) while at the same time providing some means of controlling the excess of material in a smaller adjoining area. *Dart control* is the means by which this is accomplished. It is the basis of all flat patterns.

It is not magic, nor wizardry, but dart control that converts a flat length of cloth into a three-dimensional form which fits the contours of the body. *Dart control always represents a relationship.* It is the difference between a larger measurement and a smaller one. For instance, if the bust measures 35 inches and the waistline 27 inches, the dart control necessary to shape the bodice is 8 inches. If the waist measures 27 inches and the hips 37 inches, the dart control necessary to shape the skirt is 10 inches. The greater the

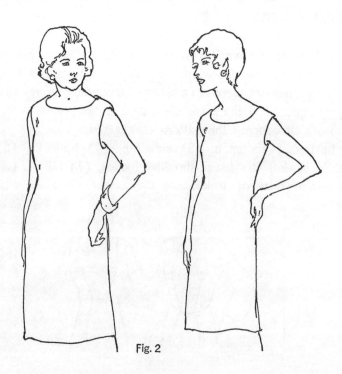

Fig. 2

difference, the larger the amount of control. The smaller the difference the smaller the amount of control.

It is not whether a figure is short or tall, heavy or slim, which determines the amount of shaping or dart control. It is always the *relationship between two adjoining measurements*. For example, a petite figure with a 22-inch waist and 27-inch hips needs 5 inches for the skirt dart control. So does a heavy figure with a 38-inch waist and 43-inch hips (Fig. 2).

There is this, too: the larger the amount of stitched dart control, the greater the resulting bulge. The smaller the amount of stitched dart control, the less the resulting bulge. This means that the shaping will be greater in those areas of the body that have the greatest need. Gentler shaping is reserved for those areas where the needs are less.

All of this vital information—the amount and the placement of the dart control—is contained in the five pieces of a sloper (basic pattern or foundation pattern) (Fig. 3).

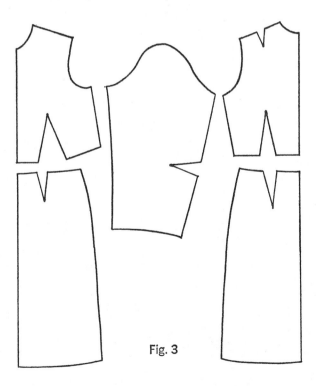

Fig. 3

Note that the total amount of dart control is divided three ways—front, back, and side. In the bodice, since the bust needs the most shaping, the largest amount of control is placed in front. In the skirt, since the buttocks require the most shaping, the largest amount of control is placed in back. If you place the front and back bodices and skirts side by side so that the center fronts and center backs are parallel to each other, you can readily see the dart control on the side seams (Fig. 4).

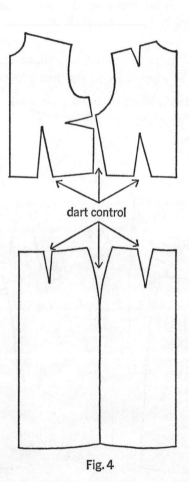

dart control

Fig. 4

DESIGN BY DARTS

The fascinating thing about dart control is that while the amount of it is constant (established by standard or personal measurements) it may appear in a variety of places. You've undoubtedly seen designs which utilize bodice and skirt dart control in any one of the positions indicated in Fig. 5.

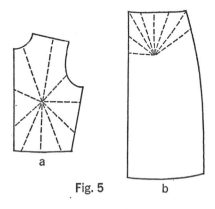

Fig. 5   a   b

Be it bodice, skirt, or sleeve, darts may radiate in any direction with the dart point as the pivot.

The shifting of the dart control to a new position in no way alters the amount of control. It does alter the shape of the pattern piece and, of course, the design of the garment. To have a dart in a new place makes a new design (Fig. 6).

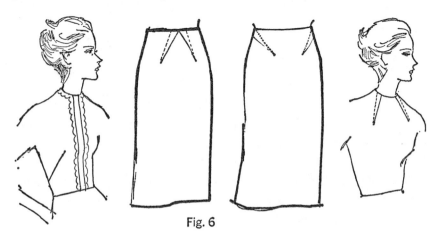

Fig. 6

The simplest and most usual form in which dart control appears is in darts. Material is stitched to take in an amount needed to fit the smaller dimension. As it tapers off the high point (the dart point), it releases enough material to fit the larger dimension (Fig. 7a).

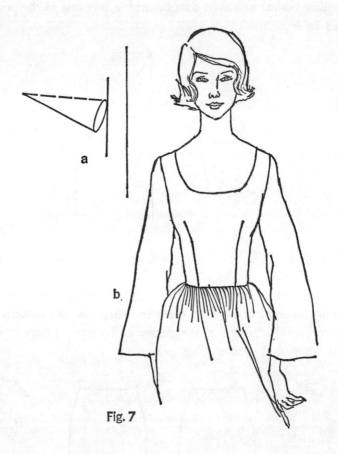

Fig. 7

In many designs (Fig. 7b), the simple waistline dart is used in the same position and in the same amount as in the sloper. It is elementary but effective shaping.

You may not get any superior shaping by shifting the dart to another position but you will get some welcome variety. Wouldn't it be dreary to have the same old waistline dart in all one's dresses?

Shifting the dart control to a new position is the first and easiest way to design by darts.

HERE'S WHAT YOU'LL NEED TO GET STARTED

Some of these tools are already in your sewing equipment. A few special ones can be purchased at an art store, a dressmaker's supply store, or even a well-equipped notions counter of a general store. These are by no means all the tools which a pattern drafter uses but will be quite sufficient for those who don't make their living at it (Fig. 8).

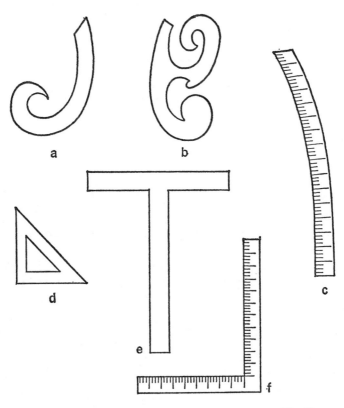

Fig. 8

For doing the exercises in this book with quarter scale models	*For developing full-scale patterns*
Colored construction paper for the patterns and a notebook of white, unlined paper for the record.	Blank paper tough enough for the construction and final patterns; shelf paper (join pieces for width) or wrapping paper are both good and easily obtainable; tissue paper is less bulky for a final pattern but more of a problem in pattern construction.
Soft paper napkins for testing fullness or drapery	Unbleached muslin or cotton for testing the pattern; use the same degree of firmness as intended for the design; test fullness and drapery in voile or other soft fabric.

Scissors—sharp and reserved exclusively for cutting paper.

Scotch tape

Several pencils of medium-soft lead sharpened to fine points, a colored pencil.

An eraser (it is possible to make mistakes).

A gauge for determining seam allowances, facings, and other small measurements.

A small ruler	a 12-inch ruler, a yardstick, an L-square (Fig. 8f), or a T-square (Fig. 8e)

In U K, 8a and b are known as French Curves. 8c may be unavailable but is less important.
Dietzgen curves (Fig. 8b) ℀16 and ℀17 (armscye) (Fig. 8a), the hip curve (curved stick) (Fig. 8c).

45-degree triangle for determining the grain of the fabric (Fig. 8d).

Tracing wheel with sharp prongs for use on paper (as opposed to the blunt-pronged tracing wheel used for marking fabric with dressmaker's carbon paper).

Scale models (Fig. 9)	Full-scale sloper (basic pattern)

SLOPERS FOR STARTING

The sloper (often called a block or foundation pattern) is a basic pattern cut to standard size from a table of standard body measurements. It contains all the necessary information about the shaping, contour seams, and ease that will make the sloper fit a particular size. It has no fullness, design details, or seam allowances. It is used as the basis for creating new designs.

In the clothing industry, the sloper is drafted in accord with a set of body measurements developed by manufacturers, distributors, and users in cooperation with the Office of Commodity Standards of the National Bureau of Standards and issued by the Department of Commerce.* While this does establish a uniform criteria, the use of the standard is voluntary.

Many manufacturers gain their reputations on particular cut and fit for what they consider a standard size. They may arrive at this judgment via personnel, experience, or sales. Americans are great name-brand buyers. If the cut and fit of So-and-So's size 10 are great for you, that's the brand you'll buy whether the sizing conforms to the standard or not.

BASIC PATTERNS ARE AVAILABLE FOR HOME SEWERS

All of the major pattern companies make basic patterns. You may find them listed in the pattern catalogues by various names— foundation pattern, master pattern, try-on pattern, shell pattern, basic-fitting pattern, etc. This pattern was drafted to a set of body measurements approved by the Measurement Standard Committee of the Pattern Industry (see page 432). The Spadea Pattern Company has its own set of measurements (see page 436).

While all pattern companies have accepted these body measurements as a base, they vary in the amounts of ease added. This makes for slight differences in basic patterns of the same size.

---

* Body Measurements for the Sizing of Women's Patterns and Apparel distributed by the Clearing House for Federal, Scientific and Technical Information, 5285 Braddock Road, Springfield, Virginia 22151.

Basic patterns as such are not available in U K. The solution for the U K reader is to buy from her favorite pattern company a simple fitted pattern with plain round neck, straight skirt and long, straight, set-in sleeves. This will serve the same purpose.

STANDARD SLOPER FOR STANDARD SIZE PATTERN

Use the commercial basic pattern for the creation of new designs in standard sizes. Any alterations to make the pattern fit an individual figure can be made after the new design has been developed. (This is the same procedure as if you had bought the pattern instead of creating it.)

PERSONALIZED SLOPER FOR INDIVIDUAL PATTERN

Many home sewers prefer to create their designs from an individual basic pattern made to their measurements and fitted to their figures. This type of basic pattern has built into it all the many little departures from the standard that say, "You."* Designs developed from a personalized basic pattern need no further alterations.

SCALE MODELS FOR THE EXERCISES IN THIS BOOK

Simply because it is a more practical way to do the exercises in this book we will use the quarter-scale models in Fig. 9. Trace and cut out the necessary five pieces: bodice front, bodice back, skirt front, skirt back, and sleeve. Use heavy paper, Manila tag, or lightweight cardboard. These slopers are going to get a lot of use; they are the basis of all new designs.

* Complete directions for making an individual basic pattern will be found in *How To Make Clothes That Fit and Flatter,* by this author, published by Doubleday & Company, Inc.

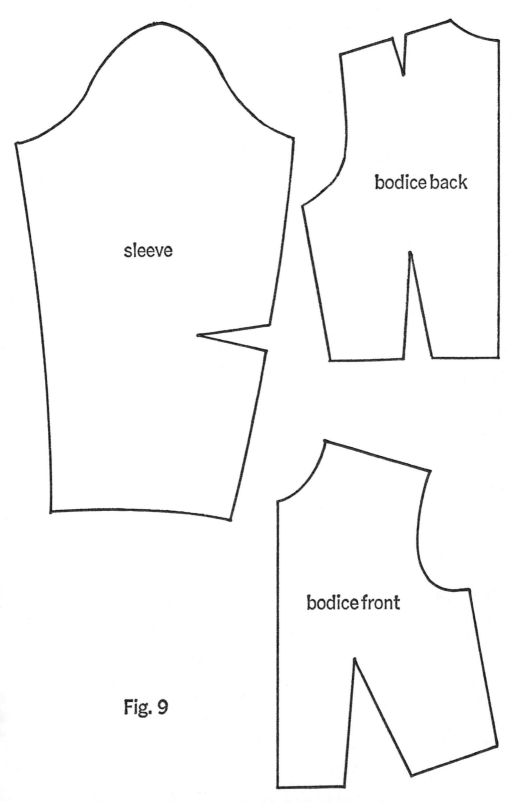

sleeve

bodice back

bodice front

Fig. 9

Quarter-scale slopers for your convenience

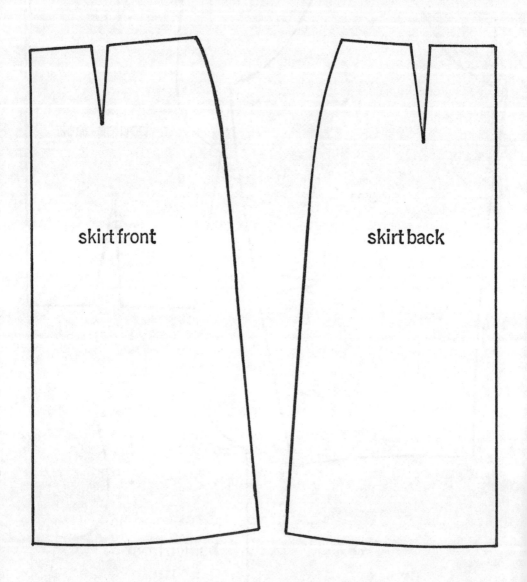

skirt front

skirt back

Quarter-scale slopers for your convenience

Fig. 9

Even when you feel confident enough to produce full-scale patterns, you will find it convenient to develop the new patterns to scale. After all the problems have been solved in miniature, it is easy enough to transfer the information to life size.

HOW TO SHIFT THE SLOPER DART CONTROL TO NEW POSITIONS

The French underarm dart is a favorite for understandable reasons. The direction of the dart line suggests the lift one associates with a high youthful figure (Fig. 10).

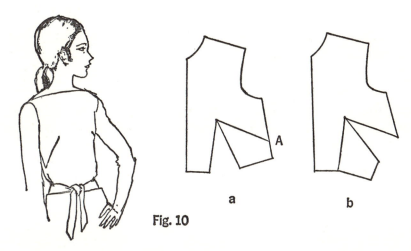

a   b

Fig. 10

1. Trace the bodice-front sloper.

2. Cut out the tracing and the dart. (You may want to make a batch of these cut-out bodices to keep handy for the following exercises.)

3. Locate the position of the new dart on the side seam. This may be a point anywhere up from the waistline 2 inches to 2½ inches. Any dart above this becomes an underarm dart. Mark the point A.

4. Using a ruler, draw a line from point A to the dart point (Fig. 10a). This is the new dart line.

5. Slash the dart line to the dart point. Start the slashing at the side seam.

6. Close the original dart and fasten it with Scotch tape. Notice that the waistline dart control is shifted to the new position (Fig. 10b). It automatically contains the right amount of dart control.

THE BULGING BLOCK

Are you surprised at the magic? Does this new dart that looks so different actually create the same shaping? For an answer try this little experiment with a bulging block.

1. Using one of your bodice-front slopers, close the waistline dart and fasten it with Scotch tape. This produces half a bodice front shaped to fit a quarter-scale figure. Instead of a flat block pattern, it is now a bulging block.

2. Take your newly created French underarm dart pattern. Close the dart and fasten it with Scotch tape. Now you have another bulging block.

3. Superimpose one block over the other. Though the position of the darts is different, the shaping (bulge) has changed not at all. *Shifting the dart control in no way changes the size, fit, or bulge of the pattern.*

The dart that emerges from the armhole is an interesting one (Fig. 11).

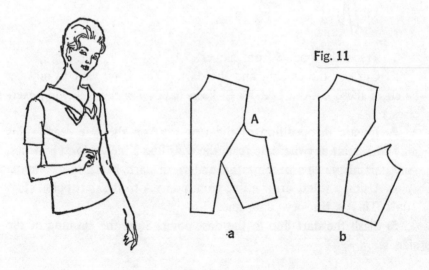

Fig. 11

A

·a   b

1. Trace the bodice-front sloper.

2. Cut out the tracing and the dart.

3. Locate the position of the new dart on the armhole anywhere that appeals to your eye. Just remember that a longer line at an angle is more graceful than a squat, horizontal line. Mark the new point A.

4. From A draw a line to the dart point (Fig. 11a).

5. Slash the dart line to the dart point. Start the slashing at the armhole.

6. Close the original dart. Fasten it with Scotch tape. The correct dart control is automatically shifted to the new position (Fig. 11b).

If you need further convincing, convert this flat pattern to a bulging block and test it over your previous blocks. Once again, nothing has changed except the position of the dart.

A neckline dart is produced by the same procedure (Fig. 12)

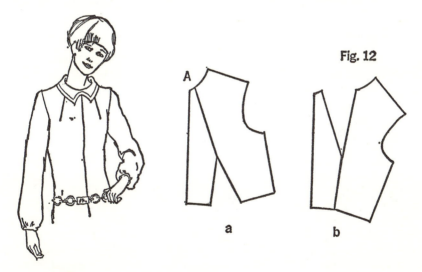

Fig. 12

1. Trace the bodice-front sloper.

2. Cut out the tracing and the dart.

3. Locate the position of the new dart at the neckline. Mark the point A.

4. Draw a line from A to the dart point (Fig. 12a).

5. Slash the dart line to the dart point. Start the slashing at the neckline.

6. Close the original dart, shifting the control to the new position (Fig. 12b). Fasten with Scotch tape.

A dart may originate *at center front* (Fig. 13)

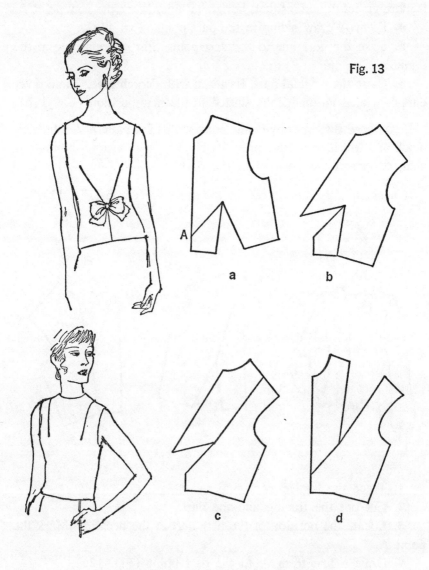

Fig. 13

A

a   b

c   d

1. Trace the bodice-front sloper. Cut out the tracing and the dart.

2. Locate the position of the new dart at center front. Mark the point A.

3. Draw a slash line from A to the dart point (Fig. 13a).

4. Slash the dart line to the dart point. Start the slashing at the center front.

5. Close the original dart, shifting the control to the new position (Fig. 13b). Fasten with Scotch tape.

SWING-AROUND-THE-SLOPER

Using this technique, you can make patterns with darts emerging from any point on the circumference of the sloper. There are only two rules which must be followed:

1. You must use the dart point as a pivot for swinging the control into its new position.

2. The new dart must start at some seam line and extend to the dart point.

One does not always have to start the shifting from the sloper waistline dart. It is possible to start with the dart in any position and shift to another. This would be true if you wished to use a pattern other than your sloper as a basis for the new design or if you changed your mind about the position of the dart in a design. For instance, to shift the center-front dart of the pattern in Fig. 13 to a shoulder dart:

1. Draw the new dart line from the shoulder to the dart point (Fig. 13c).

2. Slash the dart line to the point. Start the slashing at the shoulder.

3. Close the center-front dart, thereby shifting the control to the shoulder (Fig. 13d). The amount of dart control is in no way affected by this type of change.

As in any art, when you have mastered all the rules you may take some liberties with them. This will be discussed in later chapters.

The shifting of dart control works the same way on all the basic pattern pieces—bodice front and back, skirt front and back, and the sleeve.

HOW TO SHIFT THE SKIRT DART

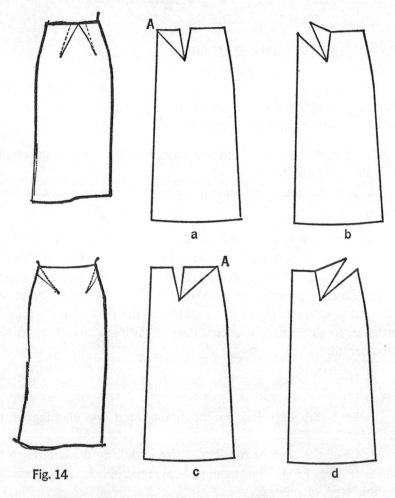

Fig. 14

1. Trace the skirt-front sloper.
2. Cut out the tracing and the dart. (Cut a batch of these slopers for future exercises so you won't have to stop each time.)

3. Locate the position of the new dart at the waistline either at center front (Fig. 14a) or at the side (Fig. 14c). Mark the point A.

4. Draw a slash line from A to the dart point.

5. Slash the dart line to the dart point. Start the slashing at the waistline.

6. Close the original waistline dart, shifting the control to the new position (Figs. 14b and 14d). Fasten with Scotch tape.

HOW TO SHIFT THE SLEEVE DART

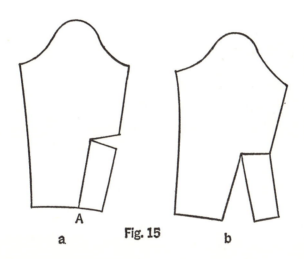

A

a   Fig. 15   b

1. Trace the sleeve sloper.

2. Cut out the tracing and the dart. (Cut a batch of these slopers for future exercises.)

3. Locate the position of the new dart at the wrist (either one-third or one-fourth of the way up from the back underarm seam). Mark the point A.

4. Draw a slash line from A to the dart point (Fig. 15a).

5. Slash the dart line to the dart point. Start the slashing from the wrist.

6. Close the elbow dart, shifting the control to the new position (Fig. 15b). Fasten with Scotch tape.

CURVED DARTS

Darts need not always be straight lines. They may be curved for interest. For instance, a French underarm dart looks quite pretty when it is a curved rather than a straight line (Fig. 16).

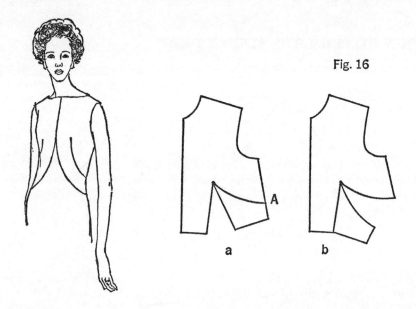

Fig. 16

a   b

1. On the cut-out sloper with the cut-out dart, locate the position of the new dart. Mark the point A.

2. Draw a curved line from A to the dart point. You may draw the line freehand for eye appeal, then true the line with an appropriate curved instrument or you may draw directly with any of the instruments that may have a curve that appeals to you (Fig. 16a).

3. Slash the curved dart line.

4. Close the original dart, shifting the control to the new curved dart (Fig. 16b). Fasten with Scotch tape.

Convert this pattern into a bulging block. Compare it with your original waistline-dart block. Does the curve make any difference in the amount of control? None, whatever. You merely have a new design that utilizes the original control.

Just for fun, go back and try all the darts you've done with curved instead of straight lines.

The curves may even be compound rather than simple (Fig. 17).

Fig. 17

ASYMMETRIC DESIGNS

All of the foregoing patterns were designed for a balanced effect, that is, half a pattern to be cut on a fold of fabric. When opened out, the darts will be exactly the same on either side of the center front or back. This is a formal or symmetrical balance (Fig. 18a). It is the one most generally used in clothing design.

Balance can be achieved in another way. The right and left sides may be different though equal. This is a balance of uneven parts, a "felt" balance, the type most seen in nature. It is called an informal or asymmetrical balance (Fig. 18b). In clothing design, this is a more sophisticated type of balance and requires great skill in handling. It is so easy to push it to a point of imbalance.

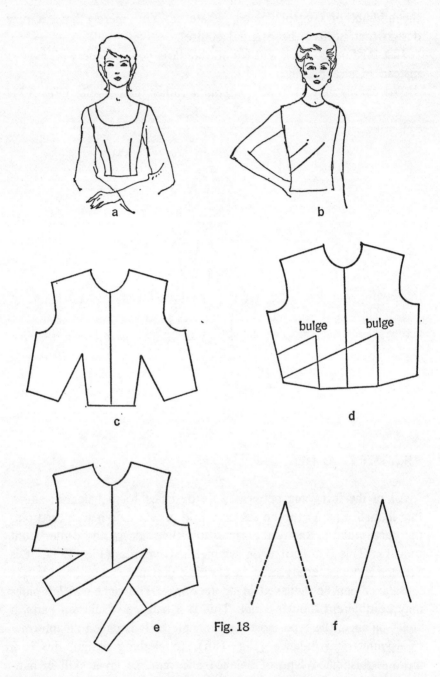

a

b

bulge bulge

c

d

e

Fig. 18

f

TO MAKE THE PATTERN FOR FIGURE 18b

1. Use two bodice-front slopers fastened at center front with Scotch tape (Fig. 18c). Asymmetric patterns must be developed from a complete sloper.

2. Close both waistline darts and fasten them with Scotch tape creating a complete bulging block.

3. Rest the bulging block on the table and draw the position of the darts on the inside of the pattern. It is easier to work on the inside of the bulge. The right dart starts at the right side seam and goes to the right dart point. The left dart starts at the right side seam and goes to the left dart point. Make the two dart lines parallel to each other; they'll look prettier that way (Fig. 18d).

4. Slash the new dart lines so the pattern opens out flat (Fig. 18e). Note that the left dart appears larger. This is only because it is longer. In reality, *the amount of dart control is equal in both darts.* Were the right dart extended to the same length as the left dart it would appear the same size (Fig. 18f).

BULGING BLOCK TO THE RESCUE

If ever you are puzzled about what to do with a dart while you are developing a new design use the bulging block method. It is an easy way to eliminate any darts that get in the way of the new style lines. There is another method for freeing the area of darts in a flat pattern while designing. Shift them temporarily to an out-of-the-way position. (See page 74.)

STRUCTURAL DESIGN VS. ADDED DECORATION

When it comes to designing (any form of designing) there are two current schools of thought. One believes in the beauty of undisguised structure, purity of line, handsome materials. The other doesn't go along with this austerity. It prefers the enrichment of additional ornamentation.

Fig. 19

Both are acceptable in clothing design. There are outstanding designers in each category. If you are a purist, then continue to be; you are in good company. Should you prefer to gild the lily—a little or a lot—you'll be right in the swing of present fashion. Often some discreet detail consistent with the structural line can provide added interest.

In Fig. 19a, the neck dart is emphasized with topstitching.

In Fig. 19b, ribbon ending in a tiny, flat bow has been superimposed on the dart concealing the structure.

In Fig. 19c, a curved welt has been inserted into the curved dart.

In Fig. 19d, both bodice and skirt close on the darts.

SHAPING SHOULD SUIT THE FABRIC, TOO

When you are using a solid-color fabric, the position of the dart control is no problem. Your chief concern in deciding dart placement is which best carries out your design idea. When you are using a figured material—a spaced print of either large or small units—a stripe, a check, a plaid; a visible vertical or horizontal weave; a diagonal weave or print—then the choice of dart position becomes more complex.

Any dart when stitched into the garment will interrupt the continuity of the fabric design. Therefore, you must choose darts which will do so with the least disturbing effect.

Consider *the simple vertical waistline dart.*

In a solid-color fabric, the dart shows clearly and effectively and can even be a part of the design (Fig. 20a).

The waistline dart in Fig. 20b cuts right into the floral motif of the fabric. How silly when this is the chief beauty of the dress. A better solution would be to shift the darts to an area that contains no design unit.

In a horizontally striped fabric, the horizontal stripes, easily matched, are little affected by the vertical waistline dart (Fig. 20c).

A chevron design results when vertically striped material is stitched in a vertical dart (Fig. 20d). Whether this is objectionable or not depends on the nature of the stripes.

Fig. 20

Fabrics with diagonal stripes are just plain difficult. When a vertical dart is stitched into the diagonal print or weave the resulting distortion is vivid (Fig. 20e). No darts or darts that follow the diagonal line of the fabric are possible solutions.

The French underarm dart with its long diagonal line is a problem in some fabrics.

In a solid color, the line is striking (Fig. 21a).

The diagonal stripe of the bias bodice of Fig. 21b can be worked into a pleasing little design.

Fig. 21

The diagonal line of the French underarm dart in a horizontal or vertical stripe, a check or plaid, results in a complete mismatching of the fabric design (Fig. 21c).

If you are planning to use a diagonal fabric, make the stripes an integral part of the design (Fig. 22).

When a commercial pattern says, "Striped, plaid, or obvious diagonal fabrics are not suitable," better heed the admonition. The professional pattern makers know whereof they speak. The pattern has been carefully tested for the effect of the darts on the fabric.

Fig. 22

THE MORAL IS CLEAR

If fabric is the inspiration for your design, use darts that will be consistent with the surface design of the material. If you start with your pattern design, choose fabric that will best conform to the position of the darts.

LOOK, MA, NO DARTS

Dart control need not be a dart! Any device will do as long as it "takes in" the amount needed to make the garment fit the smaller measurement and "lets it out" at the right place to fit the larger measurement. A pleat (Fig. 23a), gathering (Fig. 23b), smocking (Fig. 23c) will work just as well as darts and often with more interest.

a

b

c

Fig. 23

When you plan to use the dart control for gathers (or shirring or smocking) the amount of the control must be spread over a wider area. Were you to limit your gathering to the space allotted to the dart, you would have to draw up the entire amount so as not to alter the length of the original seam line. Can you imagine the impossible bunching that would result? Here is how to remedy the situation.

HOW TO SHIFT THE DART CONTROL FOR GATHERS, SHIRRING, OR SMOCKING

Waistline Fullness (Fig. 24)

1. On the cut-out bodice-front sloper with the cut-out dart, locate the outside limits of the waistline fullness. Mark the points A and B (Fig. 24a).

2. Draw slash lines from A and B to the dart point. Draw several additional slash lines on either side of the waistline dart starting at the waistline and ending at the dart point (Fig. 24a).

3. Slash all slash lines.

4. Spread all sections so the spaces between are equal (Fig. 24b).

5. Trace the new pattern. Draw the new waistline with a smooth, curved freehand line, correcting any irregularities (Fig. 24c).

6. On the new pattern make a notation that the area from A to B (indicated by the symbols o o) is to be gathered to fit the waistline measurement (Fig. 24c).

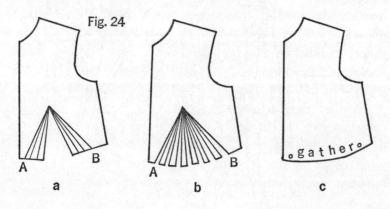

Fig. 24

a   b   c

Neckline Fullness (Fig. 25)

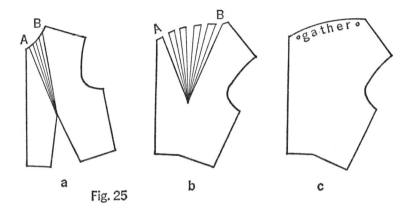

Fig. 25

1. On the cut-out bodice-front sloper with the cut-out dart, locate the outside limits of the neckline fullness. Mark points A and B on the neckline (Fig. 25a).

2. Draw slash lines from A and B to the dart point. Draw several additional slash lines between A and B (Fig. 25a).

3. Slash all slash lines.

4. Shift all or part of the waistline control to the neckline. Spread the sections so the spaces between are equal (Fig. 25b).

5. Trace the new pattern. Draw the new neckline with a smooth, curved freehand line, correcting any irregularities. Indicate the area to be gathered (Fig. 25c).

This multiple-slash line method not only produces the spread necessary for the gathers, it also provides a guide for the new seam line (the waistline in Fig. 24, the neckline in Fig. 25). Were you simply to shift the dart control to the new position by a single slash line as in the first of our exercises, you would have an opening for a dart but no way of knowing where the new seam line should be. A freehand curved line would only be guessing.

Actually the more lines slashed and the more sections spread, the more accurate the guideline. Since we are working with such a small sloper the few slash lines we have used will do. However, on a full-scale sloper, one would have to use many more.

NOTE: The only fullness in these designs is that of the dart control. There is no additional fullness. Directions for adding fullness are given in Chapter V.

Needless to say, the same rules apply to fullness in a skirt (Fig. 26) and in a sleeve (Fig. 27).

HOW TO MAKE ONE GORE OF A FOUR-GORE SKIRT By Shifting the Waistline Control to the Hem of a Skirt

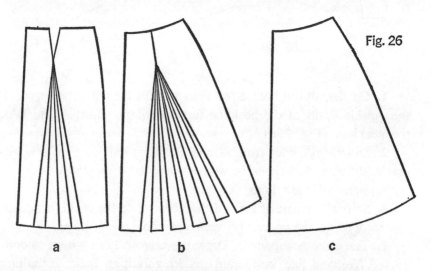

Fig. 26

a   b   c

1. On the cut-out skirt-front sloper with the cut-out dart, draw a slash line from the dart point to the hemline parallel to the center front.

2. Draw several additional lines on either side of the first slash line (Fig. 26a). (There will be room for more of them toward the side seam.)

3. Slash all slash lines.

4. Close the waistline dart, shifting the control to the hemline.

5. Spread all sections so the spaces between are equal (Fig. 26b).

6. Trace the new pattern, correcting the hemline with a smooth curve (Fig. 26c).

HOW TO CONVERT THE ELBOW DART TO GATHERS

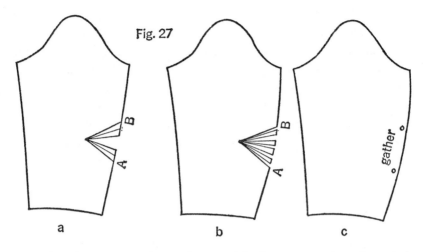

Fig. 27

a   b   c

1. On the cut-out sleeve sloper with the cut-out dart, locate the outside limits of the fullness (a total area of 2½ to 3 inches should suffice). Mark points A and B (Fig. 27a). Draw slash lines from A and B to the dart point.

2. Draw several slash lines on either side of the dart (Fig. 27a).

3. Slash and spread so spaces between sections are equal (Fig. 27b).

4. Trace the new pattern correcting any irregularities on the seam line. Note area to be gathered (Fig. 27c).

NO-DART, NO-BULGE, NO-SHAPE

A flat figure requires little dart control for shaping. What control there is can be shifted to the side seam leaving a dart-free sloper. Such a sloper gives a designer unlimited possibilities for intricate or dramatic style lines. A no-shape pattern is a marvelous way to keep an elaborate or fascinating fabric design intact (Fig. 28a).

The fashions of the past decade—designed as they were (and are) for young, undeveloped figures—have utilized this type of control extensively (Fig. 28b) (alas for the rest of us!). A no-dart pattern cut on the bias and blocked to shape over a tailor's cushion will provide just enough swell for a no-bulge figure.

This is the sloper one would use for décolleté or low-backed dresses (Fig. 28c).

a

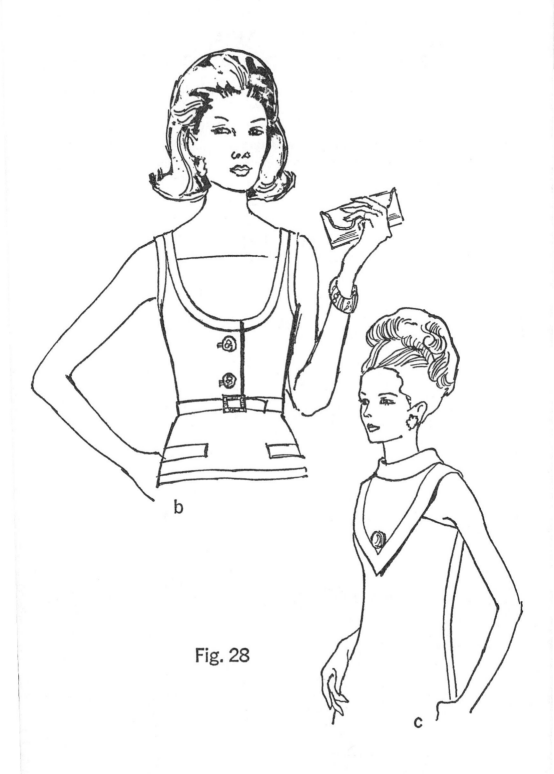

b

Fig. 28

c

HOW TO MAKE THE DART-FREE SLOPER

1. Trace the bodice-front and bodice-back slopers. Cut out the tracings *but do not cut out the darts.*

2. Starting at the ends of the dart legs, draw new darts (front and back) whose points are on the underarm curve of the armhole about 1 inch to 2 inches in from the side seams (Fig. 29a).

3. Fold in all but ¼ inch of the new dart and fasten with Scotch tape (Fig. 29b). The ¼ inch remains as a little ease.

4. Take off just enough length at center front and center back to give a pleasing slightly curved waistline.* In doing so you will be correcting the jog that results from the folding of the dart (Fig. 29b).

5. Trace the new dartless sloper (Fig. 29c).

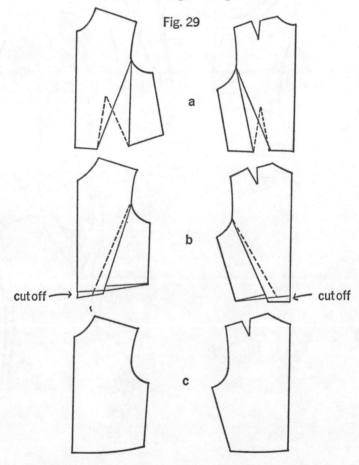

Fig. 29

a

b

cutoff →   ← cutoff

c

AN "EASY" WAY TO ELIMINATE A DART

Too many dart lines in any one area can be confusing and aes-thetically jarring. Or, perhaps a "no-dart" look is desired even though some shaping is required. If the amount of dart control is relatively small and the fabric cooperative (that is, it "eases" readily) the control may be eased into a joining seam rather than stitched as a dart. There are a number of places in a garment where this is frequently done.

The back shoulder dart can be eased into the front shoulder seam by gathering, ease stitching, or steam pressing (Fig. 30a).

The side-front bodice dart can be eased into a shaping seam at the bust by the same methods (Fig. 30b).

As can what's left of the elbow dart in a two-piece sleeve (Fig. 30c).

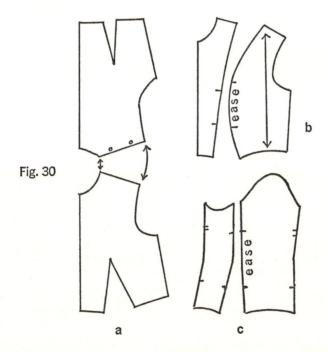

Fig. 30

a   c

---

* A bulge requires length to go over it as well as width to go around it. In re-moving the dart in this pattern, we have eliminated the bulge and reduced the width. It follows that we do not need all the length, either.

THERE'S AN ART TO A DART

Even in these first, elementary exercises you can begin to see the design possibilities of simply shifting a dart. You must admit there's an art to that dart you've been taking for granted.

Chapter II

IT'S A PATTERN!

If you run true to form, you are (after just one chapter in pattern design) overwhelmed with your prowess as a pattern maker. You can hardly restrain yourself from fishing out those patterns you've been stashing away for years and shifting all their darts. What's more, you feel certain you know how to get the dart you observed on that dress you saw in the window, or in a fashion magazine, or on that attractively dressed woman who sat beside you on the bus.

This is all very fine—but hold on! We haven't made a *real* pattern yet. What we have done needs a little work on it before it can earn that name.

FROM EXERCISE TO PATTERN

Patterns go through a step-by-step progression. All patterns start with a *sloper. The construction pattern* (the working pattern) may go through many changes before it becomes the desired design. The *final pattern* (the one we really mean when we say, "pattern") must include all the information needed for cutting and assembling the garment.

Thus far, we have worked with the first two types of patterns. We can take all of the exercises in Chapter I and convert them into final patterns by giving them the treatment described in this chapter.

REFINING THE PATTERN

How to Correct a Line Distorted by Pattern Changes

As you have discovered by now, there are many times in pattern making when the process of shifting or dividing the dart control will produce angularity (Fig. 31a), distortion (Fig. 31b), no line at all (Fig. 31c), a jog (Fig. 31d). There will be others that you will come across as your pattern making becomes more complex.

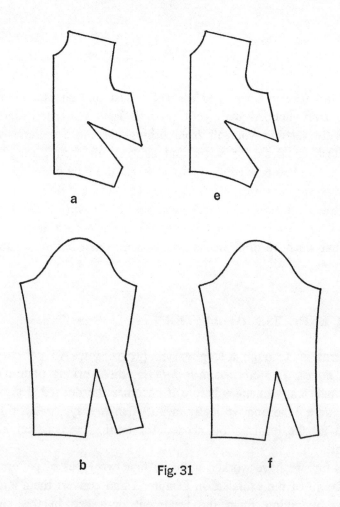

a   e

b   Fig. 31   f

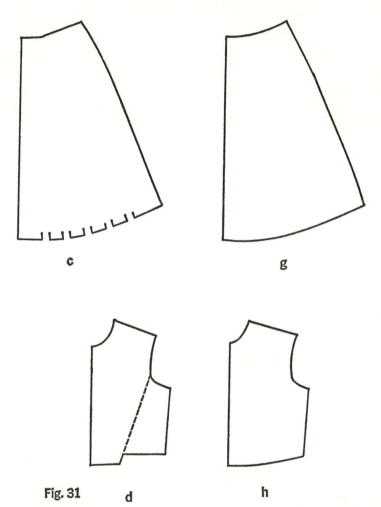

Fig. 31   c   g   d   h

Patterns are never allowed to remain this way. The angularity of the waistline seam in Fig. 31a would not fit the curve of the body. The distortion of the sleeve seam of Fig. 31b could not accurately be matched and stitched to the other sleeve seam. There is no hemline in Fig. 31c—only vague open spaces and intermittent lines of skirt. How would you know where to cut the pattern? If you left the jog in Fig. 31d, a section of your side bodice would be missing. All of these need correction.

To correct Fig. 31a (angularity) draw a curved line either free-hand or with any of the curved instruments. You need not use the entire curve of the instrument. Slide it along until you find that part of it that comes closest to the construction pattern. Use as much of the curve as you need to complete or correct a line (Fig. 31e).

To correct Fig. 31b (distortion) fold the sleeve pattern in half, matching the underarm seam at the armscye and the wrist. Correct the distorted seam by making it match the other. Either trace or cut to shape (Fig. 31f).

To correct Fig. 31c (no line) draw a curved line starting at the beginning of the original line and ending at the end of the original line. Use what lines you do have as a guide and keep the new line close to them (Fig. 31g).

To correct Fig. 31d draw a new line which fills in the missing section. Start at the beginning of the original line and stop at the end of it (Fig. 31h).

USE YOUR JUDGMENT IN CORRECTING A PATTERN

Remember that while a pattern may be designed to by-pass the body for style, it must at the same time conform to body contours in some places in order for it to fit. Style lines may be angular but circumference lines (those that go around the body) are curved, however slightly.

Make certain that joining seams match so they really can be joined.

DESIGNER'S DARTS VS. DRESSMAKER'S DARTS

The darts in your basic pattern (sloper) which extend to the high points of the curve under consideration are called *designer's darts*. As you have learned all changes in dart control are made from these darts.

Only in very small or youthful figures and only in very form-revealing garments are darts stitched to the dart point. That would be asking too much of most figures.

Generally, in dressmaking and tailoring, the darts are shortened somewhat to give a sculptured, soft effect and a little more ease. These shortened darts are called *dressmaker's darts*.

Designer's darts are used in *making a pattern. Dressmaker's darts* are used in *making a garment*.

All darts in commercial patterns are shortened darts. Should you wish to relocate such a dart you would first have to extend it to the designer's dart point.

All darts in the patterns you are creating are unshortened darts. For your final pattern, these will have to be shortened to dressmaker's darts.

HOW TO SHORTEN A DART

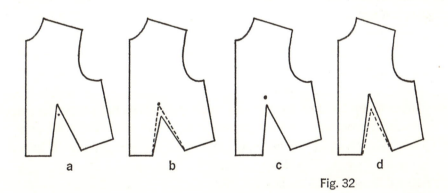

a   b   c   d

Fig. 32

1. Measure down from the dart point (Fig. 32a) the amount you wish to shorten the dart. Mark the new dart point in the center of the space.

2. Draw new dart legs starting at the ends of the original darts and ending at the lowered dart point (Fig. 32b). It is not the amount of control you wish to change, merely the length of the dart.

HOW TO LENGTHEN (EXTEND) A DART

1. Measure directly up from the dart point (Fig. 32c) the amount you wish to lengthen the dart. Mark the new dart point.

2. Draw new dart legs starting at the ends of the original darts and ending at the raised dart point (Fig. 32d).

The broken lines in Fig. 32 represent the original darts; the solid lines, the new darts.

HOW MUCH?

Here is a guide for shortening designer's darts to convert them into dressmaker's darts. Keep in mind that "standards" may be meaningless when applied to individual requirements. Shorten the darts the amount that looks best and feels most comfortable.

Bodice: The front-waistline dart is shortened ½ inch from bustpoint height,* the back-waistline dart is shortened 1 inch from the shoulder-blade height.

The underarm dart is shortened 2 inches or more from the bust point. (This dart is generally at bust-point height. Should it be on a slight angle it must end at bust-point height no matter where it originates on the side seam.) Heavy-bosomed figures may bring the underarm dart closer to the bust point for additional shaping.

A front-shoulder dart is shortened 2 inches or more from the bust point. It, too, may be brought closer to the bust point in heavy-bosomed figures. The back-shoulder dart is usually stitched to a finished length of 3 inches.

The French underarm dart is an exception. It may be stitched to the bust point except in larger figures when it is shortened ½ inch or more.

Sleeve: The elbow dart is usually stitched to a finished length of 2½ inches.

---

* The terms "height" and "point" refer to the high point of the curve.

Skirt: The skirt-front dart is shortened 2 inches from the high point of the front hipbone.

The skirt-back dart is shortened 1 inch from the high point of the buttocks.

Frequently skirt darts fit better when unshortened (or shortened very little) so that the dart releases the greatest amount of material where the figure is fullest.

A PAIR OF SHAPELY DART LEGS

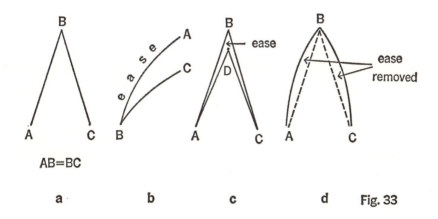

Fig. 33

Straight dart legs must always be equal in length, AB equals BC (Fig. 33a). If they are not, make them so. Wherever possible, balance the dart on grain to avoid puckering when stitched.

When the dart legs are curved, one (AB) may be a little longer than the other (BC) (Fig. 33b). Ease AB into BC. Because of the angle, it is comparatively easy to "ease" a curve.

Straight dart legs ending just short of the high point (ADC-dressmaker's dart) provide ease in the bulge area (Fig. 33c). Dart legs stitched to the dart point remove the ease (ABC) (Fig. 33c).

When the dart legs are "bowed" for closer fit (as in an evening or cocktail dress), the ease is removed (Fig. 33d).

SIGNS AND SYMBOLS

A finished pattern contains certain signs and symbols which make cutting accurate and assembling the garment easier.

Commercial patterns leave very little to chance or misinterpretation. They use not only signs and symbols but printed directions as well; "Place on Fold," "Cut Two." For your patterns you may use as many or as few markings as will be useful and understandable. Be sure to include enough information but don't overload the pattern with signs, symbols, and notations. This would only make for confusion.

Fig. 34 illustrates the markings that generally appear on a pattern. Not every pattern will need all of them. Some will need more.

There is an established system of marking. If you choose to use your own secret code, make certain that you have the legend noted somewhere. The whole idea of markings is to simplify your work, not to complicate it with deciphering woes.

THE NAME OF THE PATTERN PIECE

When the pattern piece has a simple and characteristic shape, there is no problem in identifying it. For instance, you would have no trouble recognizing a bodice front if it looked like the sloper or any of the fairly simple variations of it in Chapter 1. Intricate patterns with more unusual shapes may not be so easy to identify. There is no need for guessing if the pattern is labeled.

Write the name of the pattern clearly on it. Commercial patterns have the name printed on the pattern. Often they identify the piece by number—1, 2, 3, 4, 5, etc., or by letter—A, B, C, D, E, etc. This indicates the order in which the pattern piece is used.

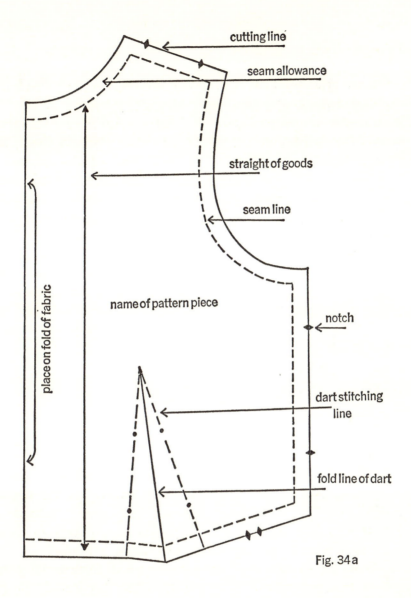

cutting line

seam allowance

straight of goods

seam line

place on fold of fabric

name of pattern piece

notch

dart stitching
line

fold line of dart

Fig. 34a

TO FOLD OR NOT TO FOLD

Patterns generally come in halves, that is half a front, half a back, etc. This makes cutting easier, faster, and more accurate (right and left sides are cut alike). It also saves space and tissue both for storing and for cutting on a normal table. It precludes tangling with yards of pattern and fabric in the layout stage.

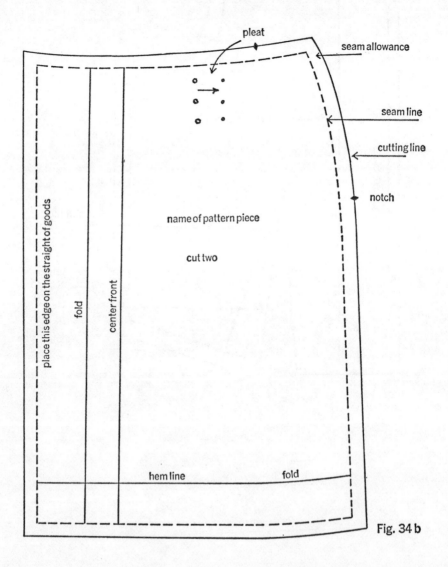

Fig. 34 b

Half a pattern may be laid on a fold to produce a complete unit when the fabric is unfolded (Fig. 34a). Two or more separate but identical pieces may be cut at the same time (Figs. 34b and 34c).

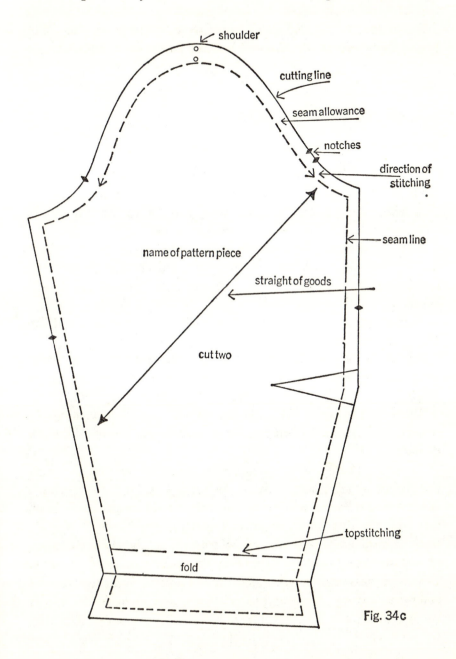

Fig. 34c

The symbol for a fold of fabric is two medium-sized perforations or two medium-sized circles (⁏) placed at the center of the fold line. You may instead write along the fold line the following: "Place on fold of fabric," or simply, "Fold of fabric."

For separate but identical pieces, write: "Cut Two," or "Cut Four," or whatever the required number.

THE GRAIN LINE (Straight of Goods)

The designer uses the "hang" of the fabric as part of the design. Because fabric is woven as it is, it hangs best with the lengthwise grain and most fabrics are used in this way (Fig. 35a).

Sometimes for a special, decorative effect a garment is cut in whole or in part (Fig. 35b) on the horizontal grain.

Both for decorative reasons or for a special kind of fit, fabric is used on the bias. Bias, being stretchable, produces a molded, clinging, form-defining fit (Fig. 35c). It is almost always used for draped effects.

In most patterns, the grain is indicated by a long line with an arrow at each end (Figs. 34a and 34c).

Sometimes the grain is indicated along one edge of the pattern with the printed or lettered direction, "Place this edge on the straight of goods." A decorative selvage is often utilized in this way (Fig. 34b).

Whatever the grain, *the grain line should extend throughout the entire length of the pattern to assure accurate placement of pattern on fabric.*

Theoretically, placing the pattern on the fabric so that the grain line is an equal distance from the selvage at both ends should guarantee that fabric will be cut on the straight of goods. It is on this principle that most commercial patterns provide a short grain line. Unfortunately, this cannot be true unless the material is anchored so firmly in correct position that it cannot slide off grain. Otherwise what may be accurate at the two points measured may be completely wrong in other places. Don't take chances. It is easy enough to draw a long grain line.

b   Fig. 35

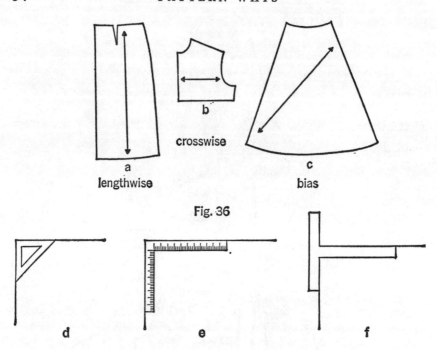

a
lengthwise

crosswise

b

c
bias

Fig. 36

d   e   f

HOW TO ESTABLISH THE LENGTHWISE GRAIN

From the center front or center back of the pattern, measure over equal distances in two or more places. Draw a line connecting these points and extending the entire length of the pattern. This places the grain parallel to the center line.

HOW TO ESTABLISH THE CROSSWISE GRAIN

At the widest part of the pattern, place the right angle (90 degrees) of your triangle against the center-front or center-back line with one leg of the triangle directly over it. "Square" a line across the entire width of the pattern (Fig. 36d). This is the crosswise grain.

A right angle or "square" may also be established by using the "tailor's square" (Fig. 36e) or a "T-square" (Fig. 36f) in the same way as the triangle.

HOW TO ESTABLISH THE BIAS GRAIN

With the triangle in the same position as for the horizontal grain (Fig. 36d) draw the diagonal line opposite the 90-degree angle or square.

STITCHING LINES—SEAMS

When you have developed the construction pattern so it is just the way you want it to be for your finished pattern, trace all the outside edges, correcting them as necessary. This is the stitching (seam) line (Figs. 34a, b, and c).

To preserve the designated shape of the cut fabric it is stitched with the grain. Often a pattern will indicate the direction of the stitching with an arrow (Fig. 34c).

STITCHING LINES—DARTS

Trace the stitching lines of all darts. Missing thus far is the stitching line at dart's end. It is drafted in the following way:

1. Fold the darts on the underside of the pattern in the position in which they will be pressed in the garment. All vertical darts are pressed toward the center; all horizontal darts are pressed down.

Here is an easy way to do it. For a vertical dart: crease the dart leg nearest the center; bring it over to meet the other dart leg (Fig. 37a). This closes the dart as if it were stitched. For a horizontal dart: crease the lower dart leg; bring it up to meet the upper dart leg (Fig. 37c).

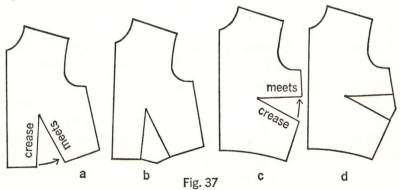

Fig. 37

2. Using the tracing wheel, trace the seam line. When the pattern is opened out, you will see a more or less pointed shape (depending on the size and position of the dart). This represents the amount of material necessary to catch the dart in the seam (Figs. 37b and 37d).

When the design calls for *pleats or folds,* the seam line of the pattern is arrived at by the same method.

Darts may be indicated by lines, perforations, or by perforations on lines (Fig. 34a). Perforations are useful when the marking must be tailor's tacks.

Narrow darts are generally indicated by a straight line bearing the instruction "¼-inch dart" or "⅛-inch dart."

DECORATIVE TOPSTITCHING

Decorative topstitching must be indicated with a line of its own. Decide how far in from a stitching line or fold line you want the top-stitching to be. Usually this is anywhere from ⅜ inch to 1 inch but it could be any measurement you determine best for your design. Set the gauge for the amount you have decided on. Slide the gauge along the pattern following the outline of the stitching line. Make a broken line to indicate the topstitching (Fig. 34c). You may label it "Topstitching" for clarity.

SEAM ALLOWANCE

Between the stitching line and the cutting line is the seam allowance. In most commercial patterns and in most places on the pattern the seam allowance is ⅝ inch. When you are making your own pattern you may make the seam allowance any amount you wish. One-half inch would do quite well for most patterns. If the pattern is designed for a sheer fabric, and/or if you plan to trim away the seam allowance after stitching, then you may use less. A heavy fabric will require more seam allowance. If you are uncertain about the fit, you will surely want more seam allowance.

In industry every fraction of an inch can add up to a great loss of yardage, hence profit. When you are designing for yourself or doing custom work, you can afford to be a little more generous with seam allowances.

THE CUTTING LINE

The cutting line (like the topstitching) is an even distance from the stitching line and follows its outline (Fig. 34a, b, and c). Where the *topstitching* was marked *in* from a stitching line or a fold, the *cutting line* is marked *out* from the stitching line to the amount of the seam allowance. Use your gauge.

NOTCHES

Notches make the assembling of a garment quicker, easier, and more accurate. Were they not there, you would have to make constant decisions about which sections are intended to be joined.

Since two edges are involved, notches come in pairs (Fig. 38). In the construction pattern notches are indicated by cross lines (Fig. 38a). In the final pattern they may be little triangular cutouts in the seam allowance (Fig. 38b) or diamond-shaped symbols on the cutting line (Fig. 38c). You may use either. If you are not certain of the fit or the fabric (a cut in some fabrics may cause them to ravel dangerously close to the stitching line) use the latter method. It's safer. Where there is no problem use the former.

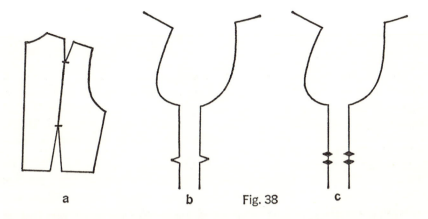

a   b   Fig. 38   c

Place the notches where you think they will facilitate the matching of seams. Notches may be used singly or in groups of two or three. Varying the number and placement of pairs of notches makes them easier to spot. Were you to use all single notches (or double or triple) and were you to place them all the same distance up or down from an edge, you'd have an awful time figuring out which seams go together.

In commercial patterns notches are numbered in the sequence of matching.

GUIDELINES

There is always a long guideline to show where the garment closes. The center front and center back are marked with long guidelines to aid in fitting (Fig. 34b).

A short guideline marks the natural waistline of a one-piece garment or a style that has a raised or lowered waistline.

SHOULDER AND UNDERARM MARKINGS

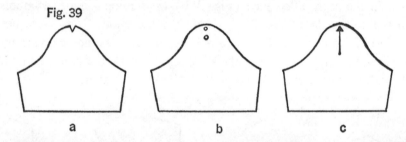

Fig. 39

a   b   c

Shoulder markings may be any of these—a notch (Fig. 39a), perforations or circles (Fig. 39b), or an arrow (Fig. 39c). The same symbol may be used to mark the underarm of a two-piece sleeve.

PLACEMENT MARKS

The manner of closing a garment must always be indicated.

For a zippered closing a notation plus notch or spot marking is used. The pattern may read, "Leave open above notch (Fig. 40a) or "Stitch to o" (Fig. 40b).

For a buttoned closing the length, size, and placement of button-holes and buttons are drawn on the garment (Fig. 40c).

Pocket and welt placement lines, stitching lines, slash marks and clipping lines are always shown (Fig. 40d).

Any *decorative detail* (band, trimming, appliqué, etc.) applied to the right side of the garment must be outlined (Fig. 40e).

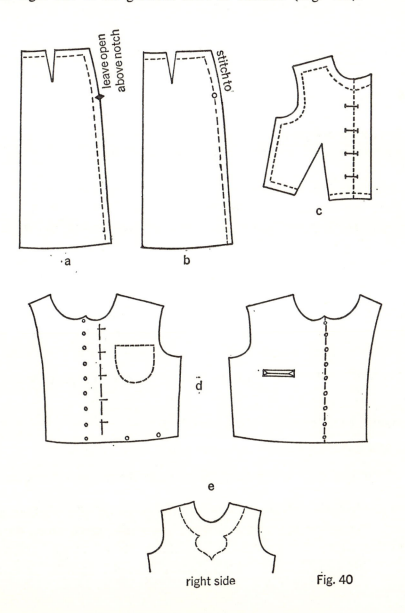

right side   Fig. 40

SPOT MARKINGS

The pattern symbols in Fig. 41 are special markings that indicate matching points in a garment. For example, the spot at which a collar joins the garment, the point where the gusset joins the underarm slash, the place on which a welt is set, etc.

Fig. 41

○ ○ △ □

FOLD LINES

Fold lines are placed wherever the material is to be folded back against itself as in a facing (Fig. 34b) or a hem (Figs. 34b and 34c).

Often the fold line of a dart is indicated (Fig. 34a).

Pleats are designated by a fold line and the line to which the fold is brought. The line may be a solid one or a series of medium and small circles (Fig. 34b). In addition, the direction of the fold may be shown by an arrow or a notation that "Pleat Meets Pleat" (Fig. 34b).

HEMS

In the finished pattern the width of the hem is always included.

Straight skirt hems are generally 2½ to 3 inches. In sheer materials they may be as deep as you would like them.

Blouse hems are 1 to 1½ inches.

Dress- or blouse-sleeve hems are 1 inch.

Jacket hems are 1½ inches. *Jacket-sleeve* hems are 1½ inches.

Coat hems are 2 to 3 inches. *Coat-sleeve* hems are 2 inches.

Flared hems on any of the above are less. The more curved the hem, the narrower it must be so that the width at the upper edge can be eased to fit without bumps, pleats, or darts. When the curve of the hem is too circular to do this successfully the hem is rolled or faced.

ANYTHING THAT WILL HELP

In addition to all of these usual signs and symbols, you are free to make any notations or write any little messages to yourself that will make the pattern easier to identify and understand, that will facilitate the layout of the pattern on the fabric, and that will make the cutting and assembling of the garment accurate.

The pattern should be so clearly marked that were you to set it aside now and pick it up again next year, you would still know how to get exactly the effect you had in mind when you designed it.

Now it might be fun to go back over some of your construction patterns and convert them into final patterns.

Chapter III

THE MORE, THE MERRIER

One dart can be good. Two darts can be better. More darts may be better yet. Only the normal restrictions of good design set the limit to the number of divisions of the dart control.

Sometimes the amount of dart control is just too much burden for a single dart. It produces too great a bulge. It greatly interferes with the continuity of the fabric design. It throws a seam line very much off grain with straining and puckering of the material as the result.

From the standpoint of fit, almost any combination of darts is better than a single dart. The more darts, the more opportunity for gradual fitting.

From the standpoint of fabric design, a division of dart control reduces the unpleasant breaking of design units.

From the standpoint of grain, a division of dart control can make the seam lines of two adjoining sections more compatible.

DIVIDE AND CONQUER

There are several ways in which dart control may be divided.

METHOD I—DIVIDED CONTROL

Any amount of the original dart control can be thrown into another position in the pattern as long as it starts on a seam line and extends to the dart point.

One of the most frequent divisions of the dart control is *a waist-line-underarm combination* (Fig. 42). In this design, the underarm dart is partly hidden by the position of the arm and the waistline dart is so reduced in size that the break in the fabric design is minimized.

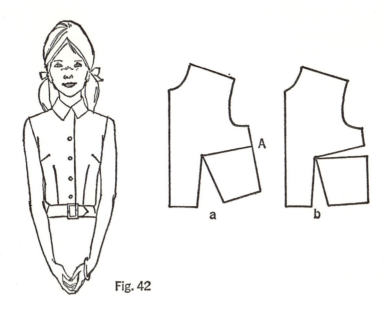

Fig. 42

1. On the cut-out bodice-front sloper with the cut-out dart locate the position of the new underarm dart—anywhere from 1½ inches below the armhole to 2½ inches above the waistline. Mark the point A (Fig. 42a). (Too close to the armhole will interfere with the setting and fitting of the sleeve. Too close to the waistline makes the dart a French underarm dart, which generally does not share honors with any other dart.)

2. Draw a line from A to the dart point (Fig. 42a).

3. Slash the new dart line.

4. Close PART of the original dart. The remaining control is automatically shifted to the new dart (Fig. 42b). Generally, most of the control remains in the waistline dart; a lesser amount is shifted to the underarm dart.

5. Complete the pattern by adding all the necessary signs, symbols, and notations.

WAISTLINE-SHOULDER DART COMBINATION

Another common division of dart control is between waistline and shoulder darts.

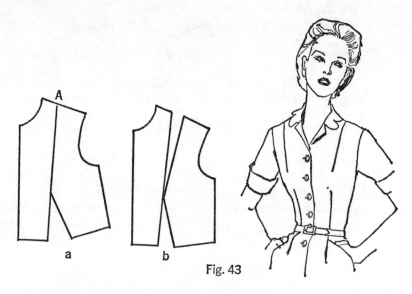

Fig. 43

1. On the cut-out bodice-front sloper with the cut-out dart, locate the position of the new shoulder dart. When there is a dart on the back shoulder, it is a fine point in design to match the location of the two. Place the front sloper against the back shoulder. Mark the position of the front shoulder dart. Label the point A (Fig. 43a).

2. Draw the new dart line from shoulder to dart point (Fig. 43a).

3. Slash the dart line.

4. Close PART of the original dart; the remaining control is automatically shifted to the new dart (Fig. 43b).

5. Complete the pattern by adding all the necessary signs, symbols, and notations.

How much dart control is shifted to a new position depends on what is appropriate for the material, what is kind to the grain, and what provides a subtle fit.

You can see how divided dart control would be a good way to handle a check or a plaid (Fig. 44).

Fig. 44

FITTED OR FULL

Stitching the full amount of dart control into any garment results in a fitted garment with a standard amount of ease.

In periods when a more relaxed look is fashionable, some of the divided dart control may appear as unstitched fullness.

For instance: In a bodice with dart control divided between waistline and underarm, the underarm dart is stitched for fit while the waistline dart is left unstitched for fullness (Fig. 45a).

In Fig. 45b, the dart control is divided between a stitched dart originating at the armhole and unstitched dart control at the waistline giving it some fullness.

The utilization of divided dart control—some stitched and some unstitched—is the basis of semi-fitted styles such as the shift or skimmer dress.

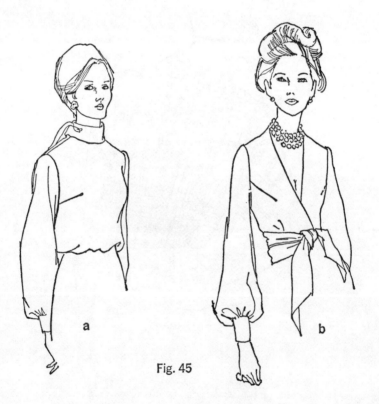

a   b

Fig. 45

HOW TO MAKE THE PATTERNS FOR FIGS. 45a AND 45b

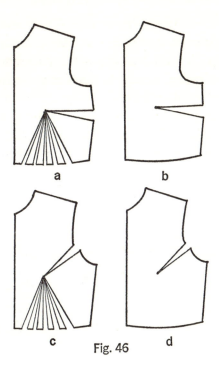

Fig. 46

FIG. *45a*

1. Divide the dart control between waistline and underarm (Fig. 46a). (The waistline dart control is handled as for gathers.)

2. Trace the pattern allowing the underarm dart to remain as a dart. Draw a line across the waistline as for a seam (Fig. 46b).

3. Complete the pattern.

FIG. *45b*

1. Divide the dart control between waistline and armhole (Fig. 46c). (The waistline dart control is handled as in Fig. 46a).

2. Trace the pattern allowing the armhole dart to remain as a dart. Draw a line across the waistline as for a seam (Fig. 46d).

3. Complete the pattern.

Sleeve dart control can be treated in the same manner.

1. On the cut-out sleeve sloper with the cut-out dart, locate the position of the new dart at the wrist. Mark point A one-third or one-fourth of the way up from the back underarm seam.

2. Draw a slash line from A to the elbow dart point (Fig. 47a).

3. Slash the new dart line.

4. Close PART of the elbow dart control. The remaining control is automatically shifted to the new wrist dart (Fig. 47b).

5. Trace the new pattern leaving the diminished elbow dart as a dart. Draw a new wrist line disregarding the wrist dart (Fig. 47c). The wrist control appears as unstitched fullness.

6. Complete the pattern.

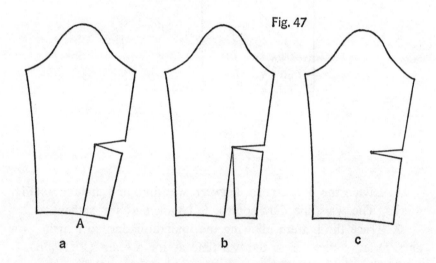

Fig. 47

a   b   c

This one-piece dress sleeve becomes the basis of the one-piece suit sleeve and the one-piece coat sleeve, both of which also require the ease provided by the unstitched fullness (see pages 391 and 392).

The division of dart control need not be limited to a two-way split. Dart control can be divided three ways, or four ways, or more. Theoretically, you could divide the control in many places around the perimeter of a sloper (Fig. 48). The question is, "Who would want to?" The resulting design would be pretty cluttered.

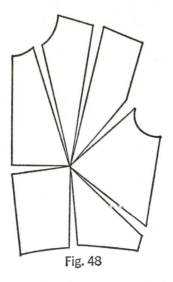

Fig. 48

METHOD II—MULTIPLE DARTS OR DART TUCKS

You will have to admit that dividing the dart control so it comes from many different directions, each vying for attention, can be very distracting (Fig. 49a). However, an equal number of darts on the *same seam line* are another matter. Repetition in a row is a time-honored method of achieving harmony and interest in design (Fig. 49b).

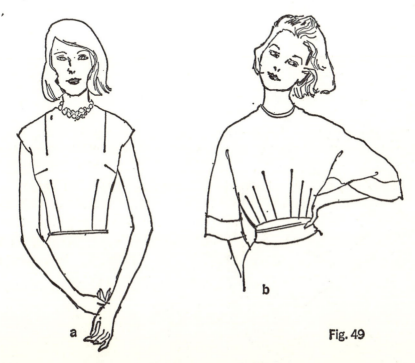

a

b

Fig. 49

Dart control may be divided into multiple darts or dart tucks.

Multiple darts like divided dart control produce a fitted garment. The shaping is more subtle than a single dart. The design may be more interesting than divided dart control (Fig. 50a).

Dart tucks are parts of darts. They begin as darts but are stitched only part way. The fullness released by this construction produces a soft, full effect (Fig. 50b) or a draped effect (Fig. 50c). Dart tucks require careful and subtle designing. There's a very fine line between a chic look and a matronly one.

Fig. 50

a

b

c

HOW TO MAKE MULTIPLE FRENCH DARTS

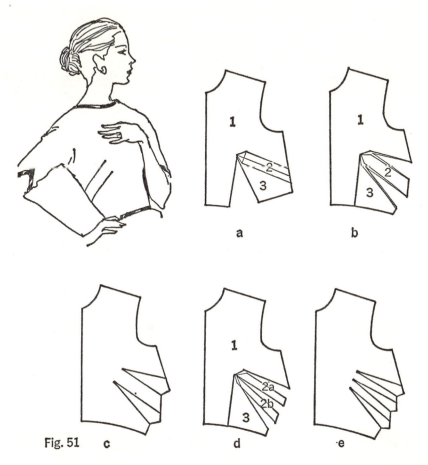

Fig. 51   c   d   ·e

1. Trace the bodice-front sloper. Cut out the tracing and the dart.

2. Draw the line for the French dart (Fig. 51a). This is a guideline for positioning the new darts.

3. Locate the position of the new darts ½ inch away on each side of the guideline. End the lines ½ inch from the dart point. This automatically shortens the darts while in construction instead of shortening them in the final pattern. Mark the ends with a cross line (Fig. 51a).

4. Connect the ends of the new darts with the dart point (Fig. 51a).

5. For clarity in developing the pattern, label sections 1, 2, and 3 as in the illustration (Fig. 51a).

6. Cut away section 2 from the rest of the bodice.

7. Close the waistline dart and fasten it with Scotch tape. This throws the dart control to the new position.

8. Place section 2 in the new dart opening so the spaces between 1 and 2 and 3 and 2 are equal (Fig. 51b). Trace the pattern.

9. Locate the new dart points in the center of each spread area at the shortened length. Draw new dart legs, making certain that each pair is equal in length. (Fig. 51b).

10. Fold the darts into position and trace the side seam (Fig. 51c).

11. Complete the pattern by adding all the necessary pattern symbols and notations.

Should you wish three French darts instead of two, slash all three French dart lines. Place sections 2a and 2b in the dart opening so that all spaces between are equal (Fig. 51d). Proceed as for two darts (Fig. 51e).

An interesting design for a dress results from utilizing related dart control in bodice and skirt (Fig. 52). The French darts of the bodice are placed at the waistline and developed as in Fig. 51. The skirt pattern is developed as directed below.

HOW TO MAKE MULTIPLE DARTS IN THE SKIRT

1. Trace the skirt-front sloper. Cut out the tracing and the dart.

2. Draw a guideline for the position of the darts. Draw new dart lines ½ inch away on each side of the guideline. End the lines ½ inch from the dart point to shorten the new darts while in construction. Connect the ends of the new darts with the dart point (Fig. 52a). (Should the skirt dart not be long enough to provide the desired angle for the new darts, extend it.)

3. Label sections as illustrated (Fig. 52a).

4. Cut away section 2 from the rest of the skirt.

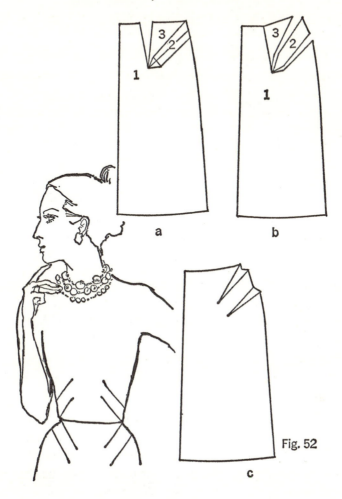

Fig. 52

5. Close the original dart and fasten with Scotch tape.

6. Place section 2 in the new dart opening so the spaces between 1 and 2 and 3 and 2 are equal (Fig. 52b). Trace the pattern.

7. Locate the new dart points in the center of each space. Draw new darts from the new dart points. Fold the darts into position and trace the side seam (Fig. 52c).

8. Complete the pattern with all the necessary signs and symbols.

MULTIPLE DARTS AT THE WAISTLINE

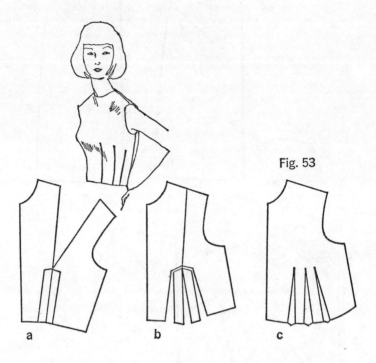

Fig. 53

a   b   c

Do you recall the exercises that utilized the bulging block as a method of eliminating the waistline dart so that we had an uninterrupted area in which to design? Here is another device that serves the same purpose. Using the flat pattern shift the dart control out of the way. Do your designing. Shift it back again to the newly designed control. It's like moving furniture out of the way temporarily so you can clean under the rug.

1. Trace the bodice-front sloper. Cut out the tracing and the dart. Shift the waistline dart control to the shoulder. Fasten with Scotch tape.

2. Locate the number and length of the new waistline darts. If you make them somewhat shorter than the sloper dart you will be shortening the darts at the same time you are dividing the control. Draw the dart lines and connect them with the dart point (Fig. 53a).

3. Slash all slash lines.

4. Close the shoulder dart, returning the control to the waistline. Fasten with Scotch tape.

5. Divide the dart control into equal darts with equal spaces between them (Fig. 53b). Trace the pattern.

6. Locate the new dart points in the center of each space at the designated height. Draw new dart legs. Make sure that each pair is equal in length.

7. Fold the darts in position. Correct the waistline and trace it (Fig. 53c).

8. Complete the pattern.

MULTIPLE ELBOW DARTS

Here is still another method for dividing the control into multiple darts using the sloper dart control in its original position.

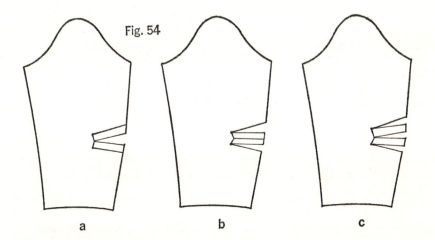

Fig. 54

a   b   c

1. Trace the sleeve sloper. Cut out the tracing and the dart.

2. Locate the position of the new darts on each side of the elbow dart and ½ inch away from it. Make the slash lines parallel to the dart legs. Since the elbow dart is already a shortened dart it needs no further shortening. Connect the ends of the slash lines with the point of the elbow dart (Fig. 54a).

3. Slash all slash lines.

FOR TWO DARTS (Fig. 54b)

4. Close the elbow dart completely, throwing the control to both sides of it. Make the new darts equal. Fasten with Scotch tape.

5. Trace the pattern. Locate new dart points in the center of each opening. Draw the dart legs. Make certain that each pair is equal in length.

6. Fold the darts to the correct position and trace the seam line.

7. Complete the pattern.

FOR THREE DARTS (Fig. 54c)

The method for developing three elbow darts is the same as for two with the exception of Step 4. Substitute the following:

Close *part* of the elbow dart, dividing the control equally in three darts.

PART OF A DART

Multiple dart tucks are developed in much the same way. Instead of stitching the darts to a point, the stitching stops part way at a designated point.

HOW TO MAKE MULTIPLE DART TUCKS AT THE SHOULDER

1. Trace the bodice-front sloper. Cut out the tracing and the dart.

2. Draw a line from dart point to mid-shoulder. Locate the position and length of the dart tucks on each side of and parallel to the line (Fig. 55a).

3. Connect the ends of the dart tucks to the dart point (the broken lines in Fig. 55a). Each entire line from shoulder to dart point (jog and all) becomes a slash line.

4. Slash the slash lines.

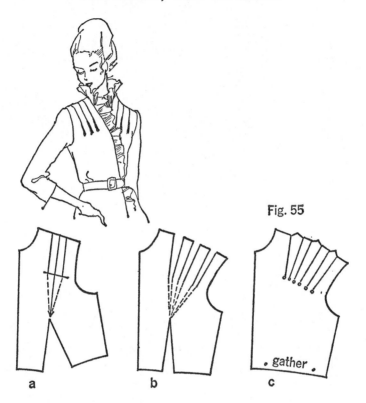

Fig. 55

a   b   c

gather

5. Close the waistline dart in whole or in part (Fig. 55b), throwing the dart control to the shoulder. Fasten with Scotch tape.

6. Arrange the sections so the spaces between are equal (Fig. 55b).

7. Trace the pattern. When you come to the dart tucks, trace only to the end of each tuck as designated in Step 2 (Fig. 55c). Notice that the dart tuck legs are *not* parallel lines. Being parts of darts, they are tapered. They must be stitched so.

8. Fold the tucks into position (the same rule as for darts). Trace the shoulder seam (Fig. 55c). Working with stiff paper in a small pattern makes this somewhat difficult because the dart tucks are so tiny. Trace the construction pattern to either tissue paper or a paper napkin. You'll find them much easier to manipulate for folds.

9. Complete the pattern.

HOW TO MAKE MULTIPLE DART TUCKS AT THE NECKLINE

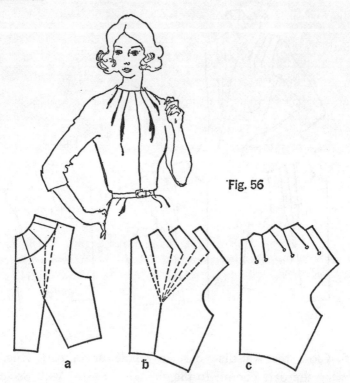

Fig. 56

1. Trace the bodice-front sloper. Cut out the tracing and the dart.

2. Lightly draw an arc as a guideline for positioning the dart tucks (Fig. 56a). Make it a distance from the neckline equal to the length you desire for the dart tucks. They may be of equal length or graduated.

3. Draw the lines for the dart tucks showing the number and the position of each one. Designate the point at which the stitching is to end (Fig. 56a).

4. Connect the ends of the dart tucks with the original dart point (Fig. 56a). All lines from neck to dart point (crooked though they are) become slash lines.

5. Slash all slash lines.

6. Close all (Fig. 56b) or part of the original dart control.

7. Spread the sections so the spaces between are equal (Fig. 56b). Fasten with Scotch tape.

8. Trace the pattern. When you come to the dart tucks, trace only to the end of each tuck as designated (Fig. 56c).

9. Fold the dart tucks in the correct position (same rule as for darts). In folding, start matching the tucks at the neckline so the original neckline is restored. Trace the neckline (Fig. 56c).

10. Complete the pattern.

The combination of *shoulder and neck dart tucks* makes an interesting design. Can you follow the diagram for producing this pattern?

Fig. 57

MULTIPLE DARTS AT CENTER FRONT

As with darts, it doesn't matter where the dart tucks are placed as long as they begin on some seam and are connected with the dart point. However, in order to improve the design, it is possible to take some slight liberties with the position of the dart point. It may be moved in any direction up to, but no more than 1 inch. Since the released fullness of dart tucks covers a comparatively wide area, the

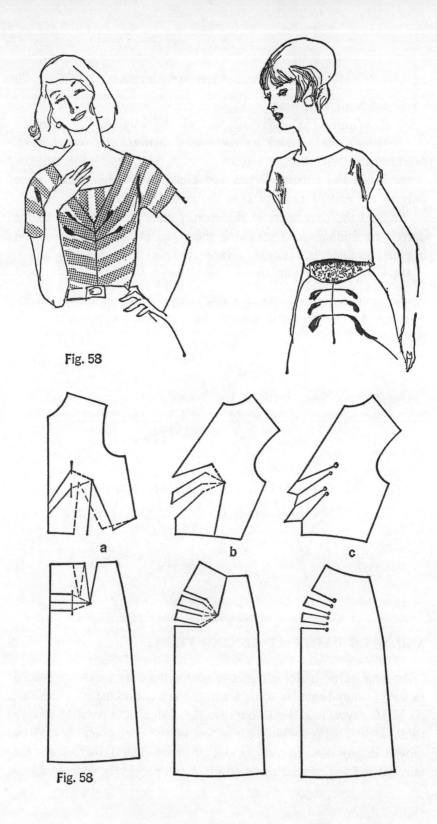

Fig. 58

a   b   c

Fig. 58

fit of the garment is not affected. One would have to be a little more careful in moving a dart.

1. Move the bodice and skirt darts closer to the side seams. Extend the skirt dart to a point in line with the widest measurement at the hips. The broken lines in Fig. 58a indicate the original dart. The solid lines show the darts in their new positions.

2. Locate the positions of the dart tucks above and below the dart point. Connect them with the new dart points (Fig. 58a).

3. Slash all slash lines.

4. Close the sloper darts. Spread the sections in the new control area (Fig. 58b).

5. Trace the pattern, showing the new dart tucks. Note that the center front of the skirt pattern becomes a curved line (Fig. 58c).

6. Complete the pattern.

SUGGESTIONS FOR NEW PATTERN MAKERS

In looking at fashions, many women lose all sense of objectivity. When a particular style doesn't fit into a personal formula for glamor, they are apt to discard it—often with unkind words.

As a pattern designer, your interest must extend to all fashions whether you would be inclined to wear them or not. Look at window fashion displays. Watch people passing. Examine the fashion magazines.

Study the darts from the standpoint of design, fit, and of appropriateness to fabric.

How has the dart control been used as design?

Why has a particular control been used on a particular fabric?

Do the darts fit the people who are wearing them? Are they in the right amount—not too much or too little considering the curves they must shape? Are they in the right place? Do they release their greatest amount of fullness where needed?

Make "shorthand" sketches of any dart treatments that interest you. The sketches don't have to be works of art. Just so you know what they mean. The rest can be done with drafting tools.

Chapter IV

HIDE-AND-SEEK DART CONTROL

Shaping by Seams

There is no disguising a dart. From the standpoint of design it is what it is: a short jab into an otherwise unbroken area. It is obvious in function and elementary in control. Many fine patterns remain on this simple level of design by darts. And, many beautiful garments are made from them, depending for their effect on handsome fabric and perfect fit.

Fig. 59

To many a designer, however, a dart is an incomplete line. Which is very frustrating. For the designer uses *line* to express his ideas as a painter uses color, or a musician the notes of a scale, or a writer words. He likes to approach the area within the silhouette as an artist approaches an empty canvas. With subtle or dramatic lines he seeks to divide the space into interesting shapes (Fig. 59).

The dress designer has one great problem that an artist does not have: he must cope with a three-dimensional figure. (Some choose to ignore this fact, hence, the many designs for the young and the flat.) The designer must find a way to shape *and* style at one and the same time. How does he do it? He incorporates the dart control in the design lines of the garment—a neat trick. When successfully accomplished, there is no better-fitting or more attractive garment.

SHAPING BY SEAMS

When a design line falls across a high point of the body, the dart control may be concealed in the seam that joins the sections. This is called a *control seam*.

In Fig. 60a, one dart leg becomes part of the style line. When the garment is joined on this line, the waistline dart control is hidden in the seam.

In Fig. 60b, part of the waistline dart control is shifted to the style line at the side seam. (The rest is used as unstitched fullness.) When the dress is stitched on this line, the shifted dart control is absorbed in the seam.

The control seam frequently works on the principle of divided control. In Fig. 60c, the dart control is divided between the armhole and waistline. When the dress is stitched on the style line, it is now the control seam that does the shaping instead of the darts.

To convince yourself that shaping can be done by seams instead of darts, Scotch tape the style lines of each of these patterns to create bulging blocks. Test the new designs over one of your previous blocks. Note that the amount of dart control and the shaping have been changed in no way—only the styling is different.

Fig. 60

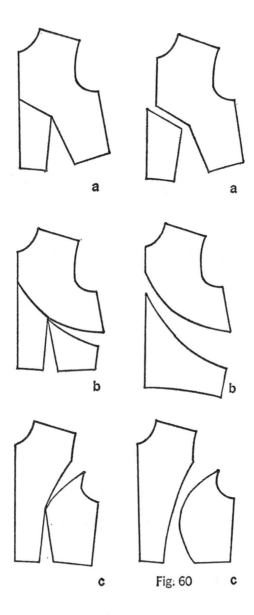

a a

b b

c Fig: 60 c

HOW TO MAKE THE PATTERN FOR A CONTROL SEAM WITH DIVIDED CONTROL
Shoulder to Waistline

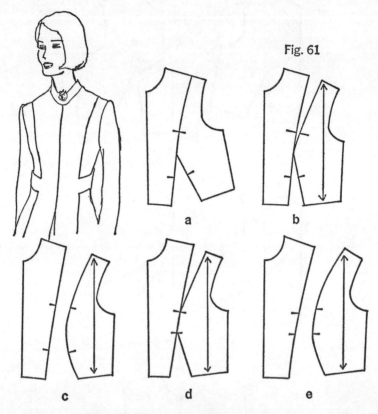

Fig. 61

1. On the cut-out bodice-front sloper with the cut-out dart, draw the style line from the shoulder to the dart point. Indicate the notches by cross lines on the style line—3 inches above and 3 inches below the dart point (opposite each other on the dart legs, Fig. 61a).

2. Slash the style line and divide the dart control. Fasten with Scotch tape. Establish the grain line in the side-front section parallel to the center front (Fig. 61b).

Since the two sections of the bodice pattern are to be separated and cut individually in fabric, you must know how to place the side sections on the grain of the fabric and at what points to match the sections.

The *notches* are best marked before the control is divided.

The *grain line* is marked *after* the control has been divided. This is most important. It is the grain line that is the clue to how much control is in each dart. If you change the position of the grain line, you change the amount of the control.

3. *For a fitted garment,* separate the two sections. Correct the angularity of the side-front seam line (Fig. 61c).

For an easier fit, shorten the darts and connect the new dart points (Fig. 61d). Place cross lines for notches at the points of the darts instead of as in Step 1. Separate the two sections of the bodice. Correct the angularity of the side-front seam line (Fig. 61e).

4. Complete the pattern.

A CONTROL SEAM FOR THE BACK BODICE

From the Shoulder

Since there are already two darts on the back bodice, there is no need to divide the waistline control. If there is a control seam on the front bodice, it is a fine point in design to make the back control seam match. Move the back shoulder dart as necessary.

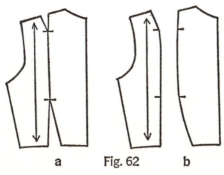

a   Fig. 62   b

1. On the cut-out bodice-back sloper with the cut-out dart, connect the shoulder dart with the waistline dart. Place notch marks at the points of the darts. Establish the grain line in the side-back section parallel to the center back (Fig. 62a).

2. Separate the two sections. Correct the angular style lines with gentle, opposing curves (Fig. 62b).

3. Complete the pattern.

For figures with high or prominent shoulder blades, extend the back waistline dart before Step 1.

From the Armhole

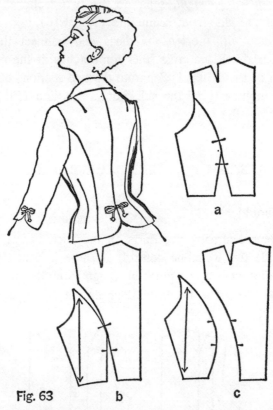

Fig. 63   b   c

1. Trace the bodice-back sloper. Cut out the tracing and the dart. Draw the style line from the armhole to the waistline dart point. Notch the style line above the dart point. Notch the dart legs opposite each other (Fig. 63a).

2. Slash the style line. Divide the dart control between waistline and armhole. Establish the grain in the side-back section parallel to the center back (Fig. 63b).

3. Separate the pattern. Trace each section, correcting the angularity of the seam lines (Fig. 63c).

4. Complete the pattern.

THE CONTROL SEAM MOVED OFF THE DART POINT

For design purposes one may take a few liberties with the position of the style line off the dart point. However, when this is done some auxiliary or compensatory shaping must be provided.

Toward the Center Front

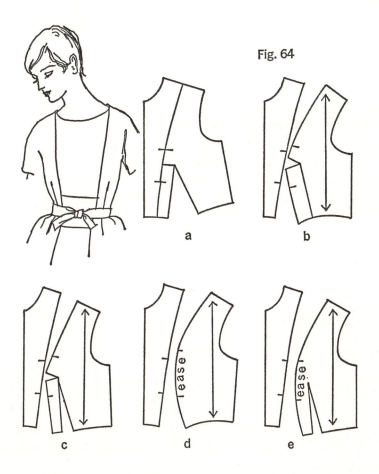

Fig. 64

1. On the cut-out bodice-front sloper with the cut-out dart, draw the style line off the dart point toward the center front—no more than 1 inch (Fig. 64a).

2. Since no shifting of dart control is possible unless the new line is connected with the dart point, draw the connecting line at right angles to the center front. Place notch marks on the style line above and below the connecting line (Fig. 64a).

3. Slash all slash lines.

4. Close all (Fig. 64b) or part (Fig. 64c) of the waistline dart, shifting some or all of the control to the style line and the connecting line. Establish the grain in the side-front bodice parallel to the center front.

5. Separate the sections. Correct any angularity. Complete the pattern.

In Fig. 64b, the dart control shifted to the connecting line is eased into the center-front section between the notches (Fig. 64d).

In Fig. 64c, a small amount of dart control on the connecting-line dart is eased into the style line between the notches. The remaining waistline control is used as a dart (Fig. 64e).

As you can see, in both cases some control is retained in the side-front section to assist with the shaping that has been moved off the high point.

Toward the Side Seam

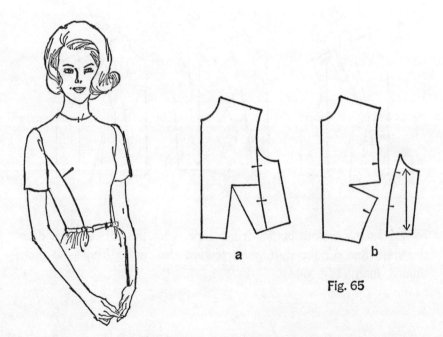

a   b

Fig. 65

1. On the cut-out bodice-front sloper with the cut-out dart, draw the style line 2 inches or more off the dart point toward the side seam. Connect the style line with the dart point. Place notch marks on the style line as indicated (Fig. 65a).

2. Cut the sections apart. Slash the connecting line. Close the waistline dart, shifting the dart control to the style line, where it is divided between waistline and armhole, and to the connecting line, where it becomes a new dart (Fig. 65b).

3. Establish the grain in the side-front section parallel to the center front (Fig. 65b). Complete the pattern.

NON-VERTICAL CONTROL SEAMS

A control seam need not be vertical. It may be diagonal (Fig. 66a) or horizontal (Fig. 66b).

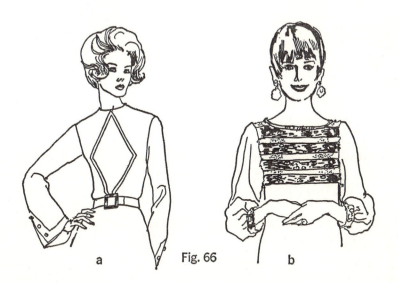

a   Fig. 66   b

Diagonal control seams produce unusual shapes such as the diamond seaming in Fig. 66a.

A horizontal control seam creates a yoke (Fig. 66b). There are many interesting design possibilities in this kind of control.

A PATTERN FOR DIAGONAL CONTROL SEAMING (as in Fig. 66a)

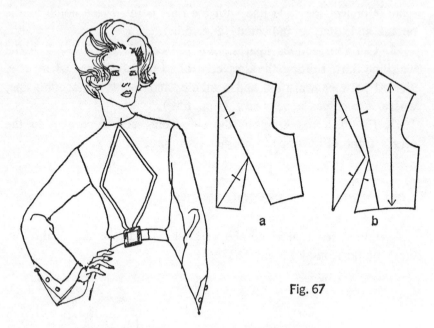

a   b

Fig. 67

1. On the cut-out bodice-front sloper with the cut-out dart, draw the style line—from neck to dart point, from dart point to center-front waistline. Place notch marks as indicated (Fig. 67a).

2. Slash the style lines.

3. Close the waistline dart, throwing the control to the style line and dividing it between neckline and waistline. Establish the grain line in the side-front bodice (Fig. 67b).

4. Complete the pattern.

If only part of the waistline dart is closed, the rest may be used as unstitched fullness.

A PATTERN WITH HORIZONTAL CONTROL SEAMING (as in Fig. 66b)

1. On the cut-out bodice-front with the cut-out dart, draw the horizontal style line at right angles to the center front. Make it pass across the dart point. Place notch marks on the style line as indicated (Fig. 68a).

2. Slash the style line.

3. Close all or part of the waistline dart, throwing the control to the seam line (Fig. 68b). If only part of the waistline dart is closed, the remaining control appears as unstitched fullness.

4. Correct the angularity of the lower-bodice seam line. Complete the pattern.

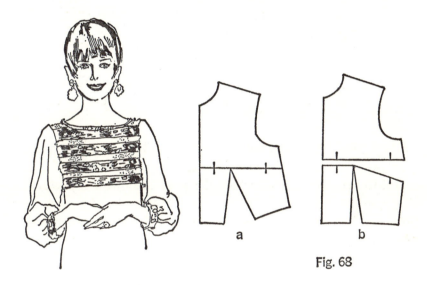

Fig. 68

FABRIC—A CONSIDERATION

The amount of dart control on the yoke seam can be placed where it will least show in the fabric.

If the yoke material is a solid color or over-all design, divide the control between the yoke and the lower bodice. This will balance the grain on either side of the seam. Each seam line then becomes curved (Fig. 69a).

If the fabric for the yoke is horizontally striped while the lower bodice is a solid color, over-all design, or a vertical stripe, straighten the yoke seam line so it is in keeping with the straight lines of the fabric. Move all of the dart control over to the lower bodice, whose curved style line will not affect the fabric design (Fig. 69b). (This is the pattern of Fig. 68b.)

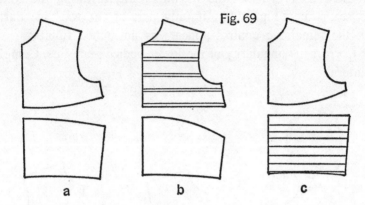

Fig. 69

a   b   c

If the yoke fabric is a solid color, over-all design, or a vertical stripe, while the lower bodice is horizontally striped, move the dart control to the yoke and straighten the seam line of the lower bodice (Fig. 69c).

The amount of the dart control remains the same whether it is placed above, below, or straddles the style line.

THE VERSATILE YOKE

The yoke is a wonderful design device. Its seaming may conceal the dart control (Fig. 70a). Where there is no control it may simply divide a bodice or skirt into interesting areas (Fig. 70b). Often, it provides a smooth, trim area in contrast to fullness in an adjoining area (Fig. 70c). It is a common device for separating a highly decorative area from a very plain one (Fig. 70d). When a yoke appears in the lower bodice, it produces a smooth, fitted midriff (Fig. 70e). When it appears in the upper part of the skirt it is a hip yoke (Fig. 70f). In its very narrowest form, a hip yoke becomes the contour belt.

a

b

c

Fig. 70

d

e

f

g

h

i

Fig. 70

There are partial yokes (Fig. 70g), yokes in one with a panel (Fig. 70h), and yokes in one with a sleeve (Fig. 70i). This has not begun to exhaust the endless possibilities and versatility of the yoke.

SOME SUGGESTIONS FOR DESIGNING YOKES

Remember that an equal division of an area is not nearly as interesting as an unequal division.

Use lines appropriate for the fabric. A solid-color fabric may have straight or curved lines. Use straight lines for stripes, checks, or plaids.

Relate the shape of the yoke to the shape of other style lines in the garment.

FOR DESIGN PURPOSES ONLY—Yokes That Do Not Involve Dart Control

On the appropriate sloper, draw the style line, place notch marks, establish the grain, cut apart.

When there is no control in the yoke seam, the entire amount of dart control may be used decoratively below the yoke.

AS GATHERS (Fig. 71a)

1. Draw the yoke style line on the bodice-front sloper. Notch the style line. Cut the yoke from the lower bodice.

2. On the lower bodice draw slash lines from the dart point to the yoke and from the dart point to the waistline.

3. Slash all slash lines. Divide the control for gathers between the waistline and the yoke style line.

4. Complete the pattern.

AS MULTIPLE DARTS (Fig. 71b)

1. Draw the yoke style line on the bodice-front sloper. Mark notches.

2. Draw the position of the darts. Connect them with the dart point.

3. Cut the yoke away.

4. Slash the dart lines to the dart point. Shift the control to the new darts, dividing it equally between them. Draw new dart legs.

5. Complete the pattern.

a   b   Fig. 71

WHEN DART CONTROL IS CONCEALED IN A YOKE SEAM

The Skirt Yoke

1. Trace the skirt-front sloper. Cut out the tracing and the dart.

2. Draw the style line of the yoke and notch it. Extend the waist-line dart to the yoke style line (Fig. 72a).

3. Cut the yoke away from the lower skirt. Close the extended dart (Fig. 72b). Note that the dart control appears in the seam that joins the yoke with the lower skirt.

4. Correct the waistline with a smooth curved line. Correct the seam line of the hip yoke (Fig. 72b).

5. Complete the pattern.

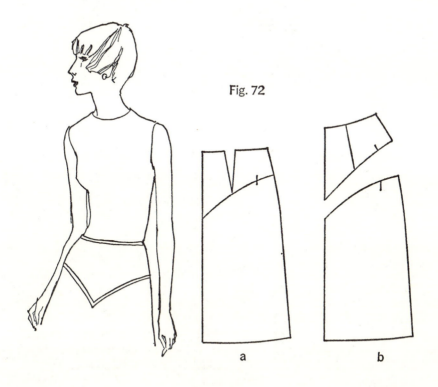

Fig. 72

a   b

A MIDRIFF YOKE

Variations of this type of yoke are understandably popular. They are a great way to emphasize a slim midriff and small waist while retaining the shaping of the upper bodice.

1. On a bulging-block bodice, draw the yoke style line* and notch it (Fig. 73a).

2. Cut away the yoke. Open the remaining dart control on the bodice (Fig. 73b). This may be used as one dart, multiple darts, or gathers.

* Whenever drawing a curved style line from the center-front or center-back position, first square a short line (⅛ inch) at the center line. This assures a smooth, continuous curve. Without doing so you may discover a point or a dip at center when the material is opened out (Fig. 73c).

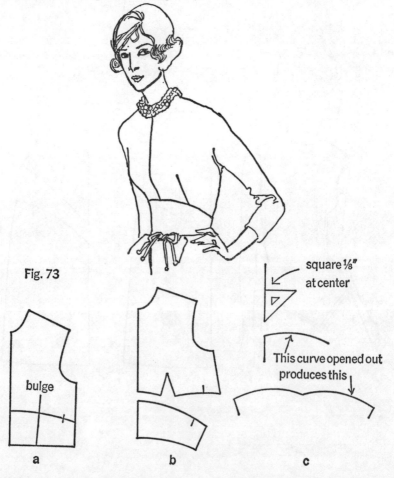

Fig. 73

square ⅛″
at center

This curve opened out
produces this

bulge

a   b   c

When the yoke is cut away, note that part of the dart control appears in the joining seam and part on the yoke side seam.

The midriff section of this unfitted dress is bodice yoke plus skirt yoke. The basis for this design is the hip-length sloper (Fig. 74).

1. Trace the hip-length sloper (see page 119). Cut out the darts. Close the waistline bodice-skirt dart and fasten it with Scotch tape. (It's easier to do this if you first slash the waistline. It can be closed at a later stage.) By doing this, you've created a partial bulging block—all that is necessary to produce the pattern for this design.

2. Draw the midriff yoke style lines on bodice and skirt. Notch the style lines (Fig. 74a).

3. Cut away the midriff yoke. Shift the underarm dart to what's left of the bodice waistline dart, thus enlarging it (Fig. 74b).

4. Slash open the vertical midriff dart but close the waistline slash. The midriff pattern should now lie flat (Fig. 74b). In this design this much midriff dart control is left as unstitched fullness.

5. Trace the bodice and midriff patterns. Close the skirt dart. Extend the remainder of the skirt pattern to full length (Fig. 74c). Add flare by the method described on page 144.

6. Complete the pattern.

Fig. 74

CALL ATTENTION TO A BEAUTIFUL MIDRIFF

Color it (Fig. 75a), bare it (Fig. 75b), embellish it (Fig. 75c). Whatever you choose to do, develop the pattern by the method used in Fig. 74.

Fig. 75

A YOKE THAT DOESN'T QUITE MAKE IT

Here is a yoke that is cut only part way from the rest of the bodice. The pattern is all in one piece.

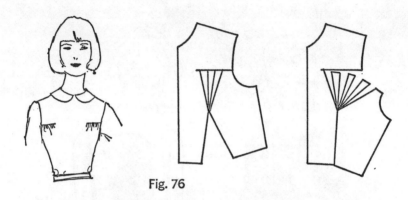

Fig. 76

The waistline dart control can be shifted all or in part to the partial yoke line. Like all dart control it may be used in this position as one dart, multiple darts, dart tucks, or gathers.

Since there is practically no seam allowance at the point where the slashing stops, it is difficult to sew designs like this. Here are two ways in which this can be overcome.

1. Reinforce the point with staystitching, slash, turn to the underside, stitch the seam tapering off the point.

2. Reinforce the point with a patch of organza stitched to the right side as a facing. Slash, turn to the underside, press. Use the organza as a seam-allowance stitching close to the previous line of stitching.

THE CONTOUR BELT

The contour belt is really a very narrow hip yoke.

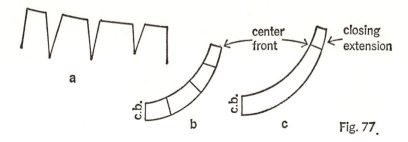

Fig. 77.

1. Trace the upper portion of the skirt-front and skirt-back slopers. Straighten the side seams (Fig. 77a).

2. Close the front, back, and side darts. Correct the waistline with a curved line. Draw the style line (Fig. 77b).

3. Cut the yoke from the rest of the skirt. Add extensions for the underlap and overlap (Fig. 77c).

4. Complete the pattern.

THE DOUBLE-CONTOUR BELT

The double-contour belt is composed of two contour belts, one for the bodice and one for the skirt, joined at the waistline. The directions for Fig. 77 will produce the skirt part. See directions for the midriff yoke (Fig. 73) for the bodice part. Join at the waistline. Close in any manner desired at the center front or center back, but be sure to make due allowance for the closing.

STITCH AND REJOIN—DESIGN POSSIBILITIES

If you have to stitch two or more sections of a garment together to form a complete front or back unit, why not make decorative use of the parts and the seaming that joins them?

Use every trick in the bag: color (Fig. 78a), texture (78b), grain (Fig. 78c), topstitching (Fig. 78d), decorative applications (Fig. 78e), insertions of lace or edgings (Fig. 78f), pipings or

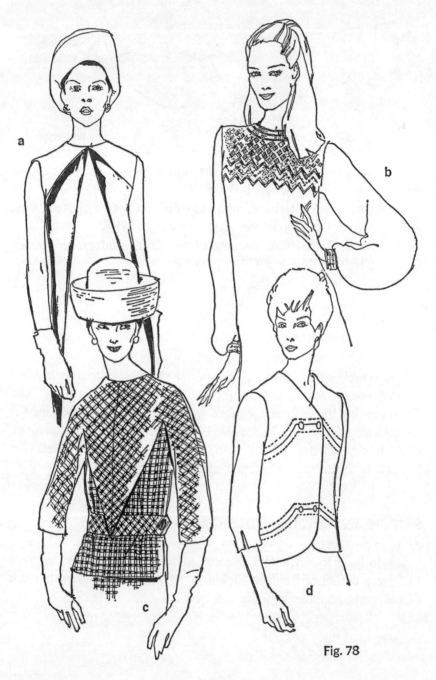

Fig. 78

bandings to apply over the seam or insert in the seam (Fig. 78g), insertions of belts, bands, pockets, welts (Fig. 78h). In fact, use anything your unleashed fancy and ingenuity can devise. The sky's the limit!

Fig. 78

REPEAT PERFORMANCE—SIMILAR SEAMS

In design a degree of repetition makes for harmony.* The eye is pleased to see a line it has met before.

In Fig. 79, each of the designs features a pair or trio of similar seam lines. One of the seams is a control seam. The other has been added for emphasis. Can you tell which carries the dart control? Yes, it is the one that comes closest to the bust point.

In Fig. 79a, the dart control appears in the lower seam. The width and shape of the band are in no way altered. The upper seam is purely decorative.

On the bodice-front sloper, draw the style lines of the band (see page 110). Make them parallel. Notch both style lines. Cut the sections apart. Shift all or part of the waistline dart control to the lower seam.

The shape of the inset band is interesting by itself. Topstitching would give even more importance to its lines. The dress would be very effective if the three sections were in gradations of the same color (a warm beige, apricot, and orange) or in contrasting colors (red, white, and blue).

In Fig. 79b, the inset band is developed in the same way. Despite the straight appearance of the lines, they are slightly curved to conform to the shape of the body.

In Fig. 79c, it is the upper seam that is the control seam. This pattern is easier to plan on the bulging block than on the flat sloper.

* Too much repetition can become monotonous. Plan just enough.

Fig. 79

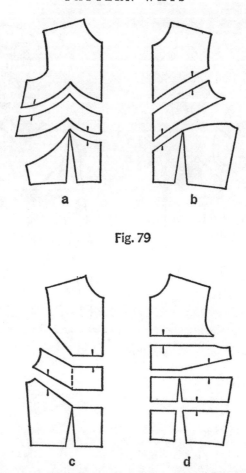

Fig. 79

Close the waistline dart. Sketch the band so the upper line touches the dart point. Mark notches. Cut the band away from the rest of the bodice. A tiny bit of the closed dart control remains forever (ignored) in the band.

In Fig. 79d, the horizontal center seam of the jacket carries part of the dart control. The rest remains as unstitched control at the waistline for the boxy design. The top and bottom seam lines merely repeat the line of the control seam for design interest.

CONTROL SEAMS IN BACK, SKIRT, SLEEVE

The foregoing discussion of control seams has dealt with the bodice front. The principles illustrated work just as well in a bodice back, in a skirt, and in a sleeve.

THE BODICE BACK YOKE

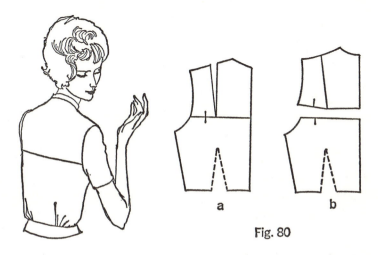

Fig. 80

1. On the cut-out bodice-back sloper with the cut-out darts, draw the style line for the yoke. Make it at right angles to the center back. Notch the style line (Fig. 80a).

2. Extend the shoulder dart to the style line (Fig. 80a).

3. Slash the style line.

4. Cut out the extended dart and close it. Note that the dart control is shifted to the control seam at the armhole (Fig. 80b).

5. Correct the shoulder line and the seam lines as necessary. Consider using the dart control of the lower bodice as dart tucks or gathers.

6. Complete the pattern.

CONTROL SEAM IN A TWO-PIECE SLEEVE

The elbow dart control of a one-piece sleeve can be divided and shifted to the control seam of a two-piece sleeve.

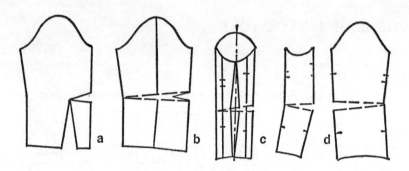

Fig. 81

1. Trace the sleeve sloper. Cut out the tracing and the dart. Shift some of the dart control to the wrist to widen it (Fig. 81a).

2. Extend the elbow dart across the width of the sleeve (Fig. 81b). Fold it out. Fasten temporarily.

3. Draw a line dividing the sleeve in half from cap to elbow, from elbow to wrist (Fig. 81b).

4. Fold each side of the sleeve so the underarm seam touches the center line at the armhole and the wrist (Fig. 81c). Fasten with Scotch tape.

5. Locate new seam lines in the underarm section—1 inch in from the fold at the armscye, ¾ inch at the elbow, and ½ inch at the wrist (Fig. 81c). Notch the seam lines. The underarm section is generally one-third of the total width of the sleeve. Adjust the above measurements accordingly.

6. Cut away the underarm section. Unfold the elbow dart to ¼ inch (not all of its control). Completely unfold the dart in the upper sleeve (Fig. 81d). As you can see, some of the dart control has been shifted to the sleeve seam, making it a control seam. Mark an area 2 to 3 inches at the elbow of the upper sleeve to be eased into the corresponding area of the under sleeve.

7. Correct the seam lines with slightly curved lines. The grain line is the center line of each sleeve section (Fig. 81e). Complete the pattern.

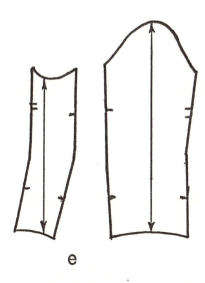

e

Fig. 81

... AND SKIRTS, TOO

The Six-Gored Skirt—three gores front, three gores back.

1. Trace the skirt-front and skirt-back slopers but do not trace the darts. Eliminate the flare by straightening the side seams from the hips to hem.

2. Draw gore lines one-third over from center front and center back and parallel to them (Fig. 82a).

3. Center the front and back darts on the gore lines and trace (Fig. 82a).

4. Place notch marks at the dart points. Establish the grain parallel to the center front and center back in each side-skirt section (Fig. 82a).

5. Cut out the pattern. Cut out the darts. Slash the style lines. The control now rests in the seams that join the gores—front, side front, side back, and back (Fig. 82b).

6. A more graceful skirt will result from a small amount of flare (1 to 2 inches) added at the hem of each control seam (Fig. 82c). The flare starts at the hips and extends to the hem.

7. Trace the pattern, correcting the control seam lines with slightly curved lines from the hips to waistline.

8. Label each section. The center gores are placed on a fold of fabric; cut two of each side gore (Fig. 82c).

9. Complete the pattern.

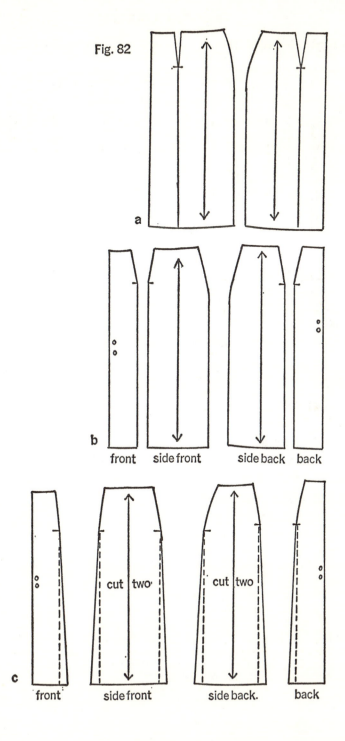

Fig. 82

a

b

front   side front   side back   back

c

cut two   cut two

front   side front   side back.   back

The Eight-Gored Skirt—four gores front, four gores back.

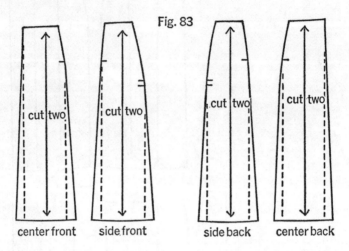

Fig. 83

center front   side front   side back   center back

Make the pattern for this skirt by the same method as the six-gored skirt with these exceptions:

1. Divide each skirt sloper in half. Move the darts to the gore line.*

2. The center front and center back become seam lines instead of folds of fabric.

3. Add flare at center front and center back to balance the flare on the opposite control seams.

4. The grain line in each gore is parallel to the original center front and center back.

5. Cut two of each section.

---

* An alternate method for handling the dart control follows: Divide the dart control so that two-thirds of the amount is placed on the gore line and one-third at the center seam. This will make for an even distribution of the control when all front and all back sections are stitched together.

A One-Sided Affair

Control seams may be asymmetric as they are in the clever seaming of this design (Fig. 84). Use a complete bodice sloper to develop the pattern. Work out each side differently.

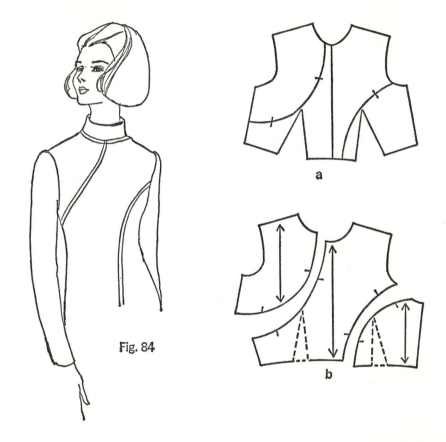

Fig. 84

1. Draw the style lines, making each touch a dart (Fig. 84a).
2. Slash the pattern on both style lines.
3. Close part of each dart (an equal amount) throwing some of the waistline control to each seam. The rest remains unstitched for some fullness (Fig. 84b).

THE HIP-LENGTH SLOPERS

Using the information in these first chapters you could (by now) make a very attractive dress. Its design would be a bodice developed from the bodice sloper. Its skirt would be a design developed from the skirt sloper. They would be joined by a waistline seam.

What if you don't want a waistline seam? What if you *do* want a seam above or below the natural waistline? For these designs you will need a hip-length or full-length sloper.

The hip-length sloper can be used for any design that extends below the natural waistline. With some modifications, it becomes the sloper to use for designing blouses, jackets, vests, coats.

The following exercises give measurements for a standard size 12 pattern.

For individual hip-length slopers, use personal measurements.

FRONT HIP-LENGTH SLOPER

1. Trace the bodice-front sloper. Cut out the tracing and the dart. Trace the skirt-front sloper. Cut out the tracing but *not* the dart.

2. On the skirt sloper, mark the front-hip depth (7 inches) and the side-hip depth (7½ inches). Draw a slightly curved line connecting the two points.

3. Cut away the hip section of the skirt. Line up the skirt and bodice waistline darts. Extend the skirt dart to the hip line and cut it out.

4. Attach the center-front skirt section to the center-front bodice section at the waistline. Attach the side-front skirt section to the side-front bodice section in the same way (Fig. 85a). Don't be surprised to find a slightly curved opening at the waistline. This is because bodice and skirt waistlines are opposing curves. (Incidentally, this is where and why a one-piece, fitted dress wrinkles.) Ignore the space in this pattern.

5. On the bodice-front sloper, shift some of the waistline dart control to an underarm dart. If the bodice waistline dart is closed to match the skirt dart, the underarm dart must really carry the burden of the shaping (Fig. 85b). If the largest amount of control remains at the waistline, the skirt dart control will end in a dart tuck rather than a dart (Fig. 85c).

6. Correct the angularity at the side waistline with a gentle curve (Fig. 85b and 85c).

The amount of dart control shifted depends on the figure requirements or the design to be developed. For example:

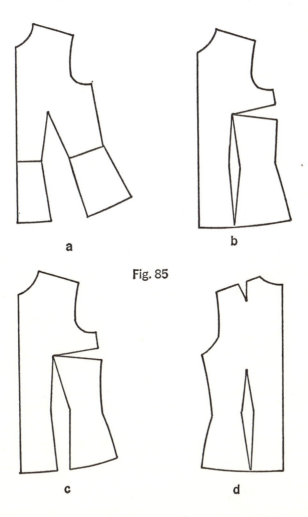

a

b

Fig. 85

c

d

FIG. *86a*

A dress with the waistline dart control left unstitched for fullness and an underarm dart that does the shaping would be designed on Fig. 85b.

FIG. *86b*

A dress with shaping in its control seams would be better designed on Fig. 85c.

BACK HIP-LENGTH SLOPER (Fig. 85d)

1. Trace the bodice-back sloper. Cut out the tracing and the waistline dart. Trace the skirt-back sloper. Cut out the tracing but do *not* cut out the dart.

2. On the skirt sloper, mark the back-hip depth (8 inches) and the side-hip depth (7½ inches). Draw a slightly curved line connecting the two points.

3. Cut away the hip section of the skirt. Line up the skirt and bodice waistline darts. Extend the skirt dart to the hip line and cut it out.

4. Attach the center-back skirt section to the center-back bodice section at the waistline. Attach the side-back skirt section to the side-back bodice section in the same way. Make the amount of the skirt dart match that of the bodice dart. If necessary, take the rest of the shaping off the side seam.

5. Correct the angularity at the side waistline with a gentle curve.

For a full-length sloper simply extend the hip-length sloper to full length.

a

Fig. 86   b

"ANYTHING YOU CAN DO, I CAN DO . . ."

Everything that was possible as a variation of dart control in the original five sloper pieces is also possible with the hip-length and full-length slopers: the shifting and division of dart control, control seams, multiple darts and dart tucks, easing, gathering, unstitched fullness—all.

FASHION-IN-THE-ROUND

Though the exercises in this chapter limited the number of divisions of dart control (after all, we were only taking our first baby steps in pattern design), in truth, the number is limitless. Any number will do to create fashion-in-the-round. Be guided by the elements of good design.

What a superbly fitting and slimming dress is the Jean Patou in Fig. 87a. See how many ways the total control has been divided in the vertical seaming. *When the center front becomes a seam line it, too, can be used for shaping.*

If you think multiple dart tucks are fuddy-duddy, just study the fascinating midriff of this Cardin design (Fig. 87b).

Notice how ingeniously the ribbon stripe of the material has been used for the shaping with multiple control seams (Fig. 87c).

These are but a tiny sampling of the infinite design possibilities of control seaming. Do they whet your appetite?

PATTERN WISE

So now you know all the ins and outs of dart control from top to bottom and all the way around. Each new design is a puzzle to be worked out. That's the fun and challenge of pattern making. It's ever different with each passing season and changing fashion. But the principles of dart control remain the same.

When it comes to dart control in design—you're now on your own!

Fig. 87

Chapter V

SLASH, SPREAD, AND SWIRL

There's nothing that makes you feel more the woman you are than yards and yards of fabric swirling as you pirouette. Be it flare or flounce, it's feminine!

Until now all of our designs—even those that appeared to be full rather than fitted—have been variations of the basic dart control. However, there are many times when more fullness is desired than is possible through the use of dart control alone.

There are two types of additional fullness: circular and balanced.

TYPE 1 CIRCULAR FULLNESS

In this type (Fig. 88a) there is a change in one edge only. The other edge maintains the original measurement. (This is the fullness of a flared or circle skirt.)

TYPE 2 BALANCED FULLNESS

In this type (Fig. 88b) there is equal change on both edges. (This is the fullness of a dirndl or knife-pleated skirt.)

Wherever found—in blouses, skirts, sleeves, collars, cuffs, peplums, capes, jabots, pants, jackets, coats, etc.—the methods of producing fullness are the same.

a

b

Fig. 88

SLASH AND SPREAD FOR CIRCULAR FULLNESS

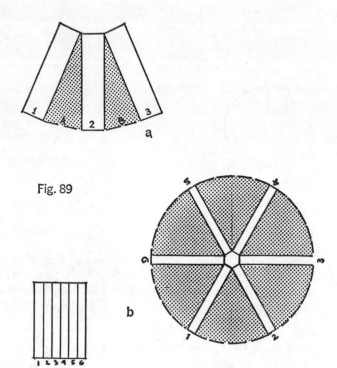

Fig. 89

1. On paper of sufficient size draw a rectangle and divide it into equal parts. The more circular the design, the more parts you will need to establish the outside line of the pattern.

2. Slash each of the dividing lines *to* one edge* but not through it. Start the slashing at the edge you want to make full.

3. While maintaining the measurement of one edge, spread the other to the desired fullness, making sure to leave equal spaces between the strips (Fig. 89a).

4. Using the strips as a guide, draw the new (full) edge with a curved line. In circularity, the fullness spreads open like a fan or a sunburst. If spread sufficiently, a complete circle is obtained (Fig. 89b).

---

* The slash must go clear across the pattern to the opposite side. Only then will it lie flat. A partial slash when spread produces bulging and straining.

SLASH AND SPREAD FOR BALANCED FULLNESS

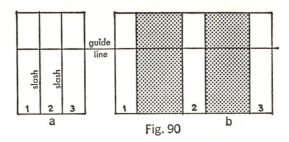

Fig. 90

1. On paper of sufficient size draw a rectangle and divide it into equal parts.

2. Draw a horizontal guideline at right angles to one side (Fig. 90a). This is necessary so that you will know how to line up the strips after they have been cut apart and separated. When shaped pattern strips are involved it is also a good plan to number them so that you will know in what order to put them together again (see Fig. 109).

3. Slash all slash lines.

4. On another sheet of paper of sufficient size (considering the projected fullness) draw a horizontal guideline.

5. Place the strips of paper in the correct order, matching the guidelines, and spread to the desired fullness (Fig. 90b). The guideline acts as a skewer on which all the little strips are speared in position. Make certain that the spaces between the strips are equal and that the strips are equidistant both top and bottom.

6. Trace the outline (across the open spaces), correcting any lines as necessary.

How much you spread the sections for any type of fullness—circular or balanced—depends on the design and the fabric you plan to use. You may have to do some experimenting before you decide just what the fullness should be.

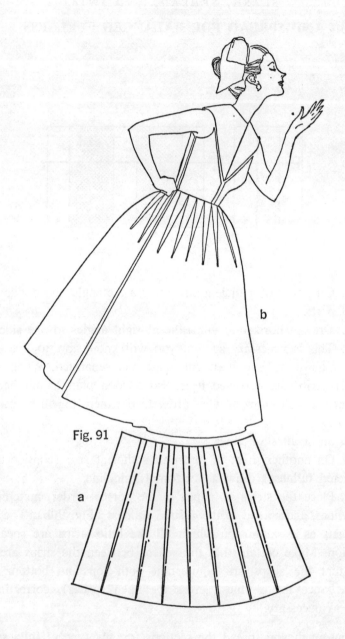

Fig. 91

A CURVE THAT COMES TO YOU STRAIGHT

It is possible to reverse the slash-and-spread procedure and still get circularity. The slash-and-overlap method is useful if you know the length of the cloth you have to work with.

1. Start with paper of the given length. Divide it into equal parts.

2. Slash each slash line. This time start the slashing at the edge you want to make smaller.

3. While maintaining the larger edge, overlap the other to the desired measurement. Make certain that the amount of the overlap is equal on each of the strips (Fig. 91a).

4. Trace the new lines, correcting the angularity with a curved line.

ANOTHER WAY TO GET A CURVE—BY DARTS

A straight length of material if sufficiently *darted* to its full width will also produce the circularity of Fig. 91a. This is a good method to use when you have a length of fabric that you do not wish to cut, for example, heirloom lace. Or, when you do not have enough material for a pattern with circular fullness (it does take more). Or, if you are using a border print.

When the darts are stitched only part way into the width, the result is a bell shape (Fig. 91b). (Curved darts produce beautiful bell shapes.)

HERE IS THE WAY TO ADD CIRCULAR FULLNESS AT A BODICE WAISTLINE

1. Start with a bodice-front pattern that has unstitched dart control at the waistline (Fig. 24). Utilize the fullness provided by the dart control as a base whenever possible (Fig. 92a).

2. Draw slash lines (Fig. 92a).

3. Slash and spread to the desired fullness. *Add half the spread at the center front* so the fullness is continuous across the entire bodice (Fig. 92b). This line becomes the new center front.

4. Trace the pattern. Unless you want a taut look to your design, *add length for blousiness* along the entire waistline (Fig. 92c). Designs with width fullness generally require added length as well.

5. Trace the pattern (Fig. 92d) and complete it.

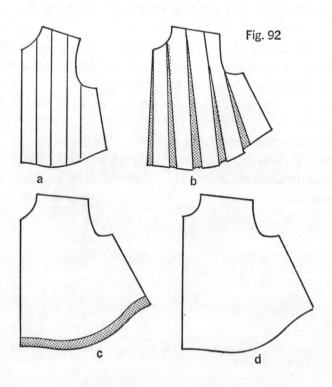

Fig. 92

a

b

c

d

Fig. 92

CIRCULAR FULLNESS ADDED AT THE WAISTLINE OF A SKIRT

Waistline fullness can be laid in folds, be tucked, or gathered to the waist measurement.

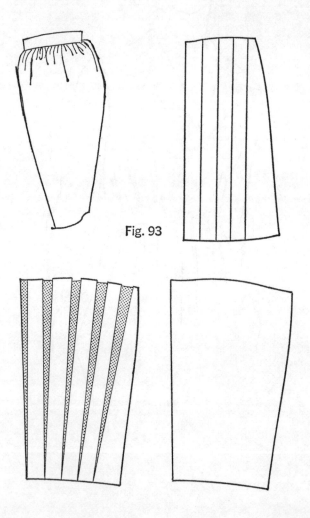

Fig. 93

Fig. 93 shows a pattern development similar to that of the bodice. No blousiness, hence no additional length is needed.

CIRCULAR FULLNESS AT THE HEM OF A SKIRT

The swinging motion of a circular skirt has made it a perennial favorite. There are several ways of achieving the circularity.

The simplest (and least) amount of fullness results from shifting the dart control to the hemline (Fig. 26).

For more flare: start with a dartless skirt sloper.

HOW TO MAKE A DARTLESS SKIRT SLOPER

1. Trace the skirt-front sloper (the back-skirt dartless sloper is developed in the same way).

2. Straighten the side seams from hem to waistline. There will be added fullness at the waistline (A) (Fig. 94a).

3. The amount that has been added at the waistline (A) plus the amount of the original dart (B) must be removed.

Dartless Sloper No. 1

4a. If the dart in the skirt sloper is not too large already, add to it the amount added at the side seam (A) (Fig. 94b). Extend the enlarged dart to the hem (Fig. 94b) and either cut it out or fold it out (Fig. 94c). Trace the pattern. Now the waistline is the correct measurement. The length is correct. The hip measurement is somewhat diminished by the folding-out but the fullness yet to be added will provide plenty of hip room.

Dartless Sloper No. 2

4b. If the dart in the skirt sloper is too large to be handled as in 4a, use the following method. Start with Fig. 94a. Draw a line across the hips. Ignoring A and B, divide the pattern into thirds lengthwise (Fig. 94d). Divide the total amount in excess of the waistline measurement (A plus B) into two equal darts centered over the slash lines and elongated to the hips (Fig. 94d). Slash the slash lines, cut out the darts, and close them. This produces a dartless sloper with considerable flare (Fig. 94e). Trace the pattern.

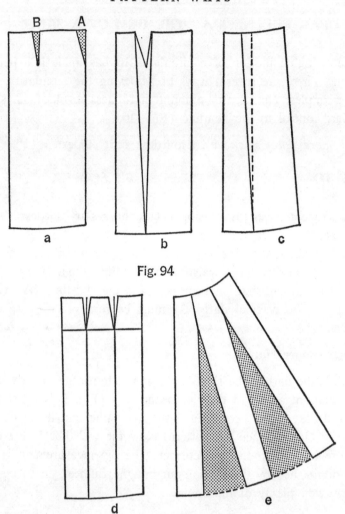

Fig. 94

ADD FULLNESS TO THE DARTLESS SLOPER

To No. 1 Sloper

1. Divide the pattern into thirds at waistline and hem.
2. Slash and spread at hem to desired fullness (Fig. 95a).
3. Trace the pattern.

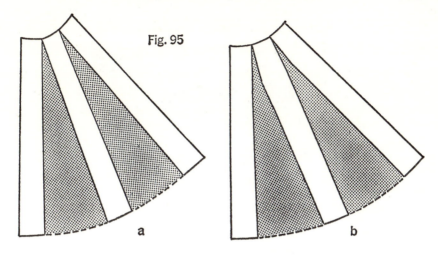

Fig. 95

a   b

To No. 2 Sloper

1. Spread the cut-apart strips to the desired fullness at the hem (Fig. 95b).

2. Trace the pattern.

AN EASY WAY TO MAKE A CIRCULAR SKIRT

Now you know the theory of adding fullness to the sweep of a skirt. For practical purposes all you really need to know is the waist measurement and the length.

HOW TO MAKE THE PATTERN FOR A SEMI-CIRCLE SKIRT

1. Start with a rectangle the sides of which are equal to the *full* front-waistline measurement and the length of the skirt.

2. Divide it into equal parts—at least six, preferably more.

3. On another sheet of paper, draw a right angle.

4. Slash the pattern. Spread the strips for circularity against the right angles so that the side seams will be on straight grain, one

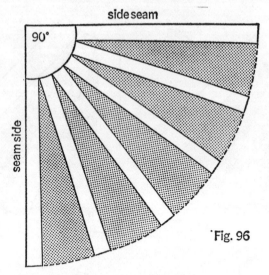

side seam

90°

seam side

`Fig. 96

vertical, the other horizontal. The center front will be on the bias (Fig. 96).

5. Trace the pattern, correcting the angularity of waistline and hemline with curved lines. Complete the pattern.

Make the pattern for the skirt back in the same way.

HOW TO MAKE THE PATTERN FOR A CIRCLE SKIRT

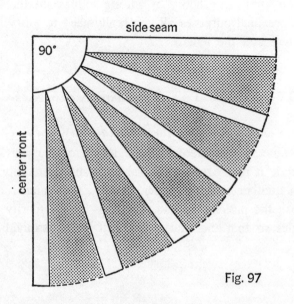

side seam

90°

center front

Fig. 97

1. Draw a rectangle (*half* the front-waistline measurement by the length of the skirt).

2. Divide it into equal parts—at least six, preferably more.

3. Slash and spread the strips for circularity against a right angle so that the center front and the side seam are on straight grain while the areas between them are on the bias (Fig. 97).

4. Trace the pattern correcting the angularity of waistline and hemline with curved lines. The center front is generally placed on a fold of fabric. When the skirt front is opened out it will be half a circle. Complete the pattern.

Develop the pattern for the skirt back in the same way.

For a Double-Circle Skirt—use a whole circle for the front and a whole circle for the back. To make this pattern you would need to quarter the waistline measurement and proceed as for the circle skirt.

For a Gathered Circle or Semi-Circle Skirt—spread the cut-apart strips for balanced fullness (the amount desired at the waistline); then spread for circularity against a square (Fig. 98).

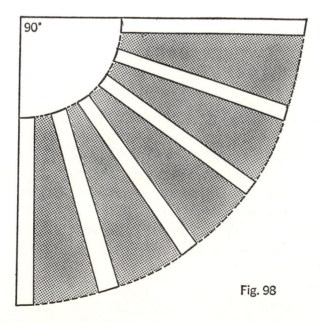

Fig. 98

CONSIDER THE FABRIC

For much fullness use very soft or very filmy materials (chiffon, tulle, net, silk, etc.).

Unless your fabric is extremely wide or the size of the pattern extremely small or the skirt very short (skating skirt), the material will need to be pieced for extra width. The piecing must look like an extension of the fabric. The added piece must be cut on the same grain. If there is a decorative weave or print, it is desirable that the motifs match. The piecing must be placed in such position that it will be lost in the folds (Fig. 99).

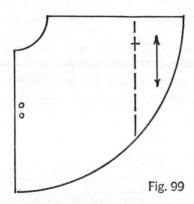

Fig. 99

A NOTE ON SKIRT WAISTBANDS

The narrower the band, the better it will hug the waist. Waistbands of 1 inch or 1½ inches are quite satisfactory. When they are wider than this, some shaping is necessary to fit the curve of the waist. A ¾-inch bias waistband works well.

The length of the waistband is equal to the waist measurement *plus* ease, *plus* an allowance for an extension (underlay or overlap), *plus* seam allowance.

FOR EXAMPLE: the length of the waistband for a 26-inch waist will be:

26 inches	—waist measurement
½ inch	—ease
1½ inch	—extension
1 inch	—two (½-inch) seam allowances
29 inches	—Total

The width will be:

2 inches	—1-inch waistband folder over
1 inch	—two (½-inch) seam allowances
3 inches	—Total

A wider waistband is drafted like a midriff band.

Waistbands are generally cut on the straight of the material. When cut on the bias a correction must be made to allow for the bias-stretch of the material. (See below—waistline measurement for circular skirts.)

CORRECTED WAISTLINE MEASUREMENT AND WAISTBAND FOR CIRCULAR SKIRT

A considerable portion of a circular skirt is bias. All bias areas stretch. There is the additional pull on the waistline of the weight of the material. Therefore, in reckoning the length of the waistline make it 1 inch to 2 inches less than the actual body measurement. How much will depend on the amount of fullness and the heaviness of the fabric.

This corrected measurement also tends to make the skirt fit more smoothly over the hips by lowering the point at which the folds or ripples start.

Stretch the new skirt waistline to fit the skirtband whose measurements are in no way changed unless the band is cut on the bias. In the latter case, the measurement for the bias band would be that of the corrected circular-skirt waistline.

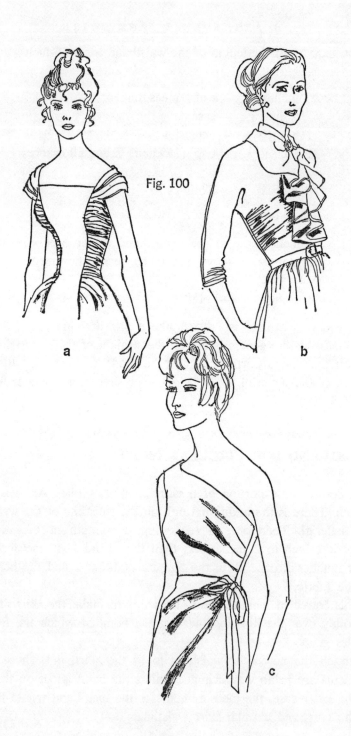

Fig. 100

a

b

c

NON-VERTICAL, NON-AXIAL, CIRCULAR FULLNESS

Additional fullness need not be vertical or balanced on an axis (both sides the same). It may be horizontal (Fig. 100a), diagonal (Fig. 100b), or asymmetrical (Fig. 100c).

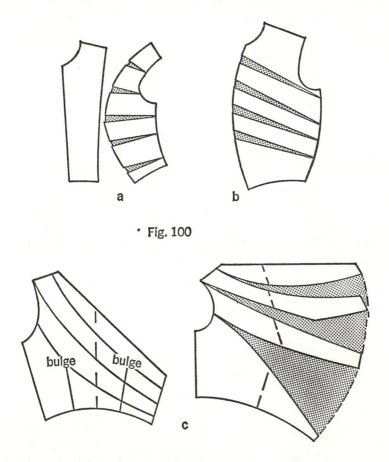

· Fig. 100

FIG. *100a* is shaped by a control seam. The additional fullness is in the side bodice.

FIG. *100b*. The dart control has been shifted to a French underarm dart consistent with the diagonal direction of the slashes. The fullness provided by the dart control is utilized as the basis for additional fullness.

FIG. *100c*. Draw the cut-away neckline on a complete bodice-front sloper. (See page 196 for directions). Close the waistline darts and Scotch tape them. Draw three slash lines from the left side seam to the opposite side as illustrated. Note that the upper slash touches the left dart point, the lower one the right. Slash and spread until the new neckline lies directly on the horizontal straight grain. In doing so, one takes advantage of the no-ripple, no-stretch straight grain for the surplice line.

HOW TO ADD CIRCULAR FULLNESS AT A NECKLINE

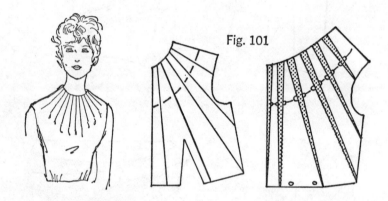

Fig. 101

In a Side-Front Skirt

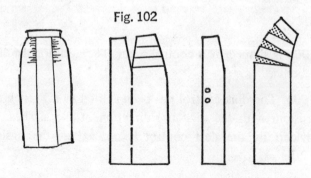

Fig. 102

At the Cap of a Sleeve

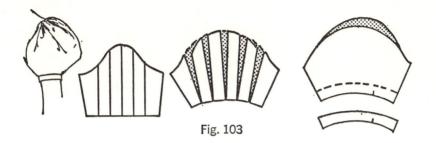

Fig. 103

At a Sleeve Band

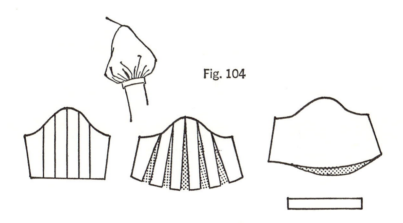

Fig. 104

Below a Bodice Yoke

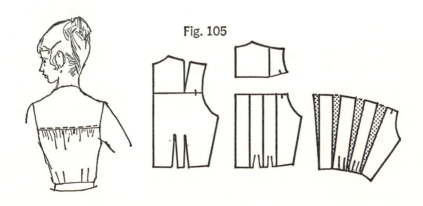

Fig. 105

Below a Hip Yoke

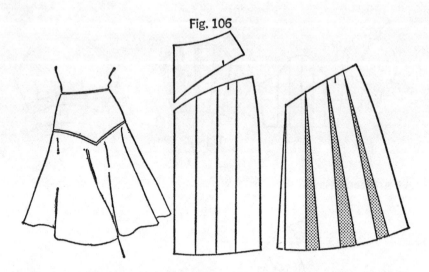

Fig. 106

Above a Midriff

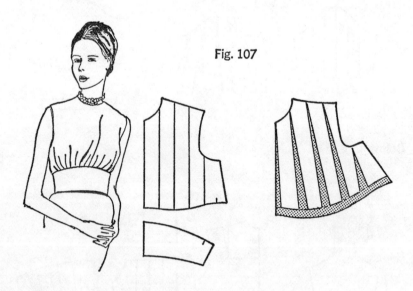

Fig. 107

To a Dart That Enters a Dart

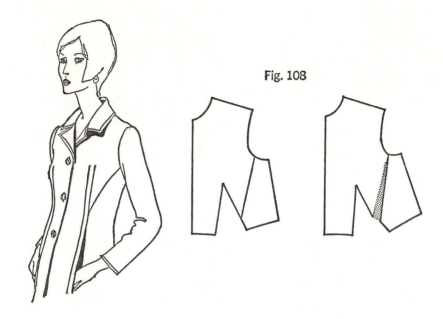

Fig. 108

HERE IS THE WAY TO ADD BALANCED FULLNESS

For a Gathered or Smocked Bodice

1. Start with the bodice pattern of Fig. 24 (unstitched dart control at the waistline).

2. Draw slash lines parallel to the center front. Draw a guideline at right angles to it. Number the sections (Fig. 109a).

3. On another sheet of paper draw a guideline of sufficient length for the expanded pattern.

4. Slash and spread for fullness (Fig. 109b):

a. Spread sections 1, 2, 3, 4 for balanced fullness.

b. Spread sections 5 and 6 for circular fullness in order to keep the fullness continuous at the waistline without enlarging the armhole.

Fig. 109

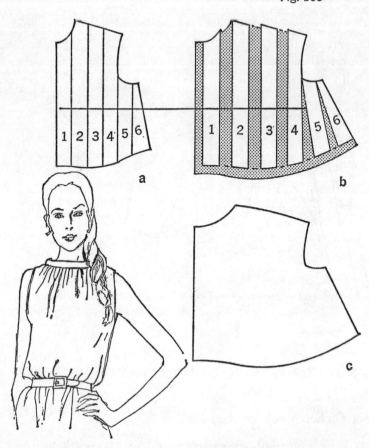

a

b

c

c. Add half the amount of the spread at the center front for continuous fullness.

5. Add length for blousiness (Fig. 109b).

6. Trace the pattern, correcting all seam lines as necessary with appropriate curves (Fig. 109c).

7. Complete the pattern.

The amount of added fullness may be anything suitable for the design and material to be used.

The bodice back is done in the same way.

For a Gathered Skirt

Cut the pattern to the following dimensions: the waist measurement times the amount of fullness (twice, three times, etc.) by the length of the skirt. Add the depth of the hem and seam allowances on all outside edges.

on all outside edges.

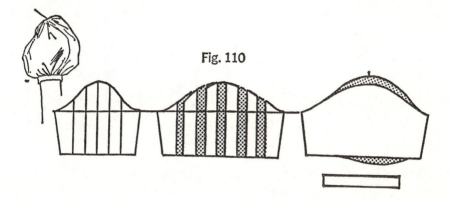

Fig. 110

For Gathers Below A Bodice Yoke

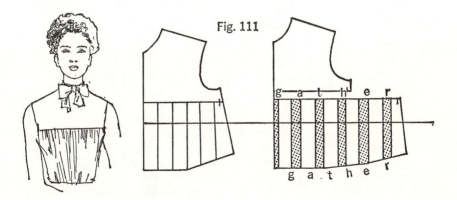

Fig. 111

For Gathers Below a Hip Yoke

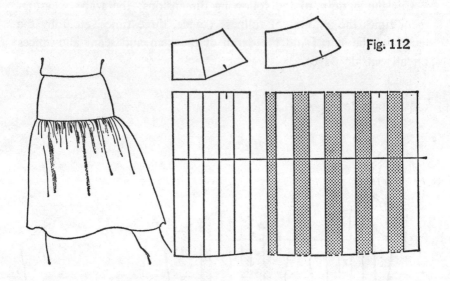

Fig. 112

For a Skirt Flounce

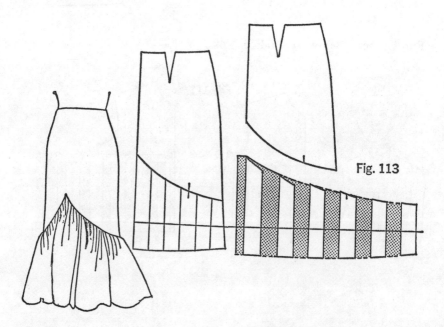

Fig. 113

For a Draped Bodice

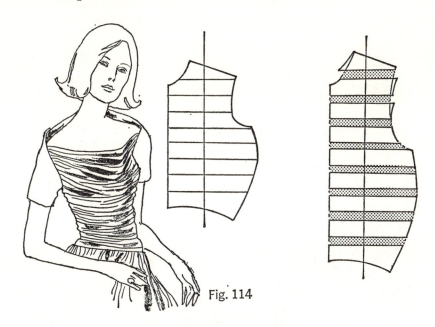

Fig. 114

For Drapery at the Center Front of a Skirt

Fig. 115

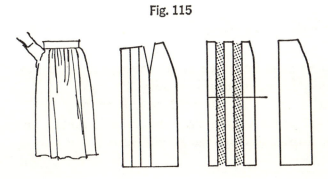

For Diagonal Drapery

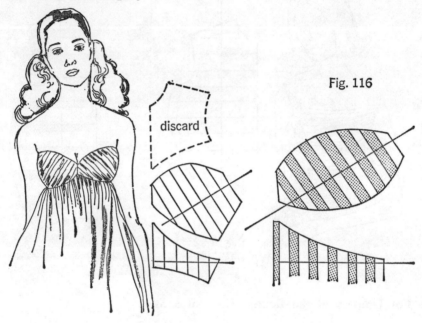

Fig. 116

discard

STAY THE FULLNESS

Fullness looks best when it is controlled in some way. Otherwise its beauty is lost in a general over-all bigness.

Often, a stay is used to hold the fullness in place. The stay is a lining cut to the pattern shape before it is slashed and spread. A stay is shaped by darts and control seams.

PLEATS FOR ADDITIONAL FULLNESS

Pleats are another way of adding fullness under control. It is easy to understand the appeal of pleats in a skirt. They add grace of movement as well as design interest.

MEET THE PLEAT

Pleats come singly, in groups, or in a series.

Fig. 117

c

d

Fig. 117

e

f

Fig. 117

Fig. 117

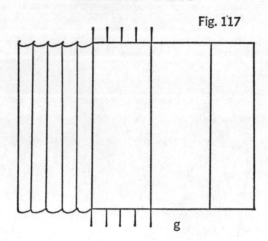

A side pleat is fabric folded to one side. The fold may be in either direction (Fig. 117a).

Knife pleats are crisply pressed, even pleats of any size folded so they all go in one direction (Fig. 117b).

When the folds of two equal side pleats meet at the center on the right side, the pleat is called an *inverted pleat* (Fig. 117c).

A *box pleat* is just the reverse of an inverted pleat (Fig. 117d). The folds turn in opposite directions on the right side and meet at the center on the wrong side.

Accordion pleats are pleats which overlap one another when closed and stand out when worn (just like an accordion). They are even top and bottom (Fig. 117e).

Sunburst pleats are very like accordion pleats with this exception: they are narrow at the top and wider at the bottom producing a flare (Fig. 117f). The fabric is pleated on the bias from one corner of the length of material.

Cartridge pleats are rounded pleats formed to resemble a cartridge belt. They are used strictly for decorative effect (Fig. 117g).

There are *make-believe pleats*. These are really feats of dressmaking. When they are used as part of the styling, the pattern maker must indicate them on the pattern.

Umbrella pleats fall in this category. The lines—pressed or stitched close to the edge like a pin tuck—suggest the rib lines of an umbrella (Fig. 132).

A tuck is a kind of pleat, too. It is a stitched fold of fabric. It may be very narrow or quite wide. Tucks may be used singly, in clusters, or in a series. The series may be of uniform or graduated width.

If you are planning to use narrow tucks (pin tucks), it is simpler to make these in the fabric first, then cut out the fabric from a simple untucked pattern (Fig. 118a).

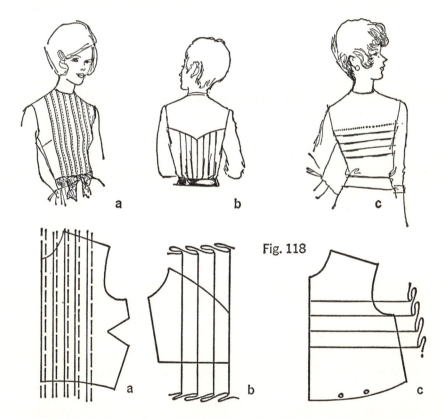

Fig. 118

When striped or plaid material is used, fold out the fabric just as you would like it to appear, pin it or baste it to position, apply a simple untucked pattern and proceed as usual (Fig. 118b).

Horizontal tucks or pleats may be handled in the same way (Fig. 118c).

Pin tucks, knife pleats, accordion pleats and sunburst pleats may be done professionally. This saves the sewer (and the pattern maker) a great deal of work.

THINGS TO CONSIDER ABOUT PLEATS

It is easier to crease, press, or stitch a pleat if it is cut on the lengthwise grain and if its fullness is balanced top and bottom.

Pleats cut on the crosswise grain tend to stand out more stiffly.

Part of a flared pleat is always off-grain. For this reason, a flared pleat is generally a soft fold of fabric. (The exception to this rule is the sunburst pleat.)

Some fabrics hold a pleat better than others. Some can be pressed to crisp edges while others are best left unpressed. It is wise to do a little experimenting with the fabric before deciding which kind of pleat to use.

To stiffen a pleat and make it stand out stitch the edges close to the fold. In soft fabrics or wash-and-wear fabrics, such stitching will ensure pleats that stay in.

Pleats stitched down from waist to hipline give a fitted look to the garment. Pleats released at the waistline make the garment look fuller.

Any seaming necessary for additional length of cloth is always concealed in the depth of a pleat.

HOW DEEP A PLEAT?

Generally, each pleat takes three times its width: the pleat (as it appears on the surface), the underfold (turn-under), the underlay (return) (Fig. 119a).

Sheer fabrics may have shallow pleats. Heavy fabrics require deep pleats.

It is possible to achieve much greater fullness by making the turn-under and the return much deeper than the pleat itself (Fig.

119b). The *kilt pleat* is an example of this type of pleating: a large pleat overlaps half the next one in a one-way series (Fig. 119c).

A good way to use a vast amount of material so it looks comparatively trim is to gather a pleated length.

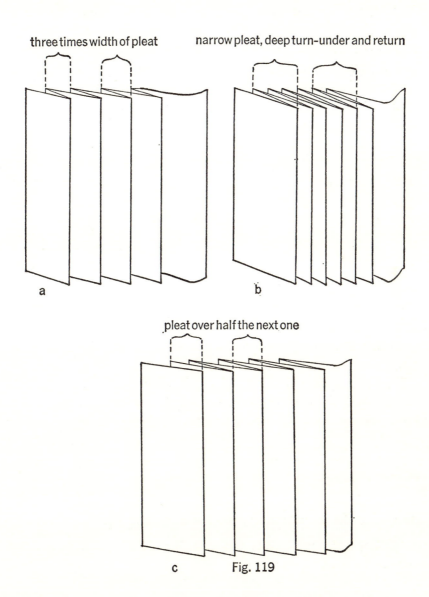

three times width of pleat   narrow pleat, deep turn-under and return

a   b

pleat over half the next one

c   Fig. 119

HOW TO MAKE A STRAIGHT KNIFE-PLEATED OR BOX-PLEATED SKIRT WITHOUT A PATTERN

A little arithmetic is needed to plan the number and size of the pleats. Use the hip rather than the waist measurement for your reckoning. Knife- or box-pleated skirts hang straight from the hips. Don't depend on the open pleats to give the necessary hip-width; they don't look pretty that way. Lay in the pleats to fit the hips. Slightly overlap each pleat from hip to waist for shaping. Keep the top fold on straight grain.

Be mindful of the fact that several inches will be taken up by the folding of the fabric and the inevitable small inaccuracies of making pleats meet.

PLEAT MEETS

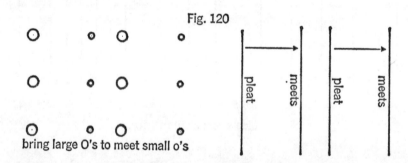

Fig. 120

bring large O's to meet small o's

Pairs of markings are needed for each pleat—one line for the fold of the pleat; the other for the line to which it is brought (Fig. 120). Either of the methods shown in Fig. 120 may be used.

PRETTY PLEATS

How to Make a Pattern For a Pleated Bodice Front

1. Use a sloper with the dart control divided between a waistline and a shortened underarm dart.

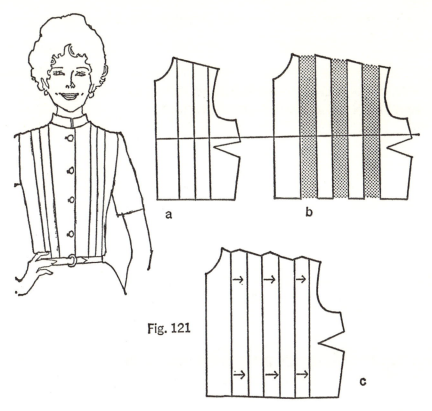

Fig. 121

Pleats in a bodice are used as a decorative detail. Do not depend on them for shaping. They lose all their charm when they pop open over the bust. The control—all or in part— must be elsewhere.

In this blouse, most of the control is in the underarm dart. The rest is used as gathers on the waistline beside the pleats.

2. Draw the lines for the pleats. (If necessary move the waistline dart over toward the side seam.) Draw a guideline at right angles to the center front (Fig. 121a).

3. Draw a guideline on another sheet of paper.

4. Slash and spread for the desired fullness of the pleats. Line up each section on the guideline (Fig. 121b).

5. Fold the pleats toward the side seam. Using your tracing wheel, trace the shoulder line and the waistline.

6. Open out the pattern and sketch in the missing lines (Fig. 121c). Complete the pattern.

THE DIAGRAMS BELOW SHOW HOW TO MAKE THE PATTERN FOR A PLEATED SLEEVE

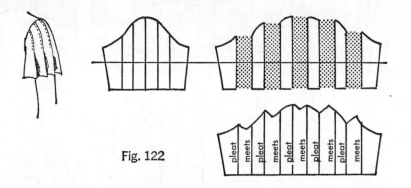

Fig. 122

A BODICE WITH AN INVERTED PLEAT BELOW A SHAPED YOKE

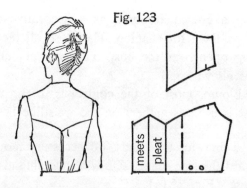

Fig. 123

HOW TO MAKE A PATTERN FOR A KNIFE-PLEATED SKIRT WITH A YOKE PANEL

FIG. *124a.* On the skirt sloper, draw the style lines for the yoke panel and the pleats. Label sections 1, 2, 3, 4. Place notch marks.

Fig. 124

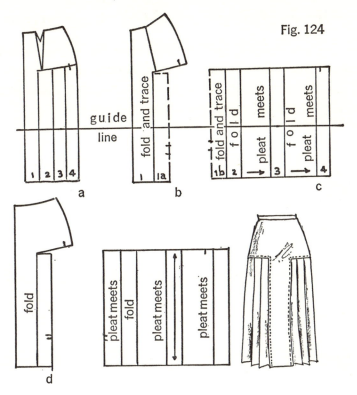

Establish the grain. Draw a horizontal guideline. Extend the dart to the yoke line.

FIG. *124b*. Cut the yoke panel from the side skirt. Close the dart, throwing the control to the yoke seam. Set aside the pattern for the moment.

FIG. *124c*. Draw a guideline on another sheet of paper. Cut the pleats apart. Spread so the spaces between the pleats are twice the width of the pleat.

FIGS. *124 b and c*. The yoke panel in Fig. 124b needs an amount added as a turn-under equal to the width of the first pleat (the broken line in the illustration). The side skirt needs an underlay of equal width added (Fig. 124c).

FIG. *124d*. The completed pattern. The yoke panel and side skirt are joined by a seam hidden under the first pleat.

THE SKIRT WITH INVERTED PLEAT

This skirt is designed so that the turn-under of the pleat is an extension of it while the underlay is a separate piece.

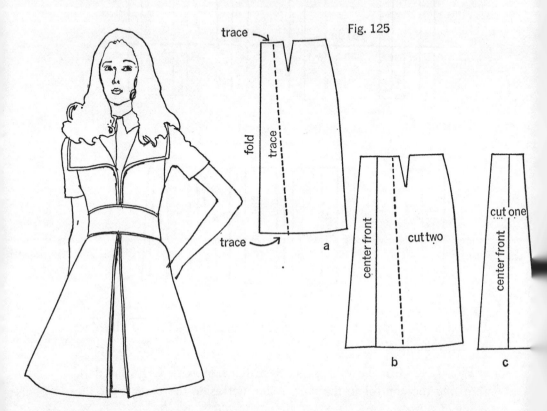

Fig. 125

THE SKIRT PLUS EXTENSION

1. On the front- and/or back-skirt sloper, locate the pleat (broken line in illustration). In this pattern the extension tapers toward the waist (Fig. 125a). This gives a deep pleat at the hemline and less material at the waistline.

2. Fold the pattern on the center front (or back). Using the tracing wheel, trace the pleat, the waistline, and the hemline.

3. Open out the pattern. Pencil the traced lines (Fig. 125b). Cut two of this pattern.

THE UNDERLAY

4. The underlay is equal to the entire pleat as it appears opened out in Step 3, Fig. 125b. Trace the underlay (Fig. 125c). Either place a sheet of tracing paper over the drawing and copy it or place a fresh sheet of paper under the pattern and use the tracing wheel. The center back or front becomes the grain line. Be sure to trace it, too.

5. Complete both parts of the pattern.

A SIDE-PLEATED DRESS

Here is a dress where the right extension becomes a soft pleat (Fig. 126). The left extension becomes the underlay.

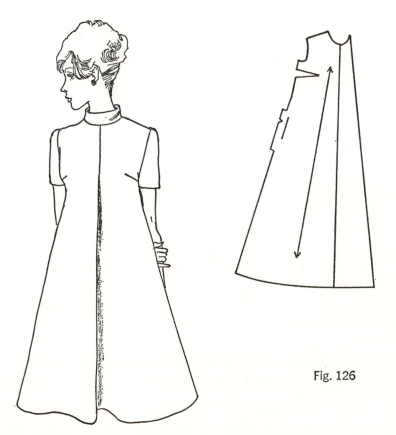

Fig. 126

WAYS OF ELIMINATING BULK IN A PLEATED GARMENT

Pleated garments add bulk to any figure because of the several layers of cloth involved. When the fullness of a pleat is released below a line of stitching, it is possible to eliminate one of the two thicknesses that comprise the underpart of the pleat above the stitching. The second thickness acts as a stay. With this construction the pleat hangs well and no outside stitching is required to hold it in place.

This can be provided for in the pattern (Fig. 127a) or be done after the stitching (Fig. 127b).

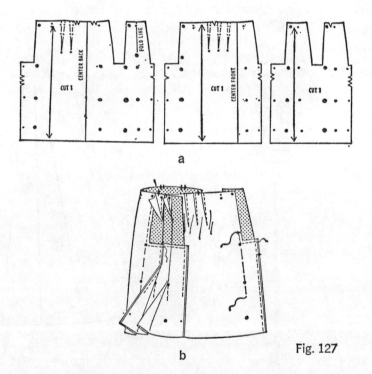

Fig. 127

When both thicknesses of the underpleat are cut away, the pleat must be anchored to the outer fabric by stitching. This is what happens in a kick pleat (Fig. 128).

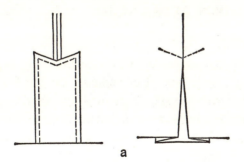

a

Fig. 128

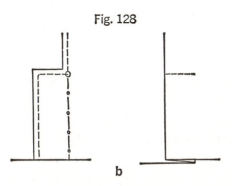

b

A kick pleat may be an inverted pleat (Fig. 128a) or a side pleat (Fig. 128b). The pattern for these designs is made in the same way as for a similar full-length pleat. The only difference is in the length. The kick pleat exists only where the action is needed.

A FLARED BOX-PLEATED SKIRT

1. Start with a pattern for a flared skirt.

2. Draw the flared box pleat centered on the flared skirt (Fig. 129a). (In this design the skirt is divided into thirds. Any reasonable number of box pleats would do as well.) Indicate the center of the pleat with a broken line. Number the sections for easy identification in the construction pattern.

3. Cut the sections apart. Spread so there is a complete pleat's width between them (Fig. 129b).

4. Trace the pattern and complete it. The folds of the box pleat meet at the broken line on the underside.

The bodice of this dress can be drafted from the hip-length slopers.

Undoubtedly you've noticed the circularity of the sleeves. Directions for making the pattern for them will be found in Chapter IX.

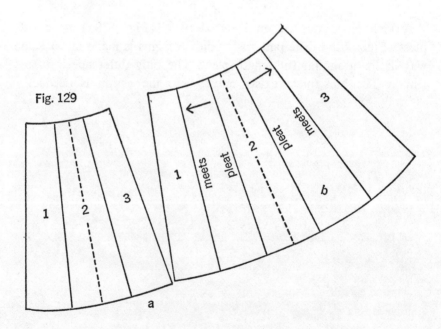

Fig. 129

MORE OF SAME

As full as this box-pleated skirt is it can be made even fuller by double or triple pleats.

Instead of spreading the sections for one pleat as in Step 3, make the spread two or three pleats.

Here is *another method* for making a flared box-pleated skirt.

Fig. 130

1. Divide the waist measurement into the number of pleats you want—say six, though it could be more.

2. Draw a rectangle that is one-sixth of the waist measurement and the full length of the skirt. Mark the position of the hips. Divide the rectangle into thirds lengthwise (Fig. 131a).

3. Slash and spread the strips so the measurement at the hips is one-sixth of the hip measurement (Fig. 131b). Proportionate flare at the hem will be automatic.

4. Trace the pattern, correcting the waistline and the hemline. This is the size of the pleat (Fig. 131c). It also becomes the underlay.

5. To Fig. 131c, add half a pleat's width on each side for the underfold (Fig. 131d).

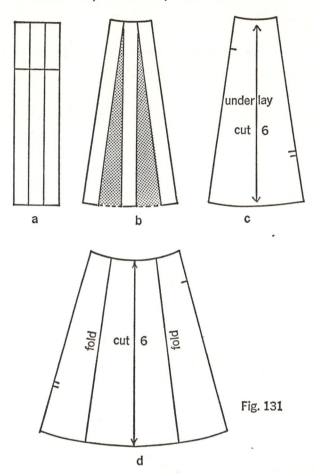

a   b   c

Fig. 131

d

6. Complete the pattern. The center line of each pleat (Fig. 131d) and each underlay (Fig. 131c) is on the straight grain. Cut six pleats and six underlays.

The advantage of this 12-piece pattern is that each pleat and each underlay is cut on straight grain. You can see how helpful this would be in striped, plaid, or checked fabric. Even solid-color fabric falls beautifully when cut so.

This flared box-pleated skirt is very graceful—fitted at the hips and plenty of swing at the hem.

ALTERNATE METHOD. You could arrange the pleats and underlays so they form a circular skirt.

MANY-GORED SKIRT

Instead of being the pleat of Fig. 131c, this section could become one gore of a many gored skirt (Fig. 132).

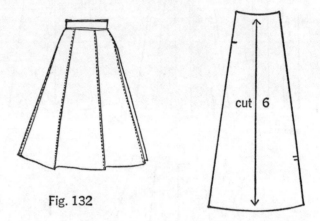

Fig. 132

Here is a way to make a gored skirt out of a circular one.

1. Start with the pattern for a flared or circular skirt.

2. Divide the waistline and the hemline into equal parts. Draw slash lines. Notch for easy assembling (Fig. 133a).

3. Cut the sections apart. Fold each gore in half. The center line is the grain line. Make certain that the gores are balanced on each side (Fig. 133b).

There are two ways of deciding the number and size of the gores or pleats.

a. Divide the entire waistline measurement into the number of pleats or gores. This produces a symmetrical skirt with each pleat or gore equal to the next both front and back.

b. Divide the front waistline measurement into the desired number of pleats and gores. Divide the back waistline measurement into the desired number of pleats and gores. Each pattern is done separately because the front measurement is larger than the back. The number of pleats may be the same but the size is slightly different.

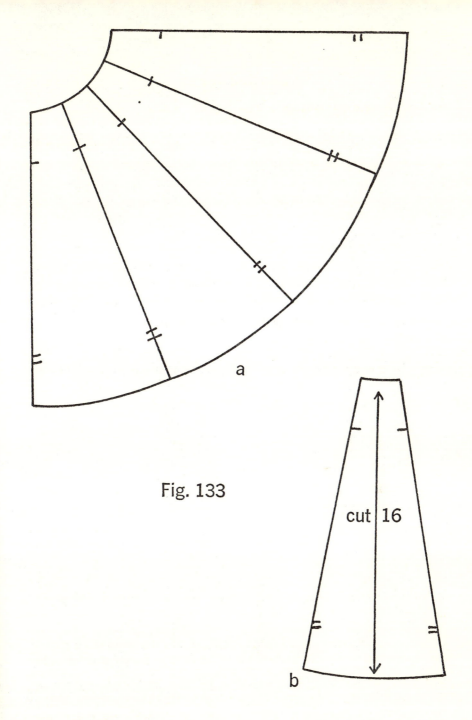

Fig. 133

cut 16

FLARE MAY BE ADDED TO EACH GORE

1. Start with a straight or flared gore, decide where the flare is to begin—at the hips, mid-thigh, knee, mid-calf, or any place between.

2. Draw a line across the gore to indicate the beginning of the flare.

> FIG. *134a*. Decide how much flare is to be added to each side of the gore at the hem. Be mindful of the fact that a few inches at each side of a many-gored skirt adds up to quite a bit of fullness in the finished skirt. Draw a curved seam line, blending it into the sides of the gores.

> FIG. *134b*. Divide the gore into thirds lengthwise. Draw the flare line across the gore. Slash and spread above the flare line

Fig. 134

to the desired fullness. Add fullness below the flare line as illustrated. Draw the side seams, correcting the angularity.

FIG. *134c.* Draw the flare line. Divide the gore below it into thirds. Slash and spread for flare. Draw the side seams correcting the angularity.

3. Add seam allowance and notches to each gore. Draw the grain line, which is in the center of each gore.

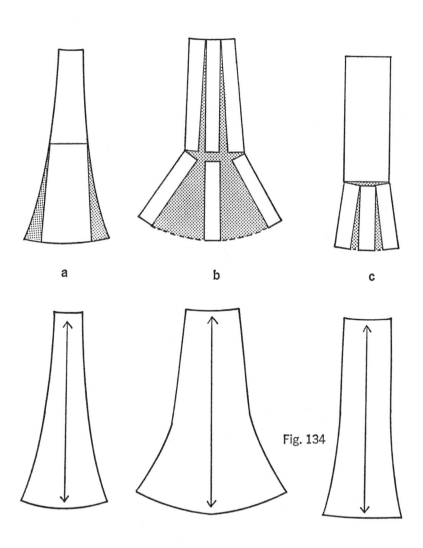

a   b   c

Fig. 134

SEAM—OR SLASH FULLNESS

Fig. 135

a

b

c

Wherever there is a seam, either straight or flared fullness may be added by way of pleats (Fig. 135a) or godets* (Fig. 135b). Even if there is no seam, a pleat or godet can be set into a slash in the fabric (Fig. 135c).

* A godet is a triangular inset of cloth placed in a seam or slash to give fullness.

GODETS

The triangular godet (Fig. 136a) is really an arc of a circle whose radius is the length of the godet (Fig. 136b). The curve of the arc supplies the hemline.

When a godet is inserted into a seam, it is pointed at the top. Were the godet to be set into a slash, it could be rounded instead (Fig. 136c). The center of the godet is generally the straight of goods. For design purposes it could be bias.

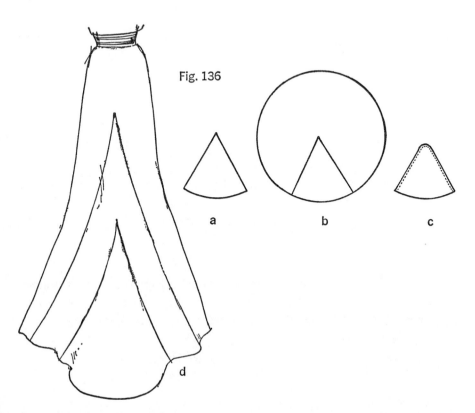

Fig. 136

a

b

c

d

Godets may be as flared as you care to make them. For a flare within a flare (a great wedding-dress train) you might even consider a godet set into the slash of a godet (Fig. 136d).

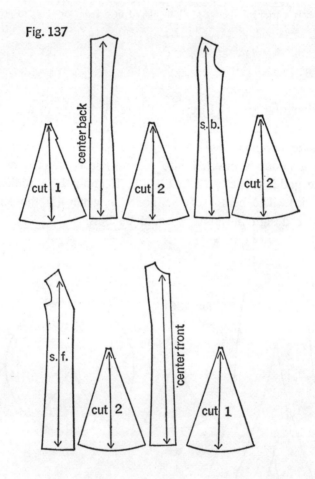

Fig. 137

Fig. 137 shows the pattern for the dress in Fig. 135b: the sections of the dress, the godets, and the markings that facilitate their joining. If you look carefully, you can see a slight difference in the length of the front and back godets. This is because there is an actual difference in front- and back-skirt lengths.

RESEARCH AND DEVELOPMENT DEPARTMENT—An Aid to Your Own Artistry and Skill

All confirmed sewers have drawerfuls of patterns as well as drawerfuls of fabric awaiting the inspiration and time for attention.

Take out some of the patterns in your collection. Study the designs. Read the descriptive matter on the back of the pattern envelope. Try to work out the pattern using your so newly acquired knowledge of dart control and additional fullness. When you have done so, examine the ready-made pattern and compare it with yours. See how close your pattern comes to that of the professional pattern maker.

More than likely, the basic structure of the patterns will be the same. Such differences as there are probably will be in the subtleties of line and proportion.

When you have lost your fear of patterns and when you have done enough of them to feel some confidence, you may surprise yourself by the artistry you will come to display.

PART II

STYLING

Chapter VI

HIGH—LOW NECKLINE

From turtle neck to waistline plunge, it's a neckline! Whether you are muffled to the ears or bared to the bosom, it's still a neckline. It's important, too. Sitting or standing, moving or at rest, your face and adjacent parts of the anatomy are the center of interest. An attractive or arresting neckline is very much a part of the picture.

SCOOPED-OUT NECKLINES

The sloper has a natural neckline, that is, one that curves around the neck from the hollow between the collar bones to the back socket bone. No matter how little or how much, any neckline which drops below this line is a dropped neckline; any neckline that rises above this line is a raised neckline.

In general, when a front neckline is low, the back neckline is high; when the front neckline is high, the back may be low. A deep décolletage, both front and back, presents the problem of keeping it in place (see page 200).

How deeply to scoop out a neckline depends on current fashion, the beauty of the neck, shoulders, and bosom, the shape of the head, the hairdo, the age of the wearer.

If the design is for your own use, past experience, some study, and a little experimentation should help you decide which style lines and which proportions are most pleasing for you.

HOW TO MAKE THE PATTERN FOR A DROPPED NECKLINE

The V Neckline (Front and/or Back)

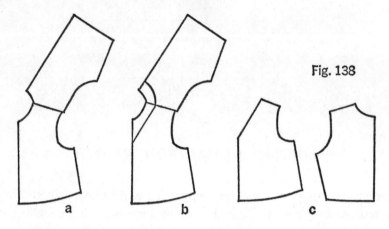

Fig. 138

a   b   c

1. Since both front and back are involved in a neckline, trace the bodice-front and bodice-back slopers. You may work with each separately or as a unit with shoulders touching (Fig. 138a). The latter has this advantage: one feels the rhythm of the line from front to back as a whole. In more complicated styling it is best to develop front and back patterns separately.

2. Decide the front drop, the back drop, and just where the neckline is to appear on the shoulders. This is your great chance to control the drop so it covers your lingerie and shoulder straps.

3. Draw the style line for the neckline (Fig. 138b).

4. Cut out the slopers. Cut away the pattern at the neckline. Discard what you don't need. Separate the front and back patterns (Fig. 138c).

It's that simple! No matter what the shape of the neckline, the method for developing the pattern is the same.

WHAT TO DO ABOUT THAT BACK-SHOULDER DART

Often, the shoulder dart is scooped out along with the neckline. If only a tiny dart is left, you don't need it (Fig. 139a). The amount of the dart can be taken off the neckline at the shoulder.

Fig. 139

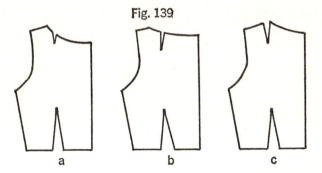

a   b   c

If a reasonable amount of dart is left after cutting away the neck-line, then this must be retained for the shoulder shaping (Fig. 139b). Like any other dart, it may be shifted to another position or to a control seam. The shoulder dart is frequently relocated to the place where shoulder and neckline meet (Fig. 139c).

Following the procedure for the V neckline, develop the patterns for the following:

THE SQUARE NECKLINE

For a better-fitting neckline, square the style line from the shoulder. Square a line from center front.

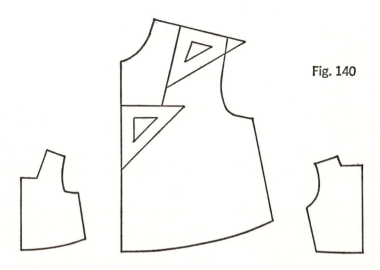

Fig. 140

AN OVAL NECKLINE

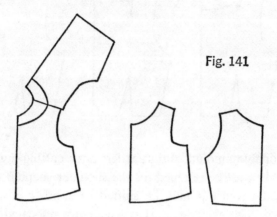

Fig. 141

Don't forget to square a short line at center front and center back before drawing the curve. The neckline will look prettier if the curve, though shallower, is continuous across the shoulders.

These three categories represent the major types of necklines. Enormous variety can be obtained by subtle variations in proportion. Make the patterns for the necklines in Fig. 142. Try to reproduce the exact line and proportion of each.

VARIATIONS OF CLASSIC TYPES

Fig. 142

Coming-and-going necklines: high in front, low in back (Fig. 143a); low in front, high in back (Fig. 143b).

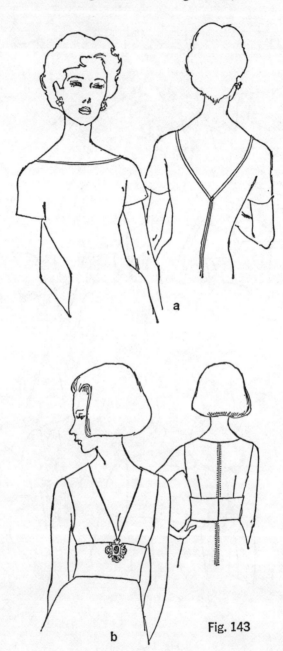

Fig. 143

Novelty necklines can be fun, too.

Fig. 144

Dropped necklines can be designed to include additional fullness.

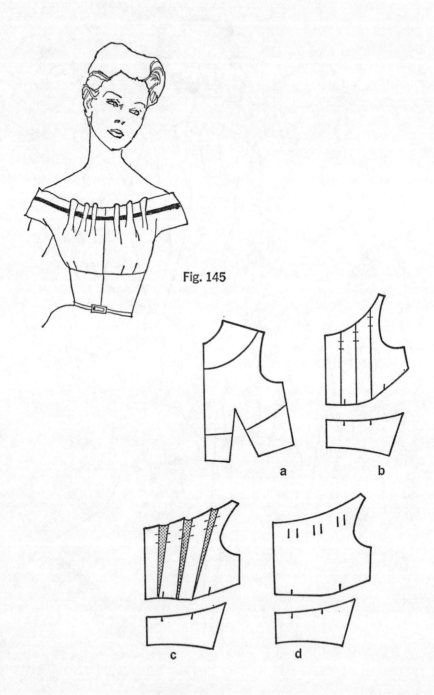

Fig. 145

In this design work out the patterns for the front and back bodices separately.

1. On a cut-out bodice-front sloper with a cut-out dart, draw the style line for the dropped neckline. Draw the style line for the midriff yoke (Fig. 145a). (In like manner, develop the pattern for the bodice-back neckline and midriff yoke.)

2. Cut out the neckline. Cut away the midriff yoke (Fig. 145b). Use the remaining dart control in the upper bodice in any way consistent with the design.

3. Draw the slash lines for the folds (Fig. 145b). Locate the position and size of the openings for the ribbon that will hold the folds in place.

4. Slash and spread for circularity to the desired fullness (Fig. 145c).

5. Trace the pattern (Fig. 145d), and complete it.

THE ASYMMETRIC NECKLINE

All of the foregoing necklines were of the formal balance variety —exactly the same on both sides. The asymmetric neckline is different on each side. Its beauty is in its informal balance. Its exaggerated and free-form style lines can be quite interesting and rather sophisticated. Here are a few asymmetric necklines (Fig. 146).

Fig. 146

In order to work out the pattern for this neckline you will need to use a complete sloper for the bodice front (or back).

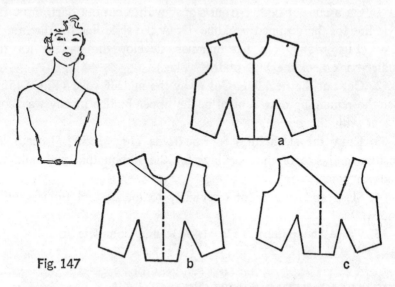

Fig. 147   b   c

1. Trace the complete bodice-front sloper. Decide where on the shoulders you would like the neckline to appear. Decide the position and the amount of the drop (Fig. 147a).

2. Draw the style line (Fig. 147b).

3. Cut out the tracing. Cut out the neckline (Fig. 147c).

4. Complete the pattern.

5. Work out the pattern for the back bodice in the same way.

FINISH WITH A FACING

All outside edges of garments need some finish. Unless the edge is finished with a binding or cording or some decorative trim, it will need a facing for a finish.

If the edge is a straight one, the facing may be an extension of the garment turned back to form a hem. The hem of a skirt is in reality a facing.

If the edge is a curved one, obviously it cannot be turned back without slashing. The resulting raw-edged fringe might be fun on some "far-out" costume but is hardly the finish for a fashionable garment. A curved facing is a separate piece of fabric cut in the same shape and on the same grain as the garment.

All outside edges—straight or curved—are subject to stress and wear. To reinforce these areas and strengthen them, the garment needs an interfacing, too. The interfacing is generally cut from the same pattern as the facing. (In tailored garments, the interfacing is often extended to include some shaping at the shoulder, the chest, and even, in some instances, the bust and hips.)

HOW TO MAKE A PATTERN FOR A FACING AND AN INTERFACING

back facing

c

a   b.

Fig. 148

1. From the new neckline on both front and back, measure down the width of the facing (1½ to 2¼ inches) in a sufficient number of places to ensure that the outside edge of the facing is parallel to the neck edge (Fig. 148a).

2. Draw the facing edge by connecting the markings. Locate the grain line (the same as for the garment). Notch the neckline. Indicate the fold of fabric (Fig. 148b).

Make a slight adjustment in the length of the facing, for it should fit the inside rather than the outside of the garment, which has a slightly larger measurement.

For necklines with a small drop, take off ⅛ inch at the shoulder (more if the fabric is heavy). Or, take off ¹⁄₁₆ inch at the shoulder and ¹⁄₁₆ inch at the center front or center back. When the center front or center back (or shoulder) are so specially shaped as to call for precision matching with the outer fabric, do this: tuck the pattern or slash and overlap it in some place where it will not affect the style line. The latter method works well when the neckline drop is a deep one.

There is another virtue to this slight adjustment. When the smaller facing is stitched to the now relatively larger outer fabric, there is sufficient material to roll the joining seam to the underside of the garment—out of sight.

3. Trace the facing pattern onto another sheet of paper (Fig. 148c). Complete it. Use the same pattern for the interfacing.

Keep facings simple in shape. Eliminate style details and darts. The width of the facing is so comparatively narrow that shaping by small darts and seams is unnecessary.

Should the garment be a sleeveless one, it is easy enough to add the armhole facing to the neck facing. Cut the pattern as one (Fig. 149).

Fig. 149

When a pattern is too cut out for a narrow facing, a complete lining cut to the bodice pattern is used instead for a finish and reinforcement. See the halter design on page 197.

FACING TO THE FORE

Rather than hiding the facing on the inside of the garment, it is possible to apply it to the outside for decorative effect.

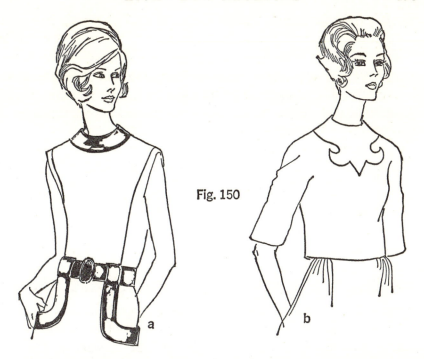

Fig. 150

Fig. 150a shows the facing as a band of contrasting color.

In Fig. 150b the facing becomes a focal point of design interest.

When the facing is applied to the outside, it must be cut slightly *larger* than the garment. This adjustment makes the facing lie flat on the surface. It also adds the size necessary for rolling the joining seam to the underside. To make the adjustment reverse the previous procedure for making the facing smaller.

The interfacing of such a decorative facing is cut without seam allowance. It is applied to the band by hand stitching at the seam line.

From this point on, whenever necessary, your patterns should be drafted with facings.

FIRST AID FOR GAPPING NECKLINES

A dropped neckline should lie flat against the body without any rippling or gapping. This can be accomplished partly by the pattern design and partly by careful cutting, handling, and sewing.

WHY THE NECKLINE GAPS

The sloper has a straight vertical line for its center front (Fig. 151a). The body, however, does not. In profile the body silhouette is more like that of Fig. 151b.* The vertical center-front line stands away from the body contour (Fig. 151c).

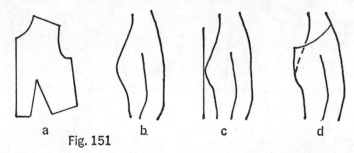

a   b.   c   d

Fig. 151

The lower portion of a bodice is generally controlled by darts (or their equivalent). The upper portion of the bodice above the bust remains as ease in the garment. In a high-necked dress this is desirable. But, in the dropped neckline the ease appears as gapping (Fig. 151d).

---

* Because of the slope from shoulder to bust, some systems of pattern making use the shoulder dart rather than the waistline dart as *the* control dart.

CORRECTION OF SLOPER FOR NARROW CHEST

Gapping can be prevented by designing a dropped neckline on a sloper with ease removed from the chest area.

Fig. 152

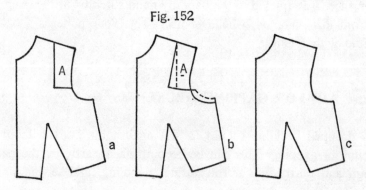

a   b   c

1. On the bodice-front sloper, draw a line from mid-shoulder toward the dart point but ending on a line with the armhole notch (where the armhole swings into the underarm curve) (Fig. 152a).

2. Draw a line across to the armhole (Fig. 152a). Label section A.

3. Slash on both lines. At the chest overlap section A to the amount of ease you wish to remove (Fig. 152b).

4. Correct the underarm curve of the armhole (Fig. 152b).

5. Trace the new pattern (Fig. 152c).

Gapping is accentuated in figures with narrow shoulders, narrow chests, and smaller-than-average busts.

CORRECTION OF SLOPER FOR NARROW SHOULDERS

Overlap section A not only at the chest but at the shoulders, too (Fig. 153a). Correct the shoulder and armhole (Fig. 153b).

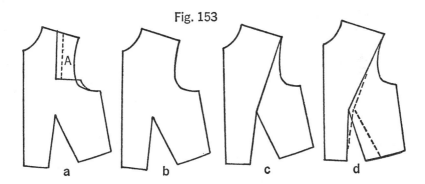

Fig. 153

a   b   c   d

CORRECTION OF SLOPER FOR
SMALLER-THAN-AVERAGE BUST

Draw a slash line from the shoulder point to the dart point (Fig. 153c); slash and overlap the pattern to the necessary amount at the dart point (Fig. 153d).

Adjust the back bodices in the same way.

THE BARE-AND-BEAUTIFUL DEPARTMENT

A minimum of coverage can mean a maximum of appeal.

Décolleté, close-fitting, and strapless dresses are designed on the sloper without ease in chest, bust, and waistline areas. Larger darts, curved darts, and darts in more places will help shape the bodice closer to the bust. Control seams do this well. On the other hand, additional fullness provides an easy, draped look.

A BASIC HALTER DESIGN

1. Place the no-ease, cut-out, bodice-front and bodice-back slopers together at the shoulders. Make them touch at the neckline. Fasten with Scotch tape (Fig. 154a).

2. Draw the neckline from center back to center front. The plunge is as deep as you dare bare (Fig. 154a).

3. Draw the lower style line from center back to side front (Fig. 154a). The line may be higher or lower than the sloper underarm.

4. Cut out the neckline. Cut out the halter. Place the remaining back sloper so its center back is parallel to the center front, the waistlines line up, and the slopers touch at the style line (Fig. 154b). Fasten in this position with Scotch tape.

5. Continue the style line from the bodice side seam to the center back in a sweeping line (Fig. 154b).

6. The pattern may be used as one piece. If so used, it must include the dart formed by the side seams for shaping (Fig. 154c). Should you desire, the pattern can be separated at the side seam (Fig. 154d).

7. In either case, add closing extensions at the center back of the halter (Fig. 154c and 154d). (See Chapter VII for directions.) Complete the pattern.

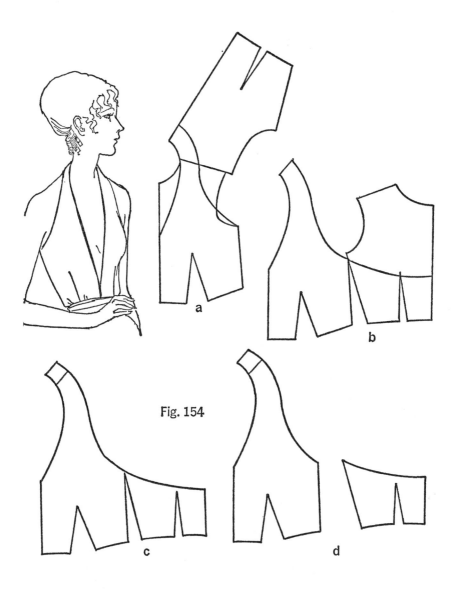

Fig. 154

ONE-SHOULDER DESIGNS

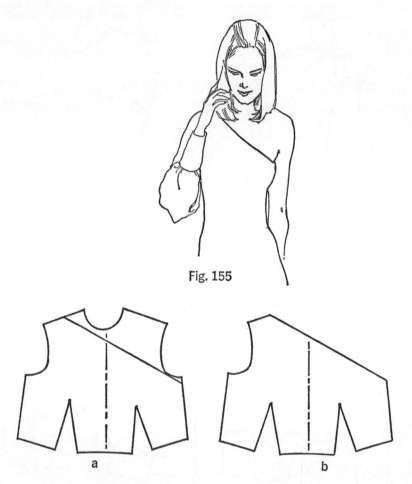

Fig. 155

1. Start with the no-ease, cut-out slopers for a complete bodice front and a complete bodice back.

2. Draw the style lines from one shoulder to the opposite side seam (Fig. 155a).

3. Cut away the neckline (Fig. 155b).

4. Complete the pattern.

STRAPLESS DRESSES

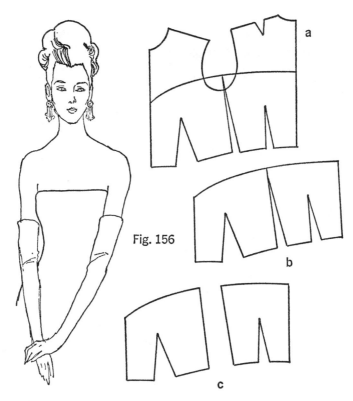

Fig. 156

1. Start with the no-ease, cut-out bodice-front and bodice-back slopers. Place them side by side as for the halter neckline (Fig. 156a).

2. Draw the style line from center front to center back (Fig. 156a). In the sloper, the underarm drops 1½ inches below the armpit for ease. Since the arm is perfectly free in a strapless dress the drop is not necessary. The underarm style line can be brought up as a continuation of the front and back style lines.

3. Cut away the pattern at the décolletage (Fig. 156b).

4. The pattern may be used as one piece, in which case it must include the dart formed by the side seams (Fig. 156b). Or, the pattern can be separated at the side seams and cut as front and back (Fig. 156c). In both cases, the garment is fitted close to the body on the side seam.

5. Complete the pattern.

The strapless construction has many interesting variations these days.

FIG. *157a.* It's simple enough to add shoestring straps that don't hold anything but your interest.

FIG. *157b.* If two straps are too much for you, add only one.

FIG. *157c.* The faced yoke and the strapless gown are held together by hardware.

FIG. *157d.* A strapless dress is harnessed to a turtle-neck collar.

FIG. *157e.* A strapless dress hung around the neck by a richly ornamented yoke band.

The more the exposure, the greater the engineering required to anchor or support the neckline.

A low V neckline can be anchored to a bra with a covered hook of boning or zigzag wiring. One end is stitched to the point of the décolletage and the other hooked into the bra.

A square décolletage can be held in place with a length of narrow elastic. It should be long enough to encircle the body from one corner of the neckline to the other. The elastic is stitched to one corner and snapped to the other.

An off-the-shoulder neckline is held within bounds with narrow elastic run through a casing stitched just inside the armhole edge of the dress from the front notch, over the shoulder, to the back notch.

A strapless dress is supported from the waistline by featherboning or covered wiring (ribbonzene) placed over the seams or darts.

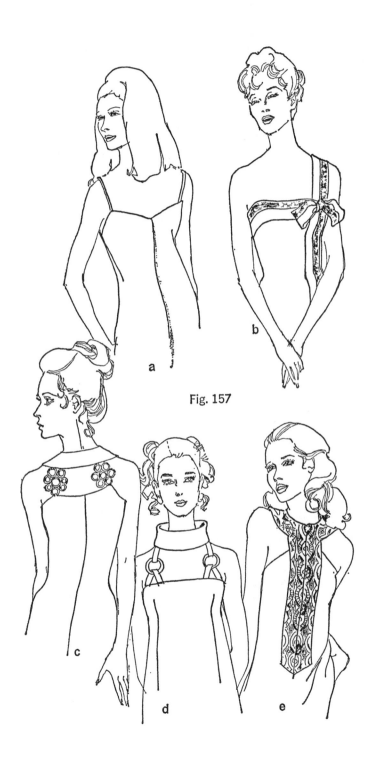

a

b

Fig. 157

c

d

e

FROM A LOW LOW TO A HIGH HIGH

Basic Raised Neckline

The raised neckline must fit not only the shoulders but part of the neck. Since the neck tapers slightly as it rises from its base, the measurement of the raised neckline is somewhat smaller than is the neckline of the sloper. The curve and size of this portion of the pattern can only be determined by careful fitting. If you are fond of this type of neckline (it's a very popular one presently) prepare a personal sloper for the neck area. Here is one way to produce the standard raised neckline.

1. Trace the bodice-front and bodice-back slopers leaving room for the raised necklines.

2. Extend both center front and back lines 1 inch (or more) (Fig. 158a). Slide the front-bodice sloper along the center-front line to the 1-inch extension and trace the front neckline again in this new position. Do the same with the back neckline (Fig. 158a).

3. Shorten each new raised neckline by ¼ inch to make it fit the smaller neck measurement at that height (Fig. 158a). (This will need careful fitting to determine the best measurement.)

4. Draw a curved line from the front raised neckline to the shoulder, blending it into the shoulder line (Fig. 158b).

5. Cut out the front neckline.

6. Place front and back slopers together, shoulders matching. Trace the new front shoulder on the back pattern so the shoulder seams will be identical (Fig. 158b).

7. Complete the pattern including the facing.

Fig. 158

RAISED NECKLINES WITH STYLE DETAILS

Raised neckline with *dropped, shaped center front or back.*

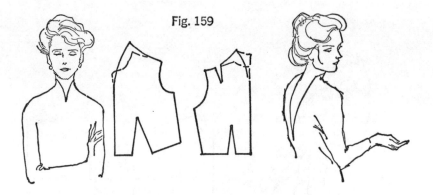

Fig. 159

On the raised neckline pattern, determine the drop in front or back. Connect the drop with the raised neckline (Fig. 159).

Raised neckline with *front fullness* at a triangular design detail.

1. On the raised front neckline pattern, draw the style line for the triangular detail. Draw slash lines (Fig. 160a).

2. Slash and spread to the desired fullness (Fig. 160b).

3. Trace the pattern (Fig. 160c) and complete it.

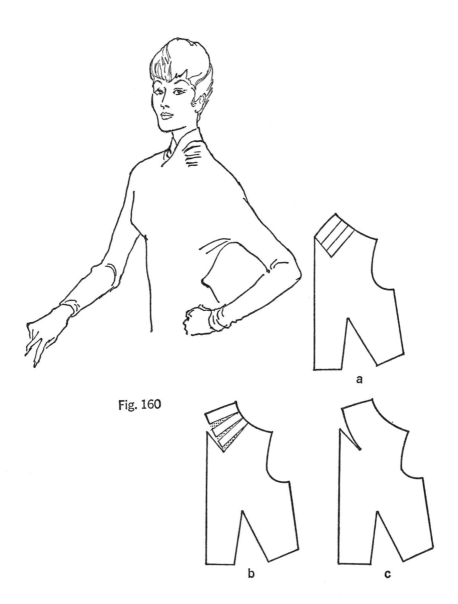

Fig. 160

THE BATEAU (BOAT) NECKLINE

The bateau neckline is high both front and back and wide at the sides ending at the shoulder seam.

1. Trace the bodice-front and bodice-back slopers leaving room for the raised neckline. Extend the center-front and center-back lines to the desired amount. Remember the position of the natural sloper neckline and don't plan too high a neckline.

2. Draw the style line to the shoulder. This may be a straight (Fig. 161a) or a curved line (Fig. 161b).

3. If the style line is curved, plan and trace the facing in the usual manner (Fig. 161c). If the style line is a straight line, the

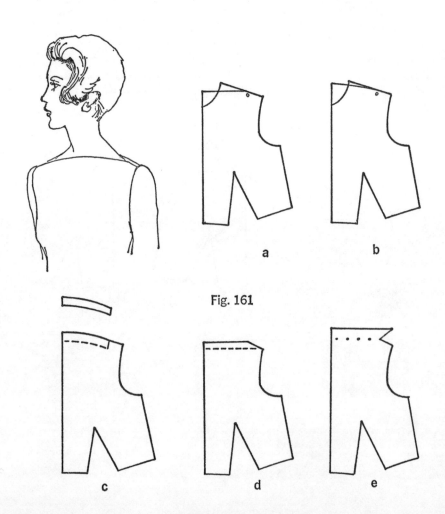

a

b

Fig. 161

c   d   e

facing may be turned back as a hem but it must include the shoulder shaping. To do this:

a. Measure down the depth of the facing along the straight neckline. Extend the facing line until it touches the shoulders (Fig. 161d).

b. Fold on the straight neckline. Using the tracing wheel, trace the lower edge of the facing, the center front, and the shoulder seam to the neckline.

c. Unfold the facing and draw in its shape (Fig. 161e).

This is the procedure used for a hem when shaping is involved in the turnback.

4. Complete the pattern.

RAISED STANDING NECKLINE

A raised standing neckline is similar to the bateau neckline except that it is raised at the shoulders as well as at the center.

1. Trace the front and back bodice slopers. Extend the center-front and center-back lines to the amount of the rise.

2. Draw the style line for the raised neckline and connect it to the shoulder with a curved line (Fig. 162).

3. Complete the pattern.

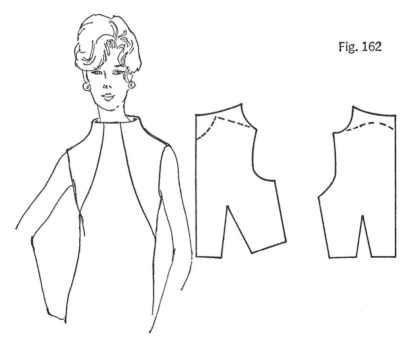

Fig. 162

DRAPERY SOFTENS THE NECKLINE—THE COWL

It's a far cry from a medieval monk's hood. Nevertheless, that's the origin of all those lovely cowl necklines.

Since the cowl is a drape, it is best cut on the bias of some fabric that will fall in soft folds—chiffon, velvet, jersey, crepe, satin.

Whether the cowl appears on the bodice front, the bodice back, a skirt, or sleeve and whether it is at the natural neckline, above it or below it, its characteristic shape is a square at center.

If the cowl is a high, single drape (Fig. 163), the dart control may appear as a waistline dart without distracting from the design interest of the cowl. When the cowl consists of drapes on a lowered neckline, a waistline dart is distracting. Use gathered fullness instead (Fig. 164). In a deep, low cowl design, the waistline dart control can be shifted and incorporated into the folds, which shape softly (Fig. 165). Were there to be dart lines so close to the drapes the result would be a great conflict of interest.

A HIGH COWL WITH A SINGLE DRAPE

1. Trace the bodice-front sloper. Extend the center front 1 inch above the neckline. Take off 1 inch of the shoulder at the neckline. Draw the new neckline from the extension to the drop (Fig. 163a).

2. Cut out the neckline, which is now a straight line. Measure down 1 inch on the shoulder from the new neckline. Label the point A. Draw a curved slash line from the center-front neckline to A (Fig. 163b).

3. On another sheet of paper draw a square (or use the corner of a sheet of paper). Slash and spread the sloper against the square as illustrated (Fig. 163c). The straight neckline rests along the horizontal line of the square. The waistline center touches the vertical line of the square. The additional fullness of the spread becomes the drape.

4. Trace the pattern leaving enough room for a facing and for the other half of a complete front. Correct the angularity of the shoulder (Fig. 163d).

5. Measure down 1½ inches from the neckline for the facing (the broken line in Fig. 163d). Fold the neckline and trace the facing. Remember to include the center front and the shoulder seam.

6. Open out the pattern and draw in the facing, which is cut in one with the bodice and turned back as a hem (Fig. 163e).

7. Bias calls for a complete pattern. Half a pattern on a bias fold may result in inaccuracies in cutting. Fold the pattern at center front and trace the other half (Fig. 163f).

8. Complete the pattern.

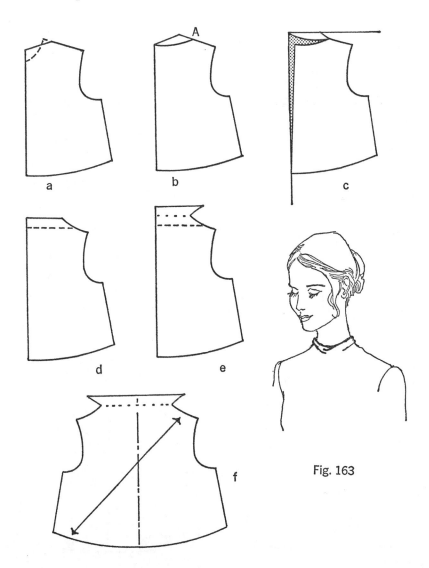

Fig. 163

A COWL ON A DROPPED NECKLINE

1. Use the sloper with gathers at the waistline (Fig. 24). Drop the neckline 1 to 2 inches at center front. From this point, draw a curved line to the shoulder in a wide sweep. Cut out the neckline (Fig. 164a).

2. Starting 1½ to 2 inches below the neckline at center front draw a slash line to the shoulder (Fig. 164a).

3. Slash and spread the pattern against a square (Fig. 164b). The neckline touches the horizontal line of the square at the shoulder. The upper line of the slash touches the vertical line of the square as does the waistline center.

4. Trace the pattern, leaving enough room to complete it. Correct the shoulder seam and the waistline (Fig. 164c).

5. Construct the facing in the same way as for Fig. 163d (Fig. 164d).

6. Trace the second half of the pattern as in Fig. 163f (Fig. 164e).

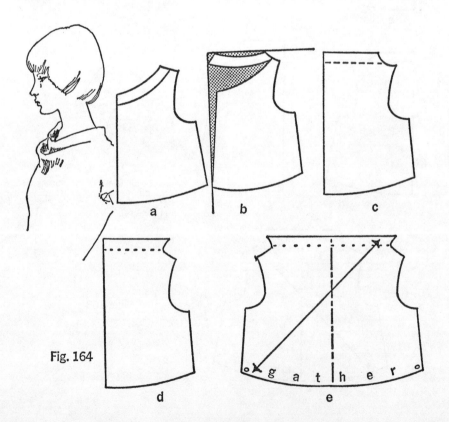

Fig. 164

A DEEP COWL NECKLINE

1. Drop the neckline on the bodice-front sloper not quite as deep as you wish it to be in the finished pattern. Some length will be added in Step 5, Fig. 165c. Cut out the neckline.

2. Close the waistline dart to create a bulging pattern.

3. Draw several slash lines from the center front to those points on the shoulder and armhole from which you would like the folds to drape. Each slash line will become a drape. Plan as many slashes as you would like drapes. Make the lowest slash line touch the dart point (Fig. 165a). (Do remember that it is possible to raise the dart point a little for design purposes.)

4. Slash each drape line. This will flatten the pattern by shifting the dart control to the center front (Fig. 165b).

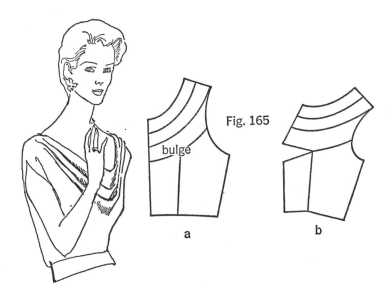

bulge

Fig. 165

a   b

5. Spread the pattern against a square (Fig. 165c). The neckline rests on the horizontal line of the square. The center front of the lower bodice rests on the vertical line of the square. The dart control becomes the lowest drape. Place the middle section between the upper and lower sections.

6. Trace the pattern. Correct the shoulder seams and the waist-line (Fig. 165d).

7. Construct the facing (Fig. 165d).

8. Trace the other half of the front pattern (Fig. 165e).

9. Complete the pattern.

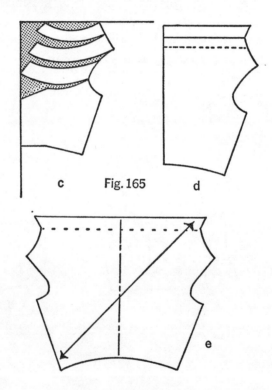

c   Fig. 165   d

e

A COWL YOKE

A cowl yoke has the advantage of being cut separately from the bodice. While the cowl is cut on the bias, the rest of the bodice can be cut on the straight of goods. This produces a fitted bodice with drapes only in the yoke.

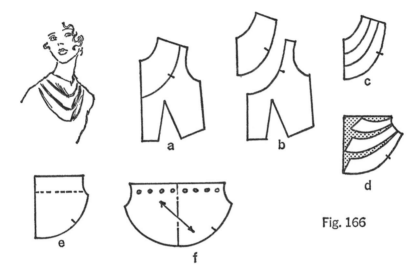

Fig. 166

1. On the bodice-front sloper, draw the style line for the yoke. Notch the style line (Fig. 166a).

2. Cup away the yoke from the rest of the bodice (Fig. 166b).

3. Draw drape lines on the yoke (Fig. 166c).

4. Slash and spread the pattern against a square (Fig. 166d).

5. Trace the new yoke pattern, correcting the shoulder line.

6. Construct the facing (Fig. 166e).

7. Trace the other half of the yoke pattern (Fig. 166f). The cut-away lower half of the bodice completes the pattern.

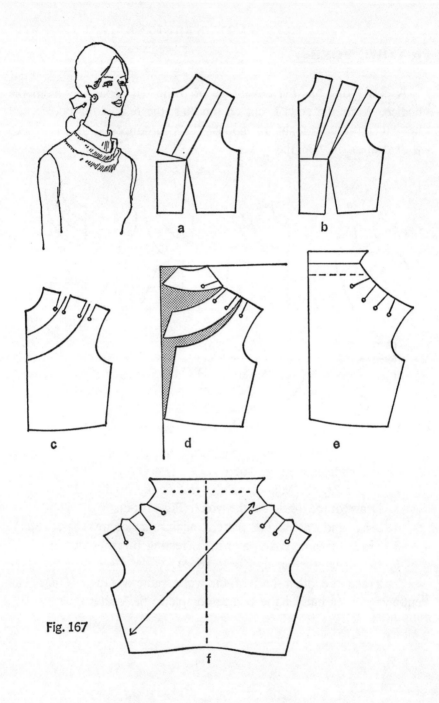

Fig. 167

FOR DEEPER, FULLER FOLDS

All of the foregoing yokes have been developed on the principle of slash-and-spread for circularity. Adding balanced fullness to the folds will make them deeper and fuller.

METHOD I—utilizes some of the dart control for the added fullness.

1. Start with a bodice-front sloper that has some of its dart control shifted to the center front.

2. Draw the lines for the pleats (fuller folds) from the center-front dart to the shoulder (Fig. 167a).

3. Slash the pleat lines. Close the center-front dart and shift the dart control to the shoulder, dividing it equally between the two pleat lines (Fig. 167b).

4. Trace the pattern to another sheet of paper. Mark the depth of the shoulder pleats (Fig. 167c).

5. Draw drape lines bringing them through the center of each pleat (Fig. 167c).

6. Slash each drape line and spread the pattern against a square as illustrated (Fig. 167d).

7. Trace the new pattern, correcting the shoulder seam and the waistline. Place pleat markings. Develop the pattern for the facing (Fig. 167e).

8. Trace the other half of the pattern and complete it (Fig. 167f).

The fullness for the pleats in Method I is only that derived from the divided dart control. You could get a little more fullness by shifting all of the waistline dart to the center front. Method II suggests a procedure for achieving as much fullness as you may desire.

Method II

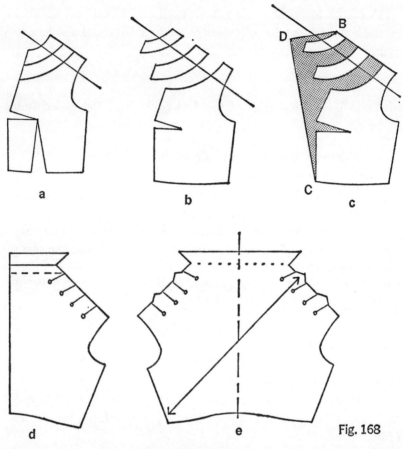

Fig. 168

1. On the bodice-front sloper with some of the dart control shifted to center front, draw drape lines. Draw a guideline parallel to the shoulder seam (Fig. 168a).

2. Draw the guideline on another sheet of paper. Slash and spread the pattern for balanced fullness (Fig. 168b).

3. Measure the length of the curved neckline. Draw a straight neckline equal to the curve. Square a line from the new neckline DB to the waistline (Fig. 168c). The new center front is DC.

4. Trace the pattern and the pleats. Correct the waistline. Construct the facing (Fig. 168d). Trace the other half of the pattern (Fig. 168e) and complete it.

OTHER COWLS

A bodice-back cowl can be very dramatic (Fig. 169a). If fashion dictates there can be cowl skirts (Fig. 169b) and even cowl sleeves (Fig. 169c).

Fig. 169

THE SKIRT WITH DEEP COWL DRAPES AT THE SIDES

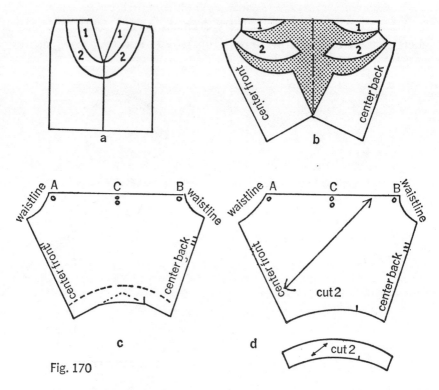

Fig. 170

1. Trace the skirt-front and skirt-back slopers. Move the dart control to the side seam. Straighten the side seam and eliminate the flare.

2. Place the skirt-front and skirt-back slopers together at the side seams. Draw the drape lines (Fig. 170a). Label sections 1 and 2.

3. Draw a horizontal line on a fresh sheet of paper large enough to take the full pattern.

4. Slash and spread the skirt against the straight line (Fig. 170b). The side seams of skirt front and skirt back touch at the hemline.

Sections 1 lies against the horizontal line.

Section 2 is placed between section 1 and the rest of the skirt.

5. Trace the entire outside line of the pattern. Correct the angularity at the hemline and the waistline. Plan the facing (broken line) (Fig. 170c).

6. Trace the skirt and the facing (Fig. 170d).

7. Complete the pattern.

NOTE: There will be seams at the center front and center back but none at the sides. Fold line AB at the center (C); stitch. Attach a covered weight at C to bring the folds into place.

THE COWL ON THE SLEEVE is constructed in the same manner as the sleeve.

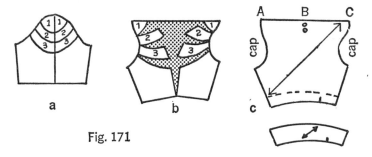

Fig. 171

1. Use a short-sleeve sloper. Divide the sleeve in half lengthwise. Draw the drape lines. Label sections 1, 2, and 3 (Fig. 171a).

2. Draw a horizontal straight line on paper large enough for the pattern.

3. Slash the center line and the drape lines.

4. Spread sections 1, 2, and 3 as illustrated (Fig. 171b). The hem of the sleeve remains closed at the hem center.

Section 1 lies against the straight line.

Sections 2 and 3 are placed so all spaces between sections are equal.

5. Trace the outside line of the pattern correcting the hemline with a curved line (Fig. 171c).

6. Construct the facing and trace it (Fig. 171c).

7. Complete the pattern.

NOTE: There will be an underarm seam and a seam at line ACB. Fold AB at C and stitch. Attach a covered weight at C.

In testing any of the cowl drapes, use a test material that will be soft enough to drape. Voile or batiste is good for this purpose.

For holding the drapery in place use spot weights—small disks that come in ⅝- to 1½-inch diameters. For uniform weighting use weighted tapes (¼-inch enclosed flat lead weights). Or, you may use lengths of muslin-enclosed shot put, the kind used for weighting draperies.

Like other designs with additional fullness, a lining stay is desirable for keeping the fullness in its rightful place. Cut the stay from the basic-fitting sloper. Tack the drapes to this undercover control at strategic points.

A little experimentation will undoubtedly be needed to achieve the effect you have in mind, but the result is so immediate and so beautiful that your new clothes will probably burgeon with cowl drapes.

Chapter VII

BUTTONS, BOWS,
AND POCKETS A'PLENTY

WHAT, NO EXIT?

We have worked out some mightily interesting designs to this point, but they all have one unfortunate feature in common—no opening which would permit you to get into them. It's somewhat like designing a house without a door or a two-story building without a staircase. It is true that some of the fuller designs with dropped necklines could be slipped over the head but that's a proceeding fraught with peril for your new hairdo! Some easier access is imperative—particularly if the dress is a fitted one.

We have seen before how designers make decorative use of structural necessity. This is especially true of closings. If a closing there must be, it may as well be beautiful. Though the simpler, less gadgety closings are always chic, there are times when your imagination can run free. The present fashion period is such a free-for-all, youthful, uninhibited one that almost anything will do for a closing.

What are the choices? A garment may be single-breasted, double-breasted, asymmetric, or surplice. It may be fastened with rope or rare buttons, with hardware or hooks and eyes, with buckles or bows. It may sport exquisitely made buttonholes or be held together by unseen snaps. It may be zipped shut in a very matter-of-fact manner. The closing can be straight, diagonal, or shaped; very simple or very intricate. Whatever the closing, it is so essential and so prominent a part of the design that it requires special thought in planning. Often, the closing can "make" an otherwise unassuming design.

DECISION, DECISION

You cannot make a pattern and then decide how to fasten the garment. *The pattern depends on the kind of closing you choose.* You must make a decision about the type of closing and the fastening.

Should you plan to use a *zippered closing* decide whether it is to be long, short, or in between; whether it will be front, side, or back; whether it will be in a construction seam, a dart, a slash, or under a pleat; whether it is to be brazenly exposed in a startling color or completely hidden in a seam that belies its existence. Inconspicuous or decorative, the zipper is the fast, easy way to get into a dress or skirt.

When you plan to use a *buttoned closing* decide how many buttons, what size they will be, and where they are to be placed. Decide whether they will be placed singly, in a series, or in groups. Decide whether the buttonholes are to be horizontal, vertical, or at an angle.

If a *novelty fastening* is your choice, decide where and how it is to be used.

THE ZIPPERED CLOSING

No need to sing the praises of the zipper for a closing. It is the easiest to account for in a pattern, the simplest to sew, and the easiest to use in a garment.

Generally a seam allowance is sufficient for the application of a zipper. To make very sure there is enough width for the overlap and underlap, you may cut the placket seam a little wider—¾ to ⅞ inch instead of the more usual ½ or ⅝ inch.

When a zipper is set into a slash in the material rather than into a seam a facing piece is necessary.

The neatest zippered closing is by the use of the new invisible zipper in a construction seam. This is simple and quick to install on the underside of a seam line. No stitching is visible from the right side (Fig. 172a).

Fig. 172   a

The two standard types of zippered closings are the regulation (Figs. 172b and 172c) and the slot seam (Fig. 172d).

In the regulation closing the zipper is hidden in a lapped seam. The overlap may be to the right or the left depending on which is easier for the wearer to use. Generally, an overlap to the right is easier for right-handed people, an overlap to the left for the left-handed. Only one line of stitching is visible.

In the slot-seam closing the zipper is concealed by two folds of material which are centered over the zipper. There are two lines of stitching, one on each side of the seam line. The repetition of vertical lines make this closing appear slimmer.

Both types of zippered closing are acceptable whatever the location of the zipper. Which to use depends on the design and the fabric. Use a slot-seam application when a symmetrical appearance is consistent with the design. It makes a trimmer opening for heavy or pile fabrics, faced, slashed, or wrist openings, openings con-

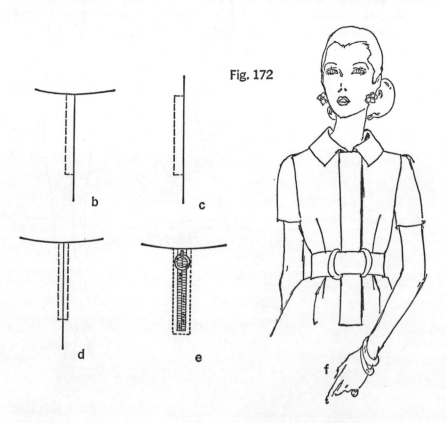

Fig. 172

cealed in box or inverted pleats. Use a lapped closing in delicate and lightweight fabrics. There is less danger of catching the cloth in the zipper.

Another type of zipper insertion exposes it for decorative purposes (Fig. 172e). If you're one who doesn't like the looks of a zippered closing but does like it's conveninece, why not hide it under a band (Fig. 172f)?

THE BUTTONED CLOSING

When a garment is buttoned its two sides must overlap each other for a secure closing. The overlap is an extension of the material beyond the closing line toward the outer edge. There is a rule which governs its width. It is this: *the extension equals the width of the button to be used* (Fig. 173a). When the garment is buttoned, there should be half a button's width between the rim of the button and the finished edge of the garment (Fig. 173b). In addition to a good overlap this bit of mathematics assures a proper setting for a beautiful button—like the jewel it is.

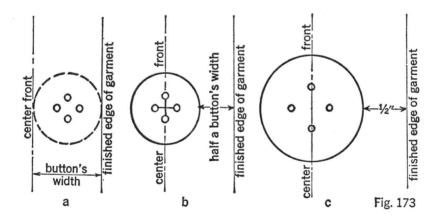

a   b   c   Fig. 173

You may use a slightly smaller button in the same space but rarely a larger one. When an outsize button is used the extension must equal at the very least half a button's width plus ½ inch (Fig. 173c).

In a garment that is buttoned to the neckline, the first button is placed a button's width from the finished edge of the neckline (Fig. 174a). When a garment has a lapel, the first button is located at the break of the collar (Fig. 174b). In a fitted garment buttons should be so placed that the garment does not pop open at the bust or gap at the waist (Fig. 174c). In an unfitted or semi-fitted garment the buttons may be widely spaced. Such designs look better when the garment is held closed between the buttons with snaps covered to match in color (Fig. 174d).

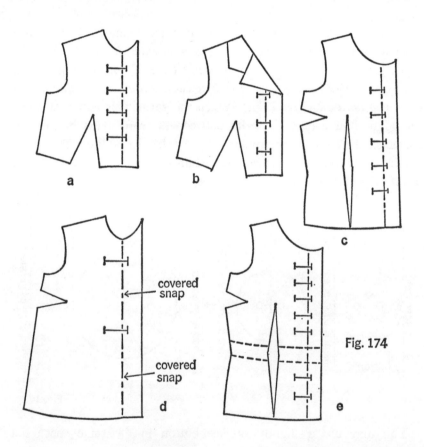

covered snap

covered snap

Fig. 174

If a belt is used at the waistline, place the buttons sufficiently above and below so they don't interfere with the belt (Fig. 174e).

Technically, button sizes are measured in "lines"—forty lines to an inch. (A forty-line button is a one-inch button.) Fig. 175 is a button gauge in actual size. It will help you determine the correct size of button required.

Fig. 175

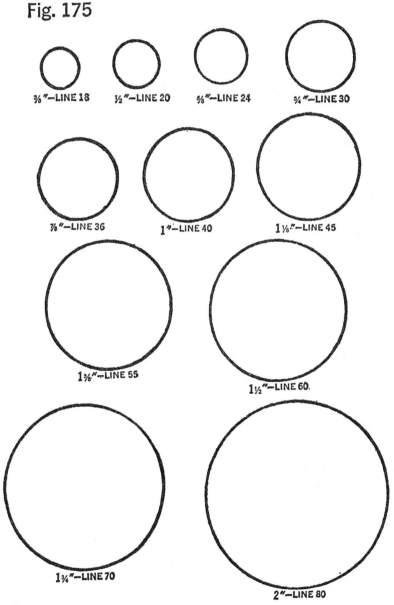

⅜"—LINE 18   ½"—LINE 20   ⅝"—LINE 24   ¾"—LINE 30

⅞"—LINE 36   1"—LINE 40   1⅛"—LINE 45

1⅜"—LINE 55

1½"—LINE 60.

1¾"—LINE 70

2"—LINE 80

Button Gauge, courtesy of B. Blumenthal & Co., Inc.—La Mode Buttons

BUTTONHOLE MARKINGS

To ensure an exact closing on the designated line, it is necessary to make an allowance for the thickness of the shank or stem of the button. The standard amount for this correction is ⅛ inch. This places the beginning of the buttonhole ⅛ inch from the closing line toward the edge of the garment (Fig. 176a). It extends inward the length of the buttonhole plus enough ease to slide the button through readily (Fig. 176a).

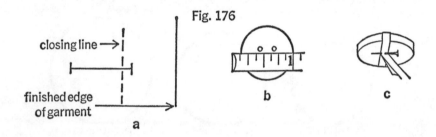

Fig. 176

closing line →

finished edge of garment

a

b

c

A buttonhole for a comparatively flat button is equal to the diameter of the button plus ⅛ inch ease (Fig. 176b). For a thick or bumpy button, the length of the buttonhole is equal to the button's width plus its thickness (height). An easy way to determine buttonhole length is to wrap a strip of narrow paper around the button at its widest part (Fig. 176c). (A very narrow tape measure would be even better.) Half the measurement is the correct size for the buttonhole.

When in doubt as to the proper length, make a test slash. Keep in mind that buttonholes tend to work up smaller than the designated length. Don't skimp on the buttonhole length. On the other hand, don't exaggerate the length; you wouldn't want a large opening with insufficient button to fill it. Aside from being unsightly, the button wouldn't stay buttoned.

Buttonholes work best when made on the horizontal or crosswise grain of the material. This is the direction of the stress on them. Buttonholes on an angle are very pretty but present a problem in the cutting and making; bias buttonholes tend to ripple. In a narrow band, the buttonhole must be made vertically on the straight grain in order to fit the space.

Making buttonholes in loosely woven or ravelly material is hazardous. Making them in knits and stretchy cloth is chancy. Bound buttonholes in transparent material reveal all the inner workings. Jeweled or rough-surfaced buttons often damage the material as they pass through a buttonhole or may, in turn, be damaged by it.

You may fake a buttoned closing by sewing a button to the right side of the garment and a snap directly beneath the button on the underside. Decorative rather than functional buttons do have their place in design (Fig. 177).

Fig. 177

HOW TO MAKE THE SINGLE-BREASTED CLOSING

1. Design the neckline on a bodice-front sloper. Cut it out. Trace it on another bodice-front sloper. Join the two at center front and fasten them with Scotch tape (Fig. 178a).

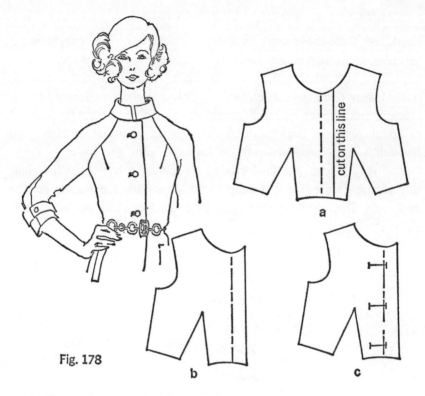

cut on this line

a

b   c

Fig. 178

2. Draw the extension line a button's width away from the center front (the closing line) (Fig. 178a).

3. Cut away the excess pattern (Fig. 178b). For a perfect closing, the extension follows the shape of the neckline.

4. Mark the position of the buttonholes (Fig. 178c). The buttons will be located on the center front of the opposite side.

This procedure can be followed wherever there is a buttoned closing—bodice back, skirt front or skirt back, sleeve opening, collar, cuff, pocket, etc. (Fig. 179).

Fig. 179

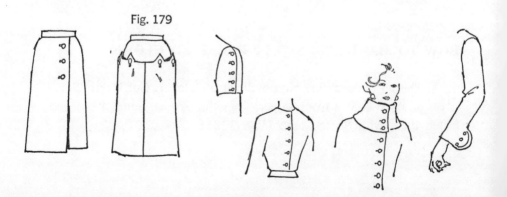

HOW TO MAKE THE FACING FOR THE
SINGLE-BREASTED GARMENT

The *facing* for the single-breasted closing may be made in one of two ways—either all in one with the extension or seamed at the edge of the extension.

(There is no particular virtue to having a seamed facing. The seam does not make it hang better. In fact, if you eliminate the seam, you may eliminate a stitching or matching problem.)

1. On the pattern with the opening extension, measure 1½ inches over on the shoulder from the neckline (Fig. 180a).

2. On the waistline, measure over 2½ to 3 inches from the center front (Fig. 180a). The above two measurements are general. You may make the facing any suitable width. Just be sure to make it wide enough to cover the buttonholes completely plus a little over.

3. Connect the two points with a slightly curved line (Fig. 180a).

For a Facing All-in-One With the Bodice

4a. Fold the pattern on the extension line and trace the neckline, shoulder line, facing line, and waistline. Unfold and draw the facing (Fig. 180b). This type of facing is used when the extension line is vertical and straight, the material wide enough, there is enough fabric for the layout, and a fold of cloth is desired rather than a seam.

Fig. 180

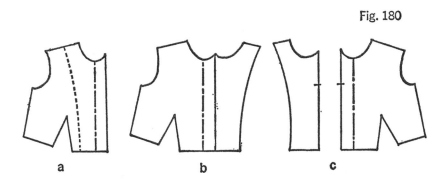

a   b   c

For a Separate Facing

4b. Place another sheet of paper under the pattern or a sheet of tracing paper over the pattern and trace the entire facing (Fig. 180c). This type of separate facing is used when the extension line is diagonal or shaped or when the material is not wide enough, or if the layout is more economical by use of a separate pattern.

For Both Types of Facings

5. Complete the pattern.

BUTTONED ON A BAND

The extension may be a band stitched to the garment on the closing line (Fig. 181a). If this is so, it is not necessary to make buttonholes. The seam line is unstitched at intervals to provide openings for the buttons. The openings must be located on the pattern (Fig. 181b).

In some designs, the closing extension is incorporated in a band (Fig. 181c) centered over the closing line. Buttonholes and buttons are placed as in a single-breasted garment.

In both of the above band designs, the rule for the width of the extension holds: a button's width from the closing line to the finished edge. It holds, too, for the dress outlined with buttons (Fig. 181d).

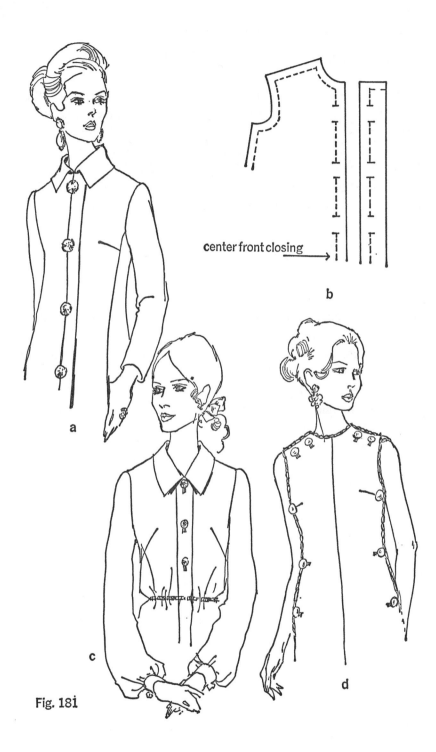

center front closing →

b

a

c

Fig. 181

d

HOW TO MAKE THE DOUBLE-BREASTED CLOSING

1. Use the entire front bodice. Mark the center line (Fig. 182a).

2. Draw the neckline and style line for the double-breasted front (Fig. 182a).

3. Cut away the excess pattern (Fig. 182b). Cut two identical fronts. This deep overlap is characteristic of a double-breasted garment. Because of the many layers of fabric, interfacing and facing over the bosom, double-breasted garments tend to make one look heavier.

4. Locate the line for the buttonhole and button placement a button's width *in* from the edge (the closing line) (Fig. 182b). The buttonholes are squared off the center line.

For the placement of the second row of buttons on the other side of the center-front line, fold the pattern on center front and trace the point of closing (Fig. 182b).

5. Locate the facing in the same way as for the single-breasted garment (Fig. 182c). Trace as a separate facing (Fig. 182d). The double-breasted garment is usually too wide for the facing to be cut all in one with the front. In this instance, were the facing to be constructed so, it would end up considerably off-grain.

6. Complete the pattern.

Fig. 182

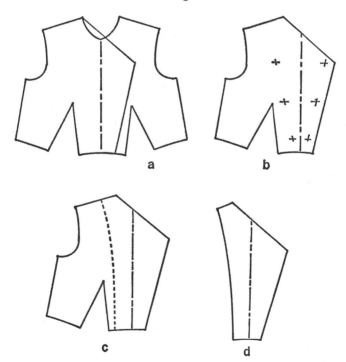

a

b

c

d

THE SURPLICE CLOSING

The easy-to-get-into surplice garment overlaps diagonally either front or back. It may be buttoned (Fig. 183a) or wrapped (Fig 183b). A cut-away surplice style can be quite intriguing (Fig. 183c).

Though asymmetric in design, both sides are cut identically. The pattern is developed as for a double-breasted closing.

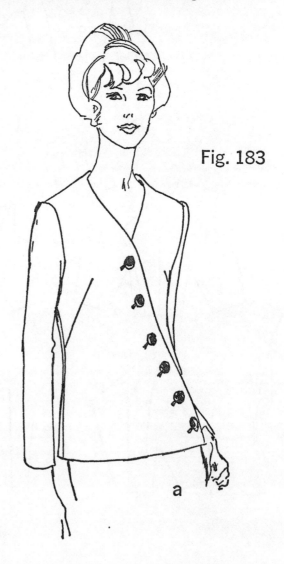

Fig. 183

a

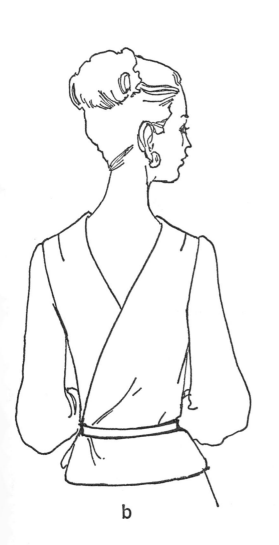

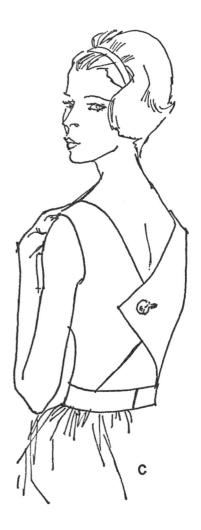

b

c

THE ASYMMETRIC CLOSING

In the asymmetric closing each side of the garment is different.

Fig. *184a*

1. Start with a complete-front pattern with a dropped neckline and the dart control on the side seam.

2. Draw the asymmetric style line and the closing line a button's width away from it.

3. With a broken line, draw the left-front extension line a button's width away from the closing line toward the right front.

4. Locate the position of the buttons and buttonholes. The buttonholes are at right angles to the center front.

5. Establish the grain in the left front parallel to the center front.

Fig. *184b*

6. Trace the complete right-front bodice. Trace the complete left-front bodice.

7. Draw the facing on each pattern parallel to the neckline and the extension. It should be deep enough to permit the finishing of the buttonholes on the underside.

Fig. *184c*

8. Trace the right and left fronts. Trace the facings.

9. Complete the pattern with all necessary signs and symbols.

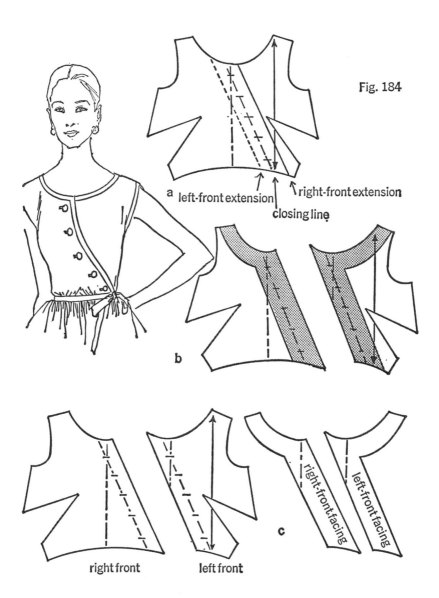

Fig. 184

a left-front extension

↑ right-front extension

closing line

b

right front   left front   c

right-front facing   left-front facing

ASYMMETRIC DESIGNS WITH DEEP OVERLAPS

There is very little overlap in the pattern for Fig. 184. Some designs call for a greater overlap, for instance, the coat-dress in Fig. 185.

1. On the complete-front sloper, draw the center-front line, the style line of the closing, and the closing line a button's width away from the style line (Fig. 185a).

2. Locate the position of the buttonholes at right angles to the closing line (Fig. 185a).

3. Trace the complete right front (Fig. 185b).

4. Trace the left-front to the center-front line (Fig. 185b).

5. Draw the facings on each pattern. The construction of the left facing is the same as for a single-breasted closing. The right-facing pattern is made in the same way as the double-breasted closing (Fig. 185b).

6. Trace the facings (Fig. 185c).

7. Complete the pattern.

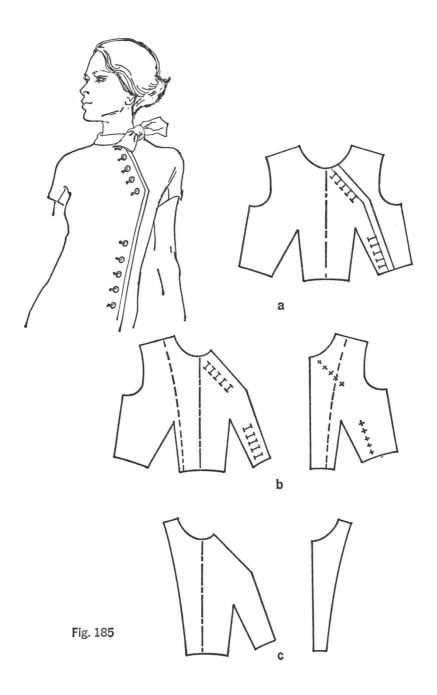

a

b

c

Fig. 185

It is possible for a single-breasted garment to have a deep over-lap, too. One way is to make the extension much wider than the diameter of the button would indicate (Fig. 186a).

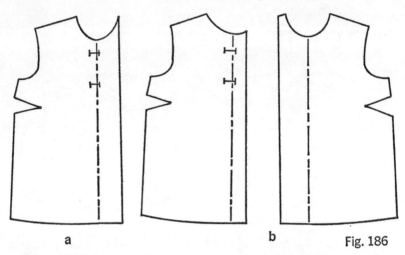

a   b   Fig. 186

Another way is to preserve the formula for the extension on the right front but design the left front with a much deeper extension (Fig. 186b). This has the advantage of preserving a single-breasted appearance while providing a deep overlap. It's a good way to solve the winter-coat overlap problem.

A RIGHT SIDE THAT DOESN'T KNOW WHAT THE LEFT SIDE IS DOING

A design need not be asymmetric for right and left extensions to be different. For example, a single-breasted design with a scalloped extension on the right front need only have a standard left front (Fig. 187).

The left front does not have to duplicate the right. It will not be seen. It has nothing whatever to do with the fit of the garment. To make both sides alike would entail a great deal of unnecessary work.

1. On a complete-front pattern, draw the style line for the right front, the closing line at center front, and the extension line of the left front (broken line) (Fig. 187a).

2. Locate the buttons and buttonholes (Fig. 187a).

3. Trace the left front (Fig. 187b).

4. Trace the right front (Fig. 187b).

5. Draw the facings on each pattern (Fig. 187b). Trace them (Fig. 187c).

6. Complete the pattern.

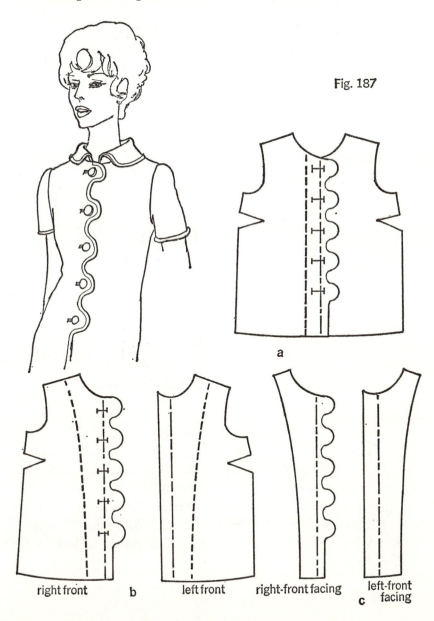

Fig. 187

a

right front b left front right-front facing left-front facing c

A wrap-around skirt is developed in a similar way (Fig. 188).

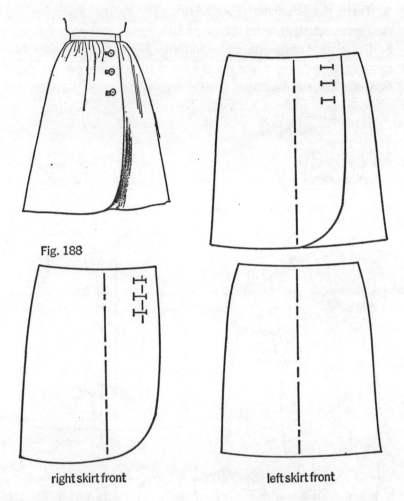

Fig. 188

right skirt front   left skirt front

THE FLY FRONT

The fly front, frequently used in sportswear, is another example of a design with different right- and left-front extensions. The closing has an extra fold of material on the right front which conceals a strip of buttonholes. The left-front extension is made in the usual manner. The two-piece fly front is easier to handle since the buttonholes can be made on a separate strip and then attached to the front extension.

THE TWO-PIECE FLY FRONT

1. Make a bodice pattern with a front extension. Trace the right and left sides separately, leaving room on the right side for the development of the fly front.

2. On the right-front pattern, construct the underfold. Make it deep enough to cover the buttonholes plus a little over (Fig. 189a).

3. Make a separate understrip pattern ⅛ inch narrower than the underfold to ensure that the understrip is concealed. Double it for a facing (Fig. 189b).

4. Complete the pattern.

NOTE: The neckline of both underfold and understrip are the same shape as the pattern design of Step 1.

Construct the one-piece-fly-front pattern in the same way as the two piece with this exception: in place of the seam that joins underfold and understrip make another fold of fabric (accordion fashion) (Fig. 189c). The double folds are held in place by stitching.

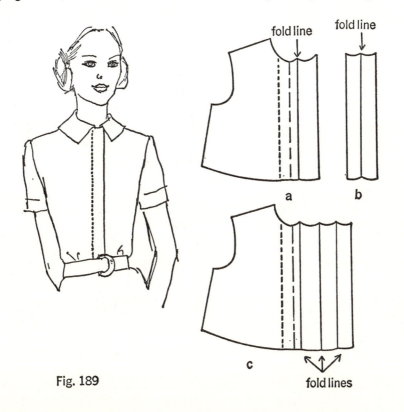

Fig. 189

THE PLACKET OPENING

A placket is an opening at the neck of a bodice, the upper part of a skirt, or the cuff end of a sleeve.

Many times a placket is finished by applying a straight strip of fabric to the edges of a seam or a slash. This is called a continuous lap. The continuous lap is more the concern of the dressmaker than the pattern maker since one does not include a pattern for the strip of fabric. The opening, however, is indicated on the pattern.

When the placket becomes part of a tailored design, then it does concern the pattern maker.

THE TAILORED NECK-OPENING PLACKET

A neck-opening placket may be snapped closed as in Fig. 190a or it may be buttoned as in Fig. 190h.

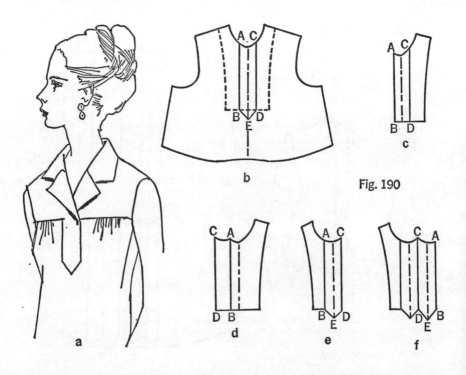

Fig. 190

1. On the complete-front sloper draw the placket. Label A, B, C, D, E (Fig. 190b).

2. Draw the facing with broken lines (Fig. 190b).

3. Trace the left facing and the placket extension (AB) minus the triangle at its base (Fig. 190c).

4. Trace the placket ABCD, cut it out, and Scotch tape it to the left facing (Fig. 190d). Placket and facing are now in one piece.

5. Trace the right facing and the entire placket (ABCDE) (Fig. 190e).

6. Trace the entire placket ABCDE once more and attach it to Fig. 190e (Fig. 190f). Placket and facing are now in one piece.

7. Cut out placket ABCD from the complete bodice (Fig. 190g).

The complete pattern for this design consists of Figs. 190d, f, and g.

Stitching directions:

Attach AB of Fig. 190f to AB of Fig. 190g; with right sides together, fold the right facing over the placket at CD; stitch the triangle BED, trim, and turn to the right side.

Attach CD of Fig. 190d to CD of Fig. 190g; with right sides together, fold the left facing over the placket; stitch across the end BD, trim, and turn to the right side.

If the placket is to be buttoned, the location of the buttonholes must be indicated.

The pattern for the tailored-sleeve placket is made in the same way.

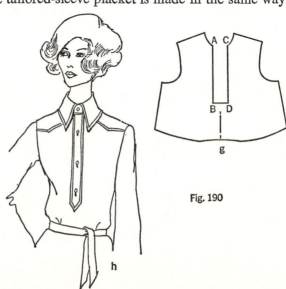

Fig. 190

WITHOUT BENEFIT OF EXTENSION

There are always contradictions in design. Take the designs in Fig. 191, for instance. They lace and loop on center front without benefit of extensions (also without benefit of completely closing if you want it that way). All that is needed on the pattern of such designs is the location of the eyelets, the loops, and the buttons.

Fig. 191

RIGHT—OR LEFT?

Pink or blue bootees are not the only way of telling which are little girls and which little boys. Little girls' clothes button right over left, little boys' clothes the opposite way.

A woman's garment usually closes right over left, both front and back. Want a surprise design element? Try lapping left over right to dramatize a style line (Fig. 192a).

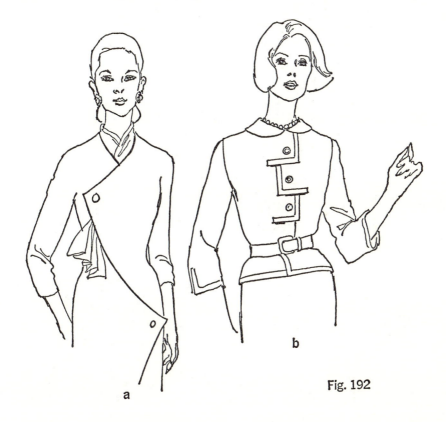

b

Fig. 192

a

An interesting counterpoint can be achieved by an alternate right and left overlapping (Fig. 192b).

Fig. 193

TABS ARE NOT TRIFLES

Tabs added to an ordinary edge can turn it into a distinctive one (Fig. 193). They may be added to any outside line of a pattern—a closing, the shoulder, the neckline, the waistline, a sleeve, a construction seam, a yoke seam, a pocket, a collar, a cuff—just about anywhere there is an edge that could benefit in interest by the addition of a tab.

How it's done:

1. Draw a tab of some interesting shape and cut it out. If you work more freely with scissors in hand, cut the tab directly. Make it curved, pointed, square, round, triangular, free-form, etc. Keep straight the side that will be attached to garment's edge.

2. Scotch tape the tab to the pattern.

3. Trace the pattern, complete with tab extension.

4. Plan a shaped facing for the shaped edge.

BUTTONS, BOWS, BUCKLES, AND BANDS

A Closing Needs a Fastening (Fig. 194)

Have you ever built a dress around some very special buttons? Have you ever sighed with relief at the thought that you could skip the buttonholes and fasten your dress modishly with buckles or bows? Have you ever been tempted to use that bizarre-looking chain your Aunt Hepzibah willed you (so fashionable now)? Have you ever been lured by outsized hooks and eyes or intricate frogs. Of course you have! Every woman who sews has a collection of such choice items tucked away somewhere waiting for just the right dress to come along. No need to wait any longer. Now, you can design one.

Fig. 194

THE POCKET PICTURE

Practical or pretty . . . used sparingly or in droves . . . so tiny you can't get more than a finger in it . . . so large they weigh you down . . . just-right-for-use ones . . . just-for-fun ones . . . in unlikely places . . . and baffling sizes . . . and surprising shapes.

FOR-REAL POCKETS

If the pocket is there for a purpose, it should be so placed and so sized that you can get a hand into it. A safe rule to follow for pocket size is this: a horizontal or diagonal opening should be as wide as the fullest part of the hand plus 1 inch; a pocket which opens vertically should be as wide as the fullest part of the hand plus 2 inches. (The hand must make a double motion to get into the pocket.) Place the pocket where it can be reached easily.

FAKE POCKETS

If a pocket is not going to be used, it may be of any size and be placed in any position consistent with the design.

PATTERN PROCEDURE FOR POCKETS

Structurally, pockets fall into two classes: those which are applied to the right side of the garment like the patch pocket and those which are inserted into a slash or seam like the welt or bound pocket or a style-line pocket.

Whatever the pocket, as far as the pattern is concerned there are several steps in developing it.

1. Draw the pocket on the pattern showing its size and position. Use solid lines to show what will appear on the surface of the garment. Use broken lines for the part that will not be seen (Fig. 195).

2. Trace off all parts that are applied to the right side.

Pockets

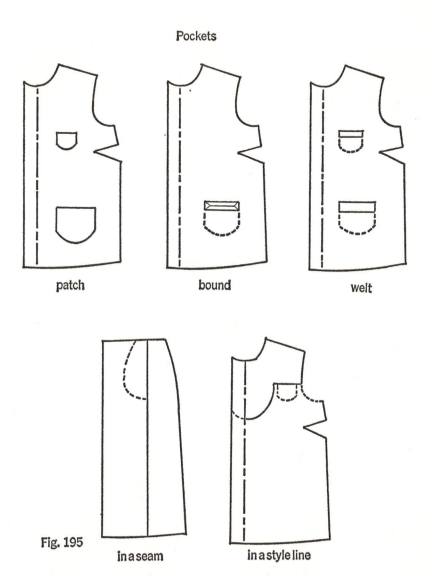

patch   bound   welt

Fig. 195

in a seam   in a style line

3. Trace off all parts that appear on the underside.

4. Make the pattern for the under pocket, the upper pocket, and any necessary facings.

5. Complete the pattern with seam allowances, grain marks, placement marks, etc.

A POCKET APPLIED TO THE RIGHT SIDE OF THE GARMENT—The Patch Pocket

Fig. 196

1. Draw the pocket on the pattern. Work out the appropriate size, shape, and proportion.

For design interest you may do anything to the patch pocket that you have learned to do with the bodice and the skirt. Divide the area into interesting shapes, add fullness, add a tab or a flap, add a band, button it, trim it, topstitch it, use the grain as part of the design.

2. Trace the pocket. Develop the pattern for any of the above details.

3. For a straight pocket edge, add the hem (in proportion to the size of the pocket.

For a shaped pocket edge, add a shaped facing.

Patch pockets topstitched in from the edge need facings slightly deeper than the distance of the topstitching from the edge.

For a lined pocket, make a lining pattern ⅛ inch smaller than the pocket. This is the allowance for rolling the seam to the underside. For heavier fabrics the amount may have to be increased.

SEWING SUGGESTIONS: Make the complete patch pocket. Slip stitch or topstitch the pocket to the garment.

NOTE: Patch pockets of lightweight material may lie fairly flat against the garment. Pockets of medium, heavy, or bulky materials need a little ease when the pocket is set so that you can get your hand into it without pulling or distorting the garment. Either make the patch pocket a little larger than that of the original drawing or ease it onto the garment in a slightly smaller space than the one allotted in the original drawing.

THE POCKET SET IN A CONSTRUCTION SEAM

This pocket may be concealed (Fig. 197a) or dramatized with topstitching (Fig. 197b).

The pocket consists of two shaped pieces stitched together and into a seam (Fig. 197c).

The *under pocket* is closest to the body (under the hand).

The *upper pocket* is closest to the outer fabric (over the hand).

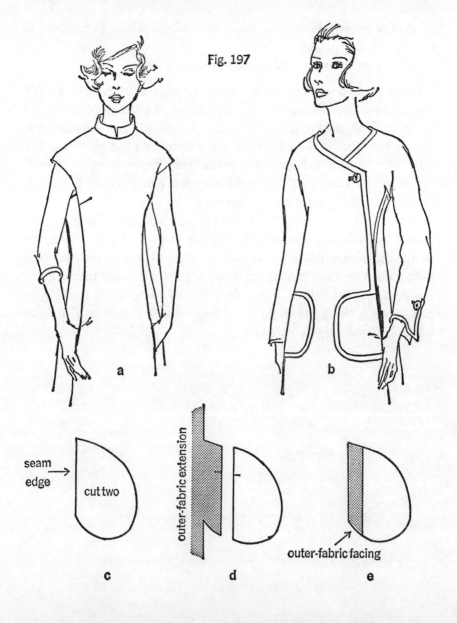

Fig. 197

seam
edge →

cut two

outer-fabric extension

outer-fabric facing

a

b

c

d

e

The pocket is least bulky when made of lining fabric but this presents a problem. The opening of the pocket reveals the material of which it is made. To preserve a continuity of outer fabric it is possible to do any of the following.

1. Add an extension to the seam allowance of the pattern at the pocket opening (Fig. 197d). Make the pocket pattern (to be cut of lining fabric) correspondingly smaller. Make the extension deep enough to conceal the lining pocket.

2. Provide a facing of outer fabric to be attached to the lining fabric (Fig. 197e).

3. Cut the under pocket of outer fabric and the upper pocket of lining material.

These suggestions are applicable also to the bound pocket, the welt pocket, and wherever a slash or opening in the garment will reveal the under fabric.

A POCKET SET IN A STYLE LINE

Fig. 198

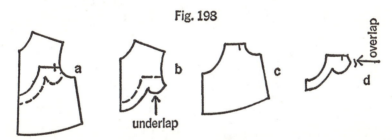

The yoke seam of Fig. 198 is utilized as a place to conceal a pocket. Any sections which need to be joined by a seam can be used in the same way.

In this pattern, the under pocket is an extension of the yoke (underlap). The upper pocket is part of the lower-bodice facing (overlap).

1. Draw the yoke. Draw the position of the underlap and overlap. Draw the pocket (Fig. 198a).

2. Trace the yoke and extension (underlap) (Fig. 198b).

3. Trace the lower bodice (Fig. 198c).

4. Trace the facing and pocket (overlap) (Fig. 198d).

Sewing directions: Stitch the overlap to the lower bodice. Top-stitch the pocket. Stitch the underlap to the overlap. Topstitch the lower bodice to the yoke from pocket on. Stitch the pockets. The patterns for Figs. 199a and 199b are developed in the same way.

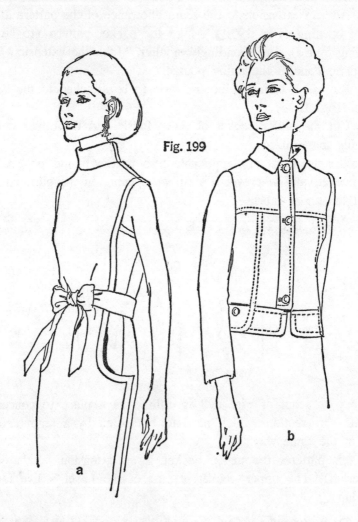

Fig. 199

a

b

THE POCKET IN A SLASH

The Bound Pocket—Classic Variety

The classic-variety bound pocket is an oversize buttonhole to which the pocket is attached on the underside. Since the under pocket is bound to be exposed, make it of outer fabric or lining material with a facing of outer fabric.

To make very sure the under pocket never shows try a zippered pocket (Fig. 200a).

Fig. 200

a   b   c

The Bound Pocket—Contemporary Variety

Cardin has designed some wonderful new bound pockets that bear no resemblance to the classic variety (Fig. 200b) except that they're bound, too. The slash becomes a cut-out, the binding large and welted. Obviously this pocket requires an under pocket of outer fabric.

Cardin's porthole pocket (Fig. 200c) is faced and topstitched rather than bound. What an exciting feature on a simple dress!

THE WELT POCKET—PART APPLIED, PART SET-IN-A-SLASH OR SEAM

The welt pocket has it both ways. The welt is applied to the surface *and* set in a slash (Fig. 201a) or seam (Fig. 201b).

1. Draw the welt as it will appear on the right side of the garment. Draw the pocket as it will appear on the underside.

2. Trace the welt. A straight-edge welt can be doubled on a fold. For a shaped welt, cut two, adding ⅛ inch (or more) to the upper welt as an allowance for rolling the seam to the underside.

3. Trace the pockets. For a one-piece pocket, cut twice the length of one pocket pattern plus an allowance for the depth of the opening. For a two-piece pocket cut two pockets, one of which has the allowance for the depth of the pocket added to it.

4. Complete the pattern.

The position of the welt must be shown on the garment pattern.

SEWING SUGGESTIONS*: Make the welt and stitch it to position on the garment. Place the pocket in position over the welt and stitch. Slash the opening and pull the pocket through to the wrong side. Stitch the pockets. Slipstitch the ends of the welt to the garment.

THE FLAP POCKET

Reverse the position of the welt and you have a flap pocket (Fig. 201c).

SEWING SUGGESTIONS: Make the flap. Stitch it into the upper binding of a bound pocket or stitch it to position ½ inch above the opening of a patch pocket (Fig. 201d).

A flap or a welt may be inserted in an existing seam—perhaps the same seam in which the pocket is inserted (Fig. 201e).

---

* For detailed sewing instruction for stitching all pockets consult *The Complete Book of Tailoring* by this author, Doubleday & Company, Inc.

Fig. 201

Fake Flaps and Fake Welts

From a design point of view these (Fig. 201f) do as well as the real thing. Plan and construct them in the same way as the real flaps and welts. Just omit the pockets. Apply them to the right side of the garment.

In addition to the pattern for the flap or welt, be sure to indicate its position on the garment pattern.

Chapter VIII

COLLARS TO CAPES

A collarless neckline, be it ever so interesting, is difficult to wear. It calls for a firm chin, a smooth and slender neck, and a good set to the shoulders—all attributes, alas, of the young and the beautiful. This leaves so many of us out. Give us, please, a soft bow, a gay scarf, our faithful pearls and, at the very least, a flattering collar.

FOR THE REST OF US

Fortunately there are many collars to choose from—little ones and big ones, tailored ones and frilly ones, dramatic ones and modest ones—something for everybody.

There are more considerations than fashion and style preference. Consider lines that are flattering to the shape of the face. Reserve a nice balance between the collar and the rest of the silhouette. How does one's new hairdo take to the lines of the collar? If the collar is to be worn under a jacket or a coat, choose one that will accommodate to that.

A WORD FOR IT—TERMS USED IN COLLAR CONSTRUCTION

A collar has parts and each part has a name.

Fig. 202

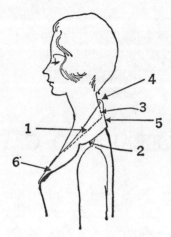

1. *The neckline:* This is the part of the collar that fits around the neck. Usually, the neckline of the collar is stitched to the neckline of the garment. The plastron collar is an exception; it is worn separately like a necklace.

2. *The style line:* This is the outer edge of the collar. As with any other style line this may be anything the designer wishes it to be. The style line always finds that part of the shoulders that equals it in measurement, pushing the rest into a stand. As the outer edge of the collar shortens, the stand increases. As the outer edge of the collar lengthens, the stand decreases.

3. *The stand:* The stand is the amount the collar rises from the neckline to the roll line.

4. *The roll line:* The roll line is the line along which the collar turns down (when it does).

5. *The fall:* The fall is the depth of the collar from the roll line to the style line. The fall must be deep enough to hide the neckline seam.

6. *The break:* The break is the point at which a collar turns back to form a lapel.

COLLARS, CURVES, AND STANDS

Any collar that conforms to the shape and length of the neckline lies flat (Fig. 203a). This may be very little better than a collarless neckline. A collar looks prettier when there is even a slight roll. To do this, the neckline of the collar must be shortened. As the collar is stretched to fit the unshortened neckline of the garment, it is pushed into a soft roll.

In the patterns which follow in this chapter, the shortening is accomplished by raising the neckline ⅛ inch (Fig. 203b). (The broken line is the original neckline. The solid line is the raised and shortened neckline.)

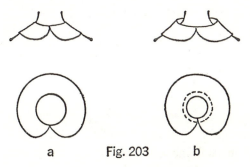

a   Fig. 203   b

When the neckline of a collar curves in a direction opposite to the curve of the neck or the bodice neckline, its style line pushes the collar into a stand (Fig. 204a).

The shallower the opposing curves, the lower the stand (Fig. 204b). The deeper the opposing neckline curves, the higher the stand (Fig. 204c).

When a collar neckline is more curved than the neckline of the garment, it will ripple (Fig. 204d).

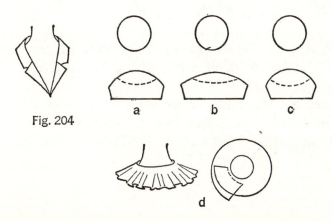

Fig. 204   a   b   c

d

The ring collar is a straight band whose neckline is the exact length of the garment neckline (Fig. 205a). Because of its straight shape and equal length, it stands away from the neck.

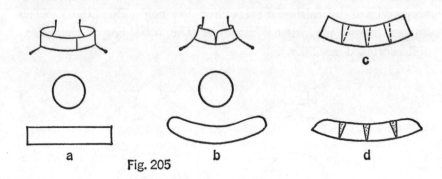

Fig. 205

The Chinese collar, too, is a standing collar but its curved shape has a smaller measurement at the upper edge, which makes it fit closer to the neck (Fig. 205b). (Remember the raised neckline? The same principle is at work here.)

A ring collar can be changed to fit more like a Chinese collar: slash and overlap the pattern to the desired degree of curve and neck measurement (Fig. 205c).

A Chinese collar can be straightened so it stands more like a ring collar: slash and spread the pattern to the desired degree of straightness (Fig. 205d).

BEFORE YOU BEGIN YOUR COLLAR DESIGNING

Since a collar fits around the entire neckline, use both front and back slopers to develop the pattern. For most collar patterns it is enough to trace only the upper portion of the slopers—center front, neckline, shoulders, center back, and part of the armscyes.

The neckline of the bodice must be established before you begin to draft the collar. If it is to be raised or lowered, this is done first. When there is a closing extension, this, too, is constructed before designing the collar. Current fashion features collars of all styles on lowered necklines. Close-fitting collars will fit with a little more ease if the neckline is dropped ½ inch at center front before the new neckline is drafted.

Analyze the collar for type, since each type of collar is constructed in its own characteristic way.

Collars are generally faced and interfaced. Both of these are cut on the same grain as the collar.

The upper collar should be at least ⅛ inch larger on all edges except the neck edge as an allowance for rolling the joining seam to the underside. The heavier the cloth, the more the allowance.

Bodice-front and bodice-back slopers are placed so that they meet at the neckline. Shoulders open, touch, or overlap as the directions call for this. As positioned, the back shoulder will extend slightly beyond the front armhole because of the shoulder dart. Unless otherwise directed, ignore the dart in designing the collar.

You really cannot tell how a collar will fit just by looking at half a flat pattern. It is wise to cut a full collar in muslin and fit it carefully. Make any necessary adjustments in the muslin and transfer the corrections to the pattern.

YOU CAN'T BEAT A BAND COLLAR

A surprising number of interesting collars can be made simply from a band of cloth (Fig. 206). Cut a strip of fabric in the desired length and width on straight or bias grain. Straight grain stands better, bias grain drapes better. The ends of the bands may meet, overlap, button, tie, loop. The band may double back against itself as in the turtle-neck collar or fold back at the ends as in the wing collar.

A deep band may hang softly like a cape from a deep V neckline or, when stiff, encircle the shoulders like a fichu. A long band may be gathered into a flounce, be pleated, or laid in soft folds.

Fig. 206

A BIAS FOLD BECOMES A COLLAR

The collars in Fig. 207 are all made of bias strips of material, cut to the correct length and width and folded lengthwise. The raw edges are attached to the neckline of the garment, the folded edge is out. Because of its bias cut, the outer edges can be manipulated to fit well wherever the band falls on the body (provided it is not too deep).

It is possible to do a little shaping by steam pressing before the collar is attached. Stretch the outer (folded) edge and ease the inner (raw) edge, taking care to press with the grain.

Fig. 207

When attaching the bias-band collar to the neckline, a higher stand may be produced by stretching the neck edge of the collar to fit the neckline. A flatter collar may be obtained by easing the fullness of the collar neckline into the garment neckline.

STANDING COLLARS

The Chinese Collar (Nehru, Mao, or Mandarin, depending on your age and point of view)

This collar may be constructed in one of two ways.

METHOD I—with a separate facing

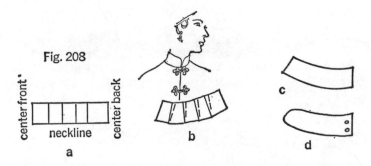

Fig. 208

center front'

neckline

center back

a

b

c

d

1. Cut a strip of paper to the length of the neckline from center front to center back. Make it the desired width (generally 1 inch to 1½ inches) (Fig. 208a).

2. Draw several slash lines. Make them a slightly longer distance from center front and center back than the width of the spaces between the slash lines. This helps the collar fit better at front and back.

3. Slash from the outer edge to the neckline. Overlap the slashed edges until the outer edge fits the neck measurement at comparable height with a bit of ease (Fig. 208b).

4. Trace the pattern, correcting the angularity (Fig. 208c).

5. Draw the center-front style line (Fig. 208d).

6. Make the upper collar slightly larger than the facing on all but the neck edge to allow for the seam roll.

7. Complete the pattern.

The slight shaping of this standing collar prevents it from poking out at back and overlapping at the front edges. The Chinese collar developed by Method II takes care of these matters in a different way.

METHOD II—a double collar on a lengthwise fold

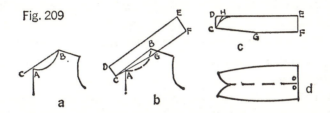

Fig. 209

1. Trace the neck and shoulder area of the bodice-front sloper.
2. Measure the neckline from the center front (A) to the shoulder (B). Draw a straight line of equal length starting at B and ending at C (Fig. 209a).

FIG. *209b*

3. Square a line from C equal to the stand of the collar (D).
4. Square a line from D to E equal to the length of the neckline from center front to center back.
5. Square a line from E to F equal to the stand of the collar plus ¼ to ⅜ inch. This deepened stand at center back sets the point from which the neckline shaping begins.
6. Square a line from F to the shoulder (G).
7. Connect G with C.

FIG. *209c*

8. Trace the collar.
9. Measure over ½ inch from D (H). Draw a line from H to C. This shortens the upper edge of the collar for fit and prevents the center front edges from overlapping. HC may be the center-front style line or become the guide for a curved style line.

FIG. *209d*

10. Trace the new collar, correcting all angularity.

11. Fold the collar on line HE and trace. Unfold and draw the collar facing in one with the collar.

12. Complete the collar.

Which of the two methods one chooses for making a pattern for a Chinese collar depends on the preferred style and the amount of available material. The curved shape of Collar I requires a little more material than the Collar II pattern, which can utilize a single straight strip of material on a fold for the entire double collar.

There is this difference, too: there are not too many style variations possible with Method I collar. When the ends of Method II collar are extended, they may button or tie in a bow, or be folded over like a cravat.

The Fichu

The fichu is a flattering collar whether stiff or draped. It is designed on a wide, deep neckline.

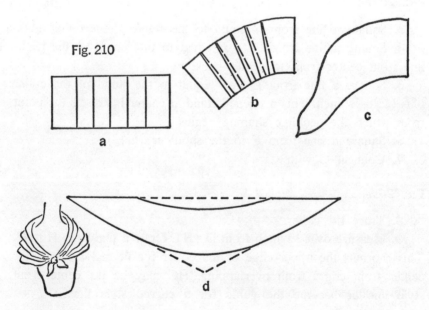

Fig. 210

a

b

c

d

1. Establish the neckline of the bodice.

2. Start with a band of paper that measures half the length around the shoulders by the desired depth of the collar at its widest point (Fig. 210a).

3. Draw several slash lines (Fig. 210a).

4. Slash and overlap to fit the neckline (Fig. 210b).

5. Add the extension for fastening. Correct the angularity. Draw the style line (Fig. 210c).

6. Trace the new pattern (Fig. 210c) and complete it.

The pattern for the fichu could be very simply worked out from a flattened triangle. Hollow out the neck and shape the style line (Fig. 210d).

Fan-Shaped Frame

The fan-shaped collar (Elizabethan, Medici) is too dramatic and impractical for ordinary wear but quite impressive for formal gowns, wedding gowns, or hostess gowns. The style must be made of material that will stand or must be stiffened with wire to make it stand.

1. Establish the neckline.

2. Cut a rectangle of paper to the desired length from center front to center back and the width of the collar at its widest point.

3. The frame may be achieved in three ways depending on the material at one's disposal and whether you start with the outer edge or with the neck measurement.

    a. Draw several slash lines. Slash and spread (Fig. 211a).

    b. Draw several slash lines. Slash and overlap (Fig. 211b).

    c. Dart the band to fit the neckline (Fig. 211c). If you use lace that you would not like to cut, use this method. If the lace is bordered, the end may be mitered to preserve the edge completely around the collar (Fig. 211d).

4. Trace the pattern. Correct any angularity. Draw any style line.

5. Complete the pattern.

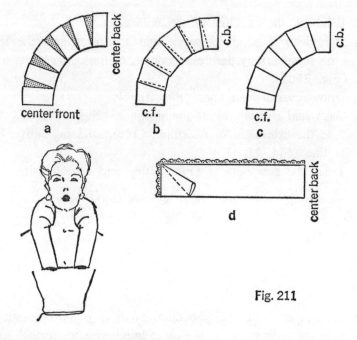

Fig. 211

VARIATIONS OF METHOD 3c

When the darts are stitched only part way up a band, the collar will stand in a line with the dart points (roll line) (Fig. 212a).

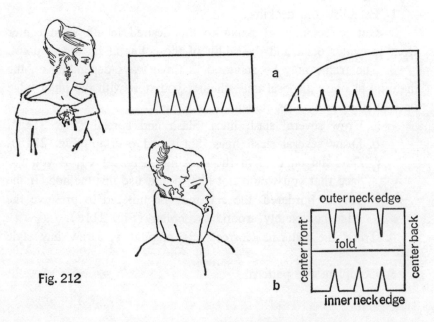

Fig. 212

For that neck-muffling collar so great on a winter coat dart both neck and outside edge, the latter not quite so much as the former (Fig. 212b). The band encircles the face and doubles back on itself.

FLAT COLLARS

Collars that lie flat around the neck may go from tiny ones of 1 inch or so to the bigness of a cape collar. Whatever the size, they are constructed in the same way.

The Plastron Collar—a temporary attachment

The very flattest collar of all is the plastron—a separate collar attached to the dress (between frequent launderings) by pins, tabs, snaps, buttons, bastings, or the law of gravity. It can be made of any interesting material in decorative shapes and garnished with trimming.

1. Place the front and back slopers together, shoulder seams touching and meeting at the neckline (Fig. 213a).

2. Make the neckline of the collar slightly smaller than the neckline of the garment by raising it ⅛ inch (Fig. 213a).

3. Draw the style line (Fig. 213a).

4. Trace the collar in one piece (Fig. 213b). If there is more than the usual slope to the shoulders, requiring a seam for shaping, trace the collar in two pieces (Fig. 213c).

5. Complete the collar. The center-front fold is on straight grain. The center front and center back are placed on straight grain in the two-piece collar.

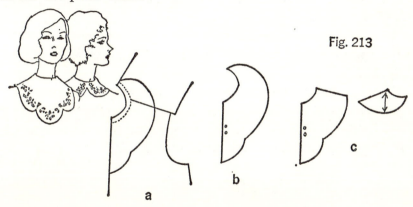

Fig. 213

a

b

c

Cape Collars

Graceful, flattering, and dramatic are the cape collars. How the patterns are developed depends on how much flare the collars have. The cape collar in Fig. 214 lies rather close to the body.

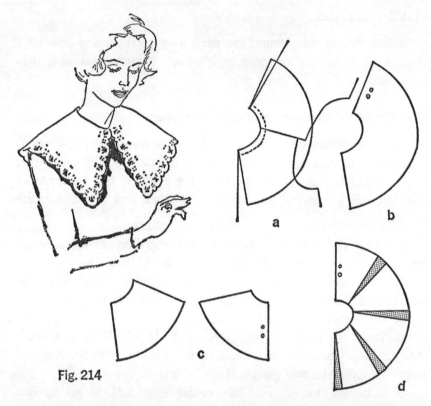

Fig. 214

1. Trace the neck and shoulder area of the front- and back-bodice slopers, shoulder seams touching and meeting at the neckline (Fig. 214a).

2. Lower the neckline for style when necessary but raise it ⅛ inch to shorten it for a soft roll after the neckline has been established (Fig. 214a).

3. From the neckline measure down in a number of places the depth of the collar. This becomes the style line (Fig. 214a).

4. Extend the collar ¼ inch at the center-back style line for ease. Taper to the center-back neckline (Fig. 214a). (In the trial muslin fitting you may find that it is necessary to slash and spread slightly at the normal shoulder line, too, for a better fit.)

5. Trace the collar (Fig. 214b).

If the shoulders slope more than usual, use a shaped shoulder seam for better fit (Fig. 214c).

If a more flared collar is desired, slash and spread for circularity (Fig. 214d).

6. Complete the pattern.

A Circular Cape Collar

1. Draw a straight line. Arrange the front- and back-bodice slopers so that the center front and center back lie along the line (Fig. 215a). The shoulder seams touch at the neckline. Trace the slopers in this position.

2. Establish the new neckline. Raise it ⅛ inch.

3. Draw the style line below the shoulders (Fig. 215a).

4. Trace the pattern (Fig. 215b) and complete it.

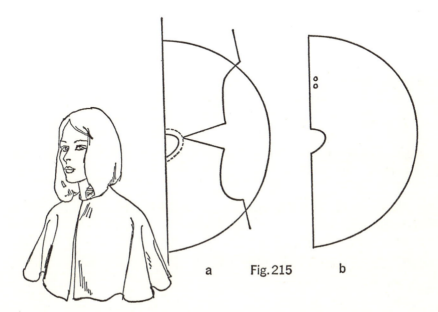

a   Fig. 215   b

In soft material, the circular collar will hang in soft folds. In stiff or stiffened material, the collar stands out sharply (Fig. 215c). (It can even be made to frame the face.) On a dropped neckline, the circular cape collar becomes the Bertha collar (Fig. 215d).

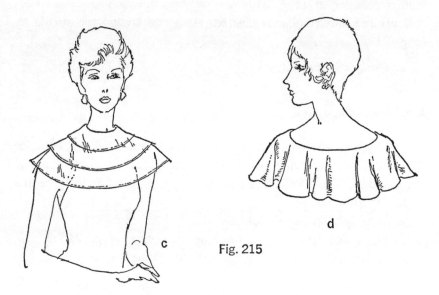

c

Fig. 215

d

The Fitted Cape Collar

1. Trace the bodice-back sloper. Eliminate the back-shoulder dart by folding it out to the waistline.

2. Draw a right angle. Place the front sloper so the center front lies along the vertical line of the right angle. Place the back sloper so that the center back lies along the horizontal line of the right angle. The shoulders touch at the armhole (Fig. 216a). Trace the slopers.

3. Establish the neckline. Raise it ⅛ inch.

4. From the neckline measure down the depth of the collar in a sufficient number of places to provide the style line (Fig. 216a).

5. Correct the dart that forms at the shoulders with curved dart legs (Fig. 216a). The collar will fit the shoulders better with a curved dart than with a straight one.

6. Trace the pattern (Fig. 216b) and complete it.

A fitted cape collar can be shaped by a control seam rather than a dart.

To make the control-seam pattern:

> a. Draw a straight line through the center of the dart and continue it to the style line (Fig 216c). Notch the seam.
> b. Cut out the collar. Cut it apart on the seam line (Fig. 216d). Complete the pattern.

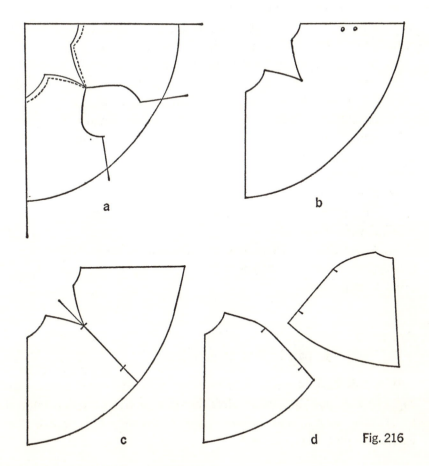

Fig. 216

A CAPE FOUNDATION PATTERN

Both the circular and fitted cape collars can be extended to become full-length capes. For a full-length cape to utilize its dart control for designing use the foundation cape pattern opposite.

1. Divide the bodice-front dart control between shoulder and waistline.

FIG. *217a*

2. Trace the front- and back-bodice slopers, leaving plenty of room.

3. Square a line from the center back to the armhole. Extend it to a distance from the armhole equal to one-quarter of its measurement (AB). Do the same with the bodice front (CD).

4. Extend the center back to the length desired for the cape (E).

5. Square a line across from E equal to one-quarter of the desired hemline measurement (F). Connect F to B.

6. Extend the center-front line (H). DH equals AE.

7. Square a line across from H to G that equals CD plus the difference between AB and EF. This will assure side seams with similar degrees of angle.

8. Connect G with C.

9. Make BF^1 equal AE. Make CG^1 equal DH. Correct the hemline with a curved line.

10. Extend the shoulder lines and the side seams until they meet. Correct the angularity with a curve for the top of the arm—1 inch over, 1 inch down.

FIG. *217b*

11. Trace the pattern and complete it.

With this basic cape pattern you can now go ahead and design capes to your heart's content. Shift the darts, convert the dart control to shaping seams, add fullness, add a collar, add pockets, add extension, etc., etc., etc.

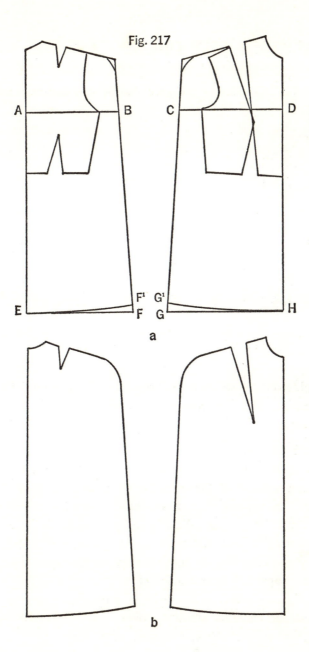

Fig. 217

COLLARS WITH A SOFT ROLL

The Peter Pan Collar and its many variations thereof

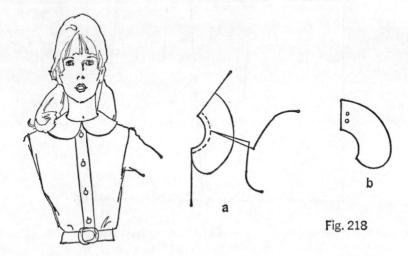

Fig. 218

Many close-fitting soft-roll collars (Peter Pan, convertible) start with a neckline that has been dropped ½ inch at the center front for more ease.

1. Trace the neck and shoulder areas of the bodice-front and back slopers in such position that the shoulder seams touch at the neckline and overlap at the armhole (Fig. 218a).

2. Establish the neckline. If the entire neckline is dropped, do this now. Raise the established neckline by ⅛ inch. Both the shortening of the neckline by raising it and the shortening of the outer edge by overlapping the slopers at the shoulders produce a soft roll. Aside from improved appearance the roll has the additional merit of hiding the seam that joins collar to garment.

3. From the neckline measure down in a number of places the width of the collar. Draw the style line (Fig. 218a).

4. Trace the pattern (Fig. 218b) and complete it.

FIG. *219a.* A Peter Pan construction on a slightly lowered neckline.

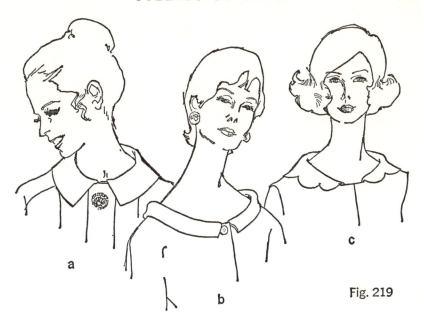

Fig. 219

FIG. *219b*. The same construction on a much lowered neckline.

FIG. *219c*. A scalloped collar that doesn't meet at center front. In designing a collar like this make sure the separation of the collar ends looks purposeful and not as if it were an accident of inadequate sewing.

The Sailor Collar

The sailor collar is still another dropped-neckline collar similar in construction to the Peter Pan collar.

1. Trace the neck and shoulder areas of the front- and back-bodice slopers as for the Peter Pan collar.

2. Drop the front neckline to a V shape. (The real middy was full enough and the V-neckline low enough to slip the head through without need of any further opening. A bib filler-in covered the too-low V.) (Fig. 220a).

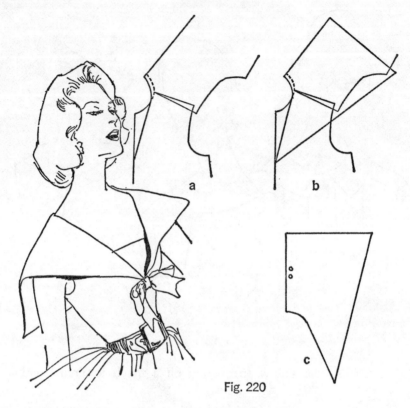

Fig. 220

3. Raise the neckline by ⅛ inch at the back only. Taper the raised neckline to the front neckline (Fig. 220a).

4. Square a line from the center back at the desired depth of the back style line to the desired width of the collar. Connect the back-collar style line with the V at center front (Fig. 220b).

5. Trace the collar (Fig. 220c) and complete it.

There is tremendous fashion appeal to this collar. In some form or another it seems perennially popular.

COLLARS WITH A DEEPER ROLL

How to Make a Flat Collar Have a Deeper All-around Roll

By the following method you may change a flat collar to one of medium or deep roll.

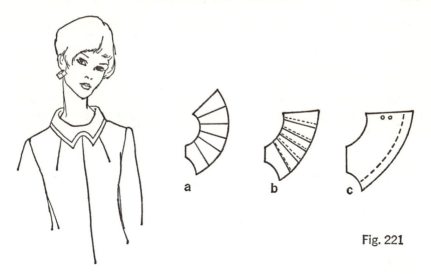

Fig. 221

1. Trace the flat collar. Draw five or six slash lines at right angles to the neckline. Begin about 1½ inches in from the center front and back (Fig. 221a).

2. Cut out the collar. Slash to the neckline. Overlap the style line—more at the back, less at the front (Fig. 221b). Note that the lapping straightens out the collar somewhat. When the straightened collar is applied to the curved garment neckline, it is pushed into a deeper stand. The amount of overlapping for the desired degree of roll (stand) can only be determined by testing in muslin.

3. Add to the width of the collar an amount equal to that used up by the newly created stand. Make certain that the fall of the collar is deep enough to hide the neckline seam. Should the style line of a collar be distorted by the addition of the stand (as it is in this design), reposition it to conform to the original design. In Fig. 221c, the scooped-out center-front style line *in its original proportions* is moved to the outside style line of the collar.

4. Complete the pattern.

COLLARS WITH A VERY DEEP ROLL

These can be drafted by the methods described for Figs. 212a and 212c. A collar on a neckband (Fig. 225a) is another way of dealing with a deep-roll design.

COLLARS WITH A DEEPER ROLL AT BACK ONLY

The Roll-Fitted Collar

This flattering collar has a medium roll at the back and fits flat at the front. (In a sense the sailor collar did this very thing.)

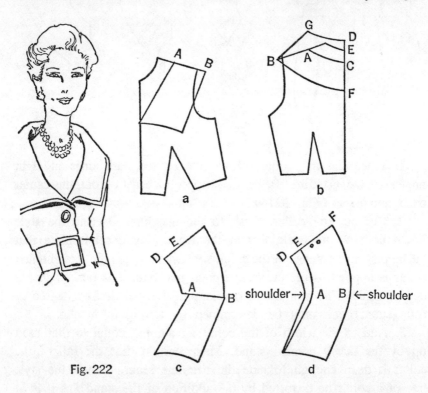

Fig. 222

FIG. *222a*

1. Trace the bodice-front sloper and establish the neckline. Draw the style line for the front collar. Label points A and B at the shoulder.

FIG. *222b*

2. Trace the bodice-back sloper but do *not* trace the shoulder dart. Establish the new back neckline (AC). Label points A and B to correspond to the bodice front.

3. From C measure up a distance equal to twice the desired stand of the collar. Label point D.

4. Mark point E halfway between C and D. This marks the position of the roll line.

5. From E measure down a distance equal to the fall of the collar. Label point F. The very least this can measure is stand plus ½ inch to cover the neckline. In this design, the fall is quite deep.

6. From D, draw a new slightly straightened neckline equal to the back neckline AC. Label point G.

7. Connect G and B with a straight line. Draw the back-collar style line from B to F.

FIG. *222c*

8. Cut out the front collar. Cut out the back collar. Join front and back collars at the shoulders, matching Bs. The back collar will extend beyond the front collar at the neckline because of the stand.

FIG. *222d*

9. Draw the neckline from center back (D) to center front, blending the curved back neckline into the straight front neckline at the shoulder.

10. Draw the roll line from the center back (E) to the center front, blending the curved back roll line into the straight front roll line at the shoulder (A).

11. Draw the style line from center back (F) to the front style line, blending the curved back style line into the straight front style line at the shoulder (B).

12. Complete the pattern.

The Convertible Collar—a medium roll collar

This is a versatile collar which can be worn open or closed and looks equally well both ways. When worn closed, the collar rolls from center back to center front and forms a V shape at center front. (Type I—Fashion Illustration 1). This distinguishes it from a roll-fitted collar that follows the curve of the neck. When worn open, the convertible collar forms lapels making it resemble the classic tailored notched collar (Type II—Fashion Illustration 2). There are several ways in which the pattern for the convertible collar can be made.

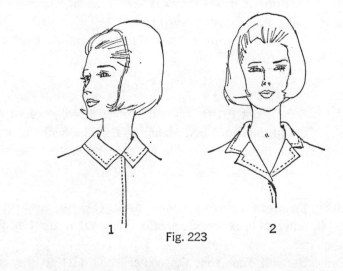

1   Fig. 223   2

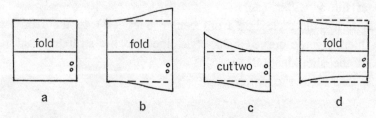

a   b   c   d

TYPE I CONVERTIBLE COLLAR (Fig. 223a)—doubled band of material with raw edges stitched to the bodice neckline.

1. Lower the neckline at center front ½ inch, making the neckline curve a more shallow one.

2. Draw a band double the width of the collar and the length of the neckline from center front to center back.

3. Complete the collar.

The straight lines of this construction are fine for striped, plaid, or checked material. The collar has one disadvantage. When worn closed, it stands away slightly from the back of the neck. Can you think why? It is because the roll line is longer than the neck circumference at the height of the stand.

TYPE II CONVERTIBLE COLLAR (Fig. 223b)—provides a better fit by using the principle described in Method II for drafting the Chinese collar, Fig. 209d.
Steps 1 and 2 are the same as for Type I convertible collar.

3. Extend the center-back line to one-half the desired stand of the collar.

4. From the back extension, draw a curved line to the center front, blending it into the original neckline of the band.

5. Fold the band along the straight outer edge and trace the pattern.

The straight line of the style line is fine for a collar planned to be worn open as a notched collar. When planned to be worn closed, the collar will fit better over the shoulders if the style line curves outward from center back to center front (Fig. 223c).

A variation of the Type II convertible collar produces a flatter, more open collar (Fig. 223d).

1. Lower the neckline at center front ½ inch, making the neckline curve a more shallow one.

2. Draw a band double the width of the collar and the length of the neckline from center front to center back.

3. Hollow out the band by drawing a curved line from center back to center front, blending it into the original neckline of the band.

Because the neckline curve of the collar is now more nearly that of the bodice, the collar will lie flatter. When cut on the bias, this type of collar will shape well around the neck and shoulders.

The Shirtwaist Collar—a convertible collar on a separate stand.

This youthful collar is a current favorite (Fig. 224). It is very effective in exaggerated style lines.

Fig. 224

HOW TO MAKE THE PATTERN FOR THIS STYLE

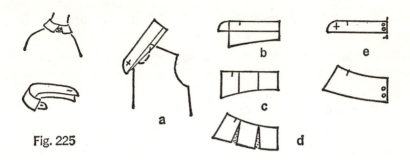

Fig. 225

The Stand (Fig. 225a)

Construct the stand like the Chinese collar of Fig. 209c. Add a front extension for buttoning.

The Fall

1. Trace the neckband. Over it, draw the collar as it will appear (neckline, center front, style line, center back). Notch the neckline (Fig. 225b).

2. Trace the fall of the collar and cut it out (Fig. 225c).

3. Draw two slash lines evenly spaced (Fig. 225c).

4. Slash and spread about ⅛ inch (Fig. 225d).

5. Trace the finished stand and fall of the collar (Fig. 225e). Complete the pattern.

The Convertible Shirtwaist Collar With Stand and Collar in One

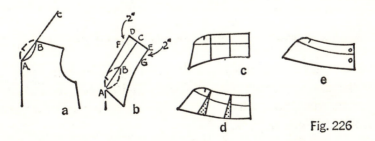

Fig. 226

FIG. *226a*

1. Trace the neck and shoulder area of the bodice-front sloper. Drop the neckline at center front ½ inch. Draw the new neckline. Label center-front A and shoulder B.

2. Connect A and B with a straight line. Extend it so the line equals the neckline measurement from center front to center back. Label the end of the line C.

3. Fold the pattern on line ABC.

4. Trace the neckline curve AB. Unfold the paper and draw the traced neckline. Notch it.

FIG. *226b*

5. From C, square a line up equal to the stand of the collar (1 inch to 1½ inches). Label point D.

6. From C, square a line down equal to the stand of the collar plus ½ inch. Label the point E.

7. From D, square a 2-inch line toward the center front. Label the point F.

8. From E, square a 2-inch line toward the center front. Label the point G.

9. From F, draw a line to the highest point of the neckline tracing.

10. Draw the style line from the center front (A) all the way around to G.

11. Trace the collar and the role line ABC (Fig. 226c).

12. Draw two slash lines evenly spaced (Fig. 226c).

13. Slash and spread ⅛ inch (Fig. 226d).

14. Trace the new pattern. Trace the roll line (Fig. 226e).

15. Complete the pattern.

The Shawl Collar—on a single-breasted garment

Will the *real* shawl collar please stand up! The bias band that looks like a shawl collar was illustrated in Fig. 207 as a separate collar. The true shawl collar is cut all in one with the bodice and is seamed at the center back.

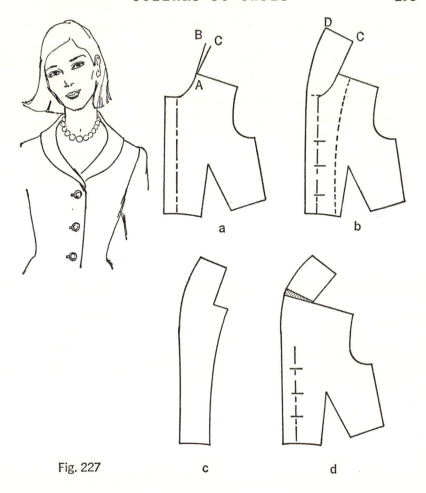

Fig. 227   c   d

1. Trace the bodice-front sloper. Label point A at the shoulder. Add a closing extension (Fig. 227a).

2. Square a line from A to half the back-neck measurement. Label point B (Fig. 227a).

3. From B, measure over ¼ to ½ inch to correct the angle of the collar. Label point C. Draw a line from C to A (Fig. 227a). CA is the back neckline now.

4. From C, square a line up equal to the entire width of the collar—that is, stand, fall, and ½ inch to cover the neckline seam. Label point D (Fig. 227b).

5. Connect D to the front extension with a curved line (Fig. 227b).

6. Draw the facing on the pattern (Fig. 227b) and trace it (Fig. 227c). Since it is the facing that becomes the upper collar, add at least ⅛ inch to the style line as an allowance for rolling the seam to the underside.

7. Test the collar in muslin. Should more ease be needed on the style line for better fit, extend the shoulder line to the style line and use it for slashing. Slash and spread ⅛ inch (or more) (Fig. 227d).

8. Complete the pattern.

The Shawl Collar—on a double-breasted garment

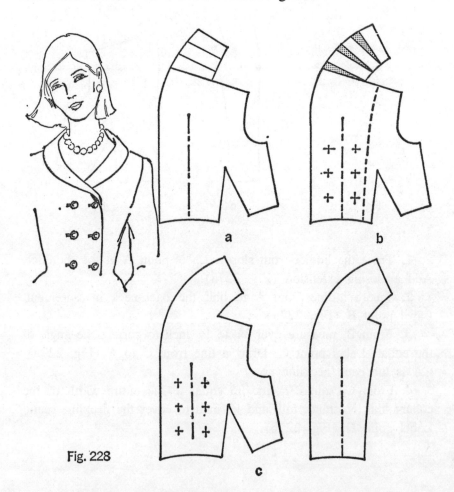

Fig. 228

The shawl collar on a double-breasted bodice is drafted in the same way with the following exceptions:

1. The extension is double-breasted (Fig. 228a).

2. From the shoulder line to the center back, the collar is slashed and spread for additional ease (Fig. 228b).

Fig. 228c shows the double-breasted shawl collar and its facing.

Notched Shawl Collar

By notching the lapel of a shawl collar, it is made to resemble the tailored notched collar. However, the construction of the two are quite different. How to tell them apart?

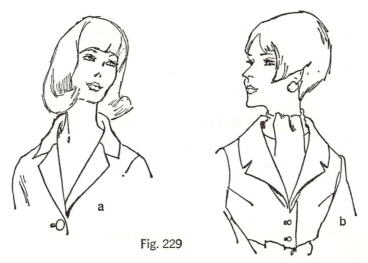

Fig. 229

The tailored notched collar always has a seam line that joins its separate collar to the lapel a little distance in from its end. This is what forms the notch. However high or low on the garment this joining seam may be, it is visible from the front (Fig. 229a).

The shawl collar and its lapel are all in one. The seam that joins right and left collars is at the center back. No seaming is visible from the front (Fig. 229b).

In the tailored notched collar, the notch is created by a set-back on the seam line. In the shawl collar, the notch is created by a cut-out on the style line.

There are other (more complex) methods of drafting the shawl and tailored notched collars but they are methods generally reserved for jackets and coats. Of course, they may be applied to dresses as well. If you prefer that type of collar and construction see page 394 for instructions.

Asymmetric Collars

You may want to have an asymmetric collar on your asymmetric closing.

STYLE I

1. Join the neck and shoulder areas of the complete bodice-front and bodice-back slopers at the right shoulder (Fig. 230a).

2. Establish the dropped neckline and the style line of the collar. Raise the neckline with a broken line (Fig. 230a).

3. Trace the collar (Fig. 230b).

4. For a deeper roll: draw slash lines around the collar (Fig. 230b).

5. Slash and overlap at the style line. Add width to the collar to compensate for the newly created stand (Fig. 230c).

6. Trace the collar (Fig. 230d).

7. Complete the pattern.

STYLE II

1. Draw a band equal to the entire back-neck measurement by the width of the collar (Fig. 230e).

2. Draw a band equal to the right-front neckline (including the extension) by the width of the collar (Fig. 230f).

3. Draw a band equal to the left-front neckline (including the extension) by the width of the collar (Fig. 230f).

4. Join the bands at the shoulder lines (Fig. 230g).

5. Trace the pattern and complete it.

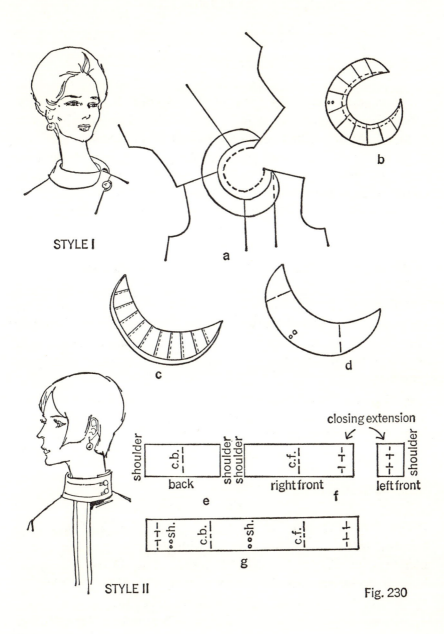

STYLE I

STYLE II

b

a

c

d

closing extension

shoulder	c.b. back	shoulder shoulder	c.f. right front	left front shoulder

e

f

sh. c.b. sh. c.f.

g

Fig. 230

CHOOSE YOUR COLLAR

"Push-button" Collars

The most difficult thing about drafting a collar is deciding which type it is—convertible or notched, notched or shawl, doubled over or faced, etc. If you are copying a picture or an actual garment or, if you are developing one of your own designs, analyze it for neckline shape, stand, roll, seaming, and style line. This will enable you to classify it as to type. Once you've done this, the rest is easy. Simply find the directions for that particular type of collar and follow them.

STRUCTURAL DESIGN VS. ADDED DECORATION

With collars, as with any other part of a garment, there arises the question as to whether the lines of the collar alone are interesting enough to carry the design or whether the assistance of trimming is needed. This is something you will have to consider with your artist's eye.

Should you decide on trimming, there is plenty to choose from: lace, ruffling, pleating, beading, embroidery, appliqués, edgings, cording, pipings, and many others.

PERHAPS SOME FULLNESS

You may be happier to leave the trimmings off and add some fullness, instead. Why not a collar with pleats (Fig. 231a), or a flounce (Fig. 231b), or one with godets (Fig. 231c). You could have rippled revers (Fig. 231d), or a jabot (Fig. 231e), or complete circles for a bit of froth at the neckline (Fig. 231f).

A thousand and one ways to design collars! Keep a scrapbook of interesting ones. You may find yourself using the ideas. Some collars are timeless.

Fig. 231

gather

a

b

c

d

e

f

Chapter IX

OFF THE CUFF—
THE SET-IN SLEEVE

OLD PRINCIPLES, NEW USES

Pattern principles are classic. The newness or today-ness of a design comes with a fresh approach to line, proportion, and detail.

There are no new principles in this chapter. There are merely the old ones used in new ways and applied to another part of a garment—the sleeve. This is one of the really satisfying aspects of pattern making: the fun of taking known rules of construction and applying them in an infinite number of variations to create new designs.

AN OLD STORY

You may do anything with a sleeve that you did with the bodice or the skirt.

The dart control may be shifted (Fig. 232a) or concealed in a control seam (Fig. 232b). It may be converted into gathers (Fig. 232c) or multiple darts (Fig. 232d). Fullness may be added— balanced (Fig. 232e) or circular (Fig. 232f). The sleeve may have a cowl (Fig. 232g). You may even add an opening extension (Fig. 232h). And so on—

Does this sound like old stuff to you? It is. You have been over it all in previous chapters. Now let us see how all this applies to a sleeve.

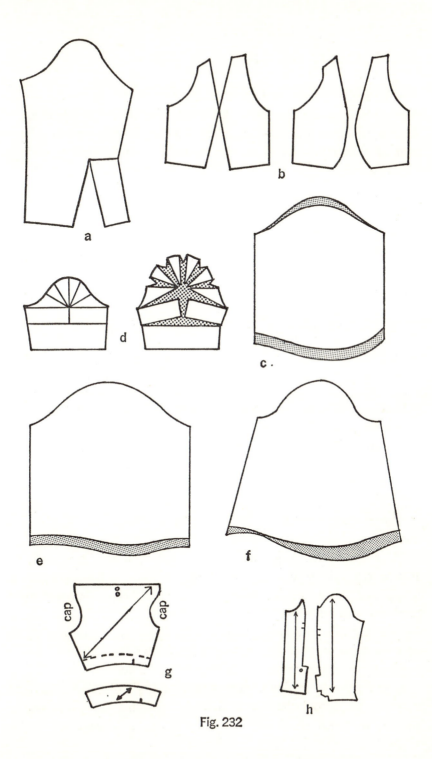

Fig. 232

THE ANATOMY OF A SET-IN SLEEVE

While more difficult to handle in sewing than the sleeve cut all in one with the bodice, the set-in sleeve has certain built-in advantages. The sleeve follows the natural "hang" of the arm while retaining freedom of movement—all this without bulk or underarm wrinkling. This is something one cannot claim for the kimono or dolman sleeve.

Fig. 233

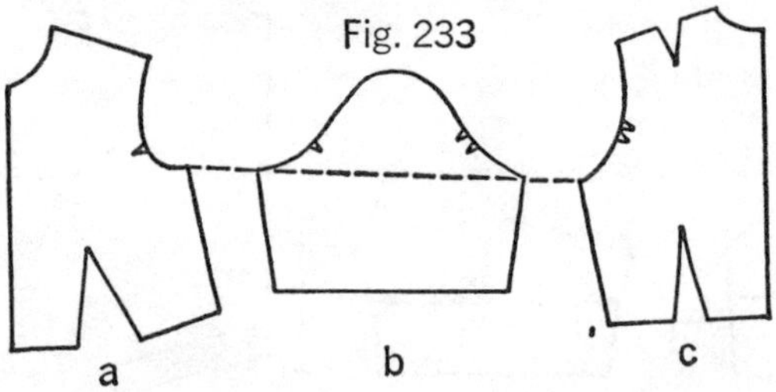

a　　　　　　　b　　　　　　c

Examine the above pattern (Fig. 233b). The part of the sleeve above the broken line is called the sleeve cap. A sleeve cap is as long as the front and back armholes (armscyes) combined plus at least 1 inch to 1½ inches of ease. (Many commercial patterns give 1½ to 2 inches of ease.) The ease is essential to accommodate the fleshiness or muscle of the upper arm and to provide room for movement. In some sleeves the ease may be minimized but rarely is it eliminated (Fig. 235).

The shape of the front armhole is different from the back armhole. It is shorter and the curve deeper (Fig. 233a). The back armhole is longer and the curve shallower (Fig. 233c). This is because most arm movement is forward, requiring an allowance in size and shape for the expanding shoulder muscle. The sleeve cap is drafted to fit each of these lengths and curves (Fig. 233b).

Make this simple test and you will see the difference (Fig. 234a).

If you are ever in doubt as to which side of a sleeve is front and which is back, fold the sleeve in half lengthwise. The front cap is deeper, the back shallower (Fig. 234a). In a below-elbow-length

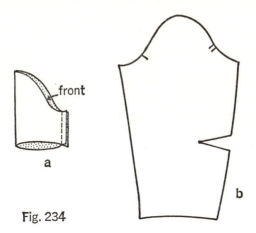

Fig. 234

sleeve, there is another way to tell front from back. The elbow darts (or their equivalent) are *always in back* (Fig. 234b).

Sleeve cap and armscye need matching notches to aid in setting the sleeve. These are placed at those points where the lines that arch over the shoulders swing into underarm curves. The sleeve cap above the notches contains the ease. The underarm curves of both sleeve and garment are the same length. The notches represent those points on the figure where arm and body meet.

HOW TO REMOVE EASE FROM THE CAP

Some sleeves are best designed on slopers where some or most of the ease has been removed. This would be so when the design calls for a smooth fit at the cap and fullness below. If there is enough fullness in the sleeve itself, the cap does not need the ease. As a bonus, you will find that removing some of the ease is a useful device when working with materials (stiff or firmly woven) that are difficult to set and stitch.

To remove the ease:

1. Draw a line across the cap of the sleeve. Draw a line at right angles to this and extending to the shoulder marking (Fig. 235a).
2. Slash both lines.

Fig. 235

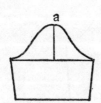
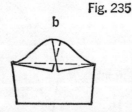
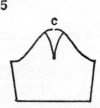

a   b   c

3. Overlap the slashed edge at the shoulder, removing all but ¼- to ¾-inch ease. Lap the cap over the lower sleeve at center. Keep the underarm in its usual position (Fig. 235b).

4. Compare the length of the new cap with the armscye. Make any needed adjustments.

NOTE: Instead of removing the ease, it can be converted into a dart (Fig. 235c). In addition to the design possibilities of any dart, this is a fine way to handle the ease in plaids, checks, and stripes that need matching with the bodice.

HOW TO COMPARE THE SLEEVE CAP WITH THE ARMSCYE

1. Start the comparison at the underarm seam. Match the underarm curve of the sleeve with the underarm curve of the armscye (Fig. 236a).

2. Using a pin for a pivot continue to match a tiny section at a time (about ⅛ inch) of sleeve and armscye from the underarm to the shoulder.

3. Mark the place where the shoulder of the bodice appears on the sleeve cap.

4. Do the same for the other side. You will find a space between the two marks (Fig. 236b). This leftover space is the ease.

5. Place the shoulder notch of the sleeve cap at the center of the space, dividing the ease equally between front and back (Fig. 236c).

NOTE: The notch should be at the crest of the curve. If it isn't, redraw the curve so that it will be (Fig. 246d). This will assure that the back sleeve cap will fit the back armscye and the front sleeve cap, the front armscye.

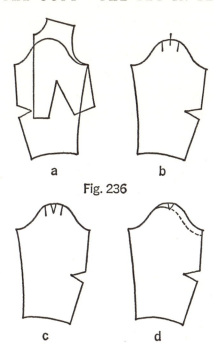

a   b

Fig. 236

c   d

THE UNDERARM CURVE

In a fitted dress, the armhole generally drops 1½ inches below the notch. This provides comfort in wearing and room for movement. The armholes of jackets and coats drop more. (See page 390.) Sleeveless dresses generally have less of a drop. (See page 351.)

There are some schools of thought that do not approve so deep a drop. They hold that a set-in sleeve set high provides greater ease of movement without the unsightly pulling up of the garment when the arm is raised. It is true (you've undoubtedly found this so) that the lower the armhole of a set-in sleeve, the more likely it is to involve the rest of the garment when the arm is in action. The problem is to strike a fine balance between comfort and movement.

Style changes are usually made on the overarm rather than the underarm (Fig. 268d). With few notable exceptions (the burnoose sleeve, page 364), underarm designs are lost to view. Additional fullness on the underarm may interfere with the comfort of the sleeve.

HOW TO DETERMINE THE GRAIN OF THE SLEEVE

Most sleeves are designed to hang with the vertical grain. Fold the sleeve in half lengthwise. The fold line is the vertical grain line (Fig. 237a).

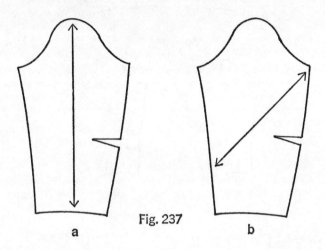

Fig. 237

a   b

Sometimes sleeves are designed on the bias (Fig. 237b). This may be for purposes of design or for fit. Bias gives easy mobility to a set-in sleeve. It "gives" with every arm motion. Expect the hemline of a bias sleeve to "bell" (gracefully) with time. Use the 45-degree triangle to determine the bias.

SET OF SLOPERS

It is a good idea to keep a set of sleeve slopers on hand for your designing. It saves time. It would be well to have:

1. a long sleeve
2. a short sleeve
3. an in-between-length sleeve

4. a two-piece sleeve
5. a sport-shirt sleeve and bodice adjusted for it
6. a shirtwaist sleeve

Directions for making these slopers follow.

THE LONG AND THE SHORT OF IT

In a dress a long sleeve ends at or just below the wrist bone.

A short sleeve is as short as the season, the fashion, and the beauty of the arms of the wearer permit.

Between the long and the short sleeves are many gradations of in-between-length sleeves.

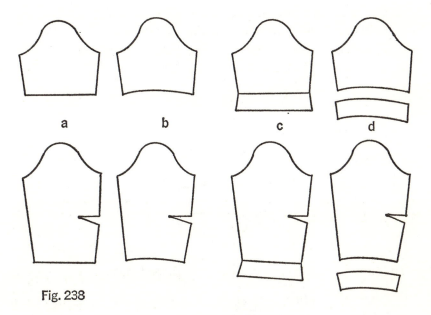

Fig. 238

1. Trace the basic sleeve sloper—above the elbow dart for the short sleeve, below the elbow dart for the in-between sleeve.

2. *For a short sleeve,* measure *down* an equal distance from the base of the sleeve cap on both underarm seams. *For an in-between-length sleeve,* measure *up* from the wrist in several places.

3. Draw the lower line of the sleeve. This may be a straight line (Fig. 238a) or a curved line (Fig. 238b).

4. If the lower line is straight, the facing may be turned up as a hem (Fig. 238c). If the lower line is curved, a separate facing must be provided (Fig. 238d).

5. Complete the patterns.

To refresh your memory about the straight hem (Fig. 239a):

a. From the hemline, measure up in a number of places the width of the hem (the broken line in the illustration).
b. Fold the pattern on the fold line of the hem.
c. Trace the width of the hem and both side seams.
d. Unfold the pattern and draw the hem.

Fig. 239

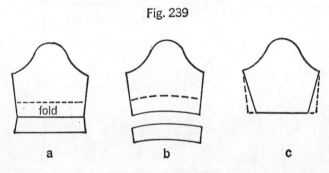

a   b   c

To refresh your memory about the shaped facing (Fig. 239b):

a. From the hemline, measure up in a number of places the width of the hem. Draw the facing (the broken line in the illustration).
b. Trace the facing on a separate piece of paper.

The standard-sleeve sloper contains at least 2 inches of ease at the biceps. This may make the short sleeve derived from it too wide to be pretty. Reduce the width at the hemline on the underarm seams. The broken lines of Fig. 239c are the original pattern; the solid lines, the adjusted pattern.

THE SPORT-SHIRT SLEEVE

Shirts, dresses, and uniforms designed to be used in action require sleeves which will not pull or ride up while in motion. To provide greater ease in movement, the sleeve cap is shortened and widened and the underarm seam is lengthened. The armscye of the bodice is adjusted to fit.

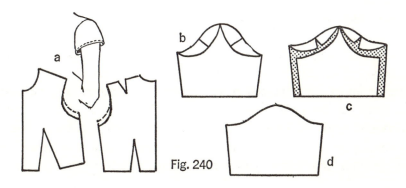

Fig. 240

1. Trace the bodice-front, bodice-back, and sleeve slopers. Use the sleeve sloper with most of the ease removed. (Leave ½ to ¾ inch.)

On the bodice front and back

2. Lower the underarm curve about 1 inch. (This may vary with your design or your need.) The lowering starts from the armscye notches. Redraw the underarm curve (Fig. 240a).

On the sleeve

3. Draw two deep curved lines from the shoulder notch to the underarm seams (Fig. 240b). These become slash lines. Draw two more straight slash lines dividing each new wing-like section in half (Fig. 240b).

4. Slash and spread so that the underarm-seam tips are raised and extended about 1 inch (or to match the underarm drop) (Fig. 240c).

5. Widen the sleeve to match (Fig. 240c).

6. Trace the sleeve pattern (Fig. 240d). Compare the new cap length with the front and back armscyes. Make any necessary adjustments.

7. Complete the pattern.

FLAT-CAP, MOVEMENT; HIGH-CAP, STYLE

The sport-shirt sleeve is designed for action and looks best when in action. The arm hangs naturally, the sleeve has a tendency to wrinkle under the arm and poke out on the overarm. The vertical grain fits as usual but because of the flattening of the cap the horizontal grain cannot. It will droop to the front and back. There is nothing you can do about this. Remember that this sleeve is designed for comfort in action rather than beauty at rest.

THE BASIC SHIRTWAIST SLEEVE PATTERN

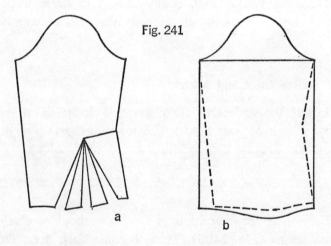

Fig. 241

a

b

1. Trace the full-length sleeve sloper. Cut out the tracing and the dart.

2. Shift the elbow dart to the wrist for gathers. Trace the pattern (Fig. 241a).

3. Draw a line across the cap of the sleeve. Square a line from each end of the cap to the length of the sleeve (Fig. 241b).

4. Draw a curved line at the wrist, making it about 1 inch longer at the deepest part of the wrist curve and blending it into the original wrist line at the underarm seams (Fig. 241b). The additional length provides room for the arm when bent.

This basic shirtwaist sleeve may be gathered into a band and slipped over the hand (Fig. 242a). Or, it may have a placket opening for easy access (Fig. 242b).

THE SLEEVE BAND TO BE SLIPPED OVER THE HAND

Make the band long enough to slip over the hand easily (knuckle circumference plus ease). Make it 1 inch to 1½ inches wide on a fold. It may be either straight or bias grain.

The width of the band added to the original full length of the sleeve provides a bit of "blousiness."

THE SHIRTWAIST SLEEVE WITH A PLACKET OPENING AND BAND

Mark the placket opening on the shirtwaist sleeve. This is in the little-finger position about one-fourth to one-third up from the back underarm seam. It is generally about 3 inches in length (Fig. 243a).

The opening may be finished with a facing (Fig. 242c), a continuous-bound placket (Fig. 242d) (done in the dressmaking stage), or a tailored placket (Fig. 242e). Directions for making the pattern for a tailored placket are on pages 246–247.

Fig. 242

front

a

b

c

d

e

The sleeve band equals the wrist measurement plus ease plus extensions for a buttoned closing. For design purposes, the band may be larger.

If the band is wider than 1½ inches, a comparable amount must be taken off the sleeve length (page 316).

A SHORTENED SHIRTWAIST SLEEVE

A sleeve band may be set on a shortened shirtwaist sleeve.

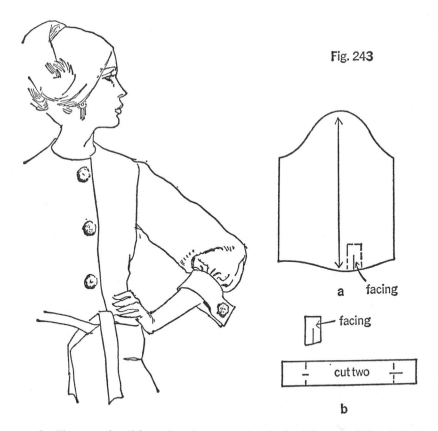

Fig. 243

a   facing

facing

cut two

b

1. Shorten the shirtwaist sleeve to the desired length (Fig. 243a).

2. Construct the pattern for the band and the facing for the opening (Fig. 243b).

THE SHIRTWAIST SLEEVE WITH A WIDE, FITTED BAND

If a sleeve band is wide and fitted to the arm, it is designed on the lower portion of the sleeve sloper. In the shirtwaist design of Fig. 244 (see Fashion Illustration), the band, like a yoke, provides a trim, fitted look that contrasts with fullness above.

HOW TO MAKE A FITTED BAND

1. On the cut-out sleeve sloper with the cut-out elbow dart, shift the dart control to the position for the sleeve opening (Fig. 244a).

2. Close the dart temporarily as for a bulging pattern. Draw the style line for the fitted band as for a yoke. Notch the style line and the underarm seam. Label sections 1 and 2 (Fig. 244b).

3. Cut the band away from the rest of the sleeve. Slash the dart line. Separate the two sections (Fig. 244c).

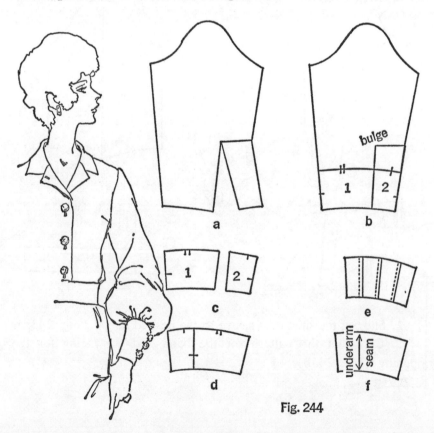

Fig. 244

4. Join sections 1 and 2 on the underarm seam so the band may be cut as one piece (Fig. 244d).

5. Remove the excess ease by slashing and overlapping the band to fit the lower arm snugly (Fig. 244e).

6. Trace the pattern (Fig. 244f). Add a closing extension. Face each band.

Directions for developing the pattern for the upper sleeve follow.

ADDITIONAL FULLNESS FOR THE SHIRTWAIST SLEEVE

Additional fullness may be added to the shirtwaist sleeve by the slash-and-spread method. The fullness may be circular (Fig. 245a) or balanced (Fig. 245b).

Additional fullness in width must be accompanied by additional length as well. This may be over-all length for general puffiness (Fig. 245c) or in varying amounts (Fig. 245d).

Make certain that both underarm seam lines are on the same angle. If not, there will be off-grain pulling and puckering when the sleeve is stitched.

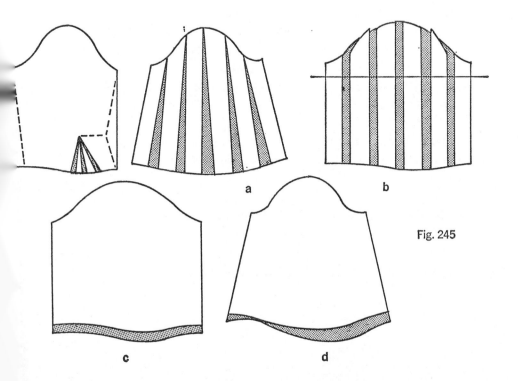

a

b

c

d

Fig. 245

THE FIVE STANDARD SLASH LINES

Generally, fullness is confined to the overarm area of the sleeve.

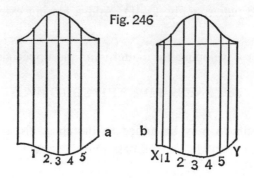

Fig. 246

FIG. *246a*

1. Draw a line across the sleeve cap.

2. Draw five slash lines at right angles to it:

   slash line #1 (front)—from the front notch on the cap

   slash line #2 (front midway)—from the front cap midway between the front and shoulder notches

   slash line #3 (shoulder)—from the shoulder notch

   slash line #4 (back midway)—from the back cap midway between the back and shoulder notches

   slash line #5 (back)—from the back notch on the cap

FIG. *246b*

When a great deal of circular fullness is to be added slash lines on the underarm are necessary, too (slashes X and Y).

SLEEVE STYLES WITH FULLNESS

Many sleeve styles are created by the manner in which the basic shirtwaist sleeve pattern is slashed and spread.

THE BISHOP SLEEVE

The bishop sleeve, derived from the Anglican bishop's robe, has additional length and width at the little-finger position. Viewed from the front, this sleeve looks like the classic shirtwaist sleeve.

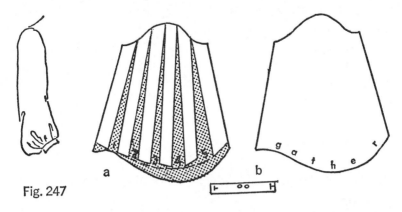

Fig. 247

1. Slash and spread the shirtwaist sleeve, adding more fullness toward the back of the sleeve and length in varying amounts as follows (Fig. 247a):

  a. add some length in equal amounts at the underarm seams.
  b. keep front (slash line ⅟1) as is.
  c. add more length at the center (slash line ⅟3).
  d. add most length at the back (slash line ⅟5).

2. Draw a compound curve connecting all points (Fig. 247a).

3. Trace the pattern (Fig. 247b). The sleeve opening is on the underarm seam.

4. Construct the sleeve band (Fig. 247b).

5. Complete the pattern.

THE PEASANT SLEEVE

The original peasant sleeve was on a dropped shoulder. Our peas-
ant-type sleeves are usually set-in sleeves.

1. Draw the vertical slash lines on the shirtwaist sloper. Draw a
horizontal guideline across the cap (Fig. 248a).
2. Slash and spread for balanced fullness (Fig. 248b).
3. Add length for puffiness at the cap and at the wrist (Fig. 248c).
4. Make the pattern for the sleeve band (Fig. 248d).
5. Complete the pattern.

FULLNESS UPON FULLNESS

Circular fullness may be added to the balanced fullness of the
peasant sleeve.

1. Start with Fig. 248b. Slash the sleeve on the guideline, dividing it into cap and lower sleeve.
2. Arrange sections 1 to 6 of both cap and lower sleeve on a
new guideline as follows (Fig. 248e):

The Cap

The sections are placed so they form a curve *above* the guideline—
sections 3 and 4 are raised 1 inch above the guideline, sections 1 and
6 touch the guideline at the underarm seams, and sections 2 and 5
are placed between 1 and 3 and 4 and 6.

The Lower Sleeve

The sections are placed so they form a curve *below* the guideline—
sections 3 and 4 are dropped 1 inch below the guideline, sections 1
and 6 touch the guideline at the underarm seams, sections 2 and 5
are placed between 1 and 3 and 4 and 6.

3. Trace the new pattern and complete it.

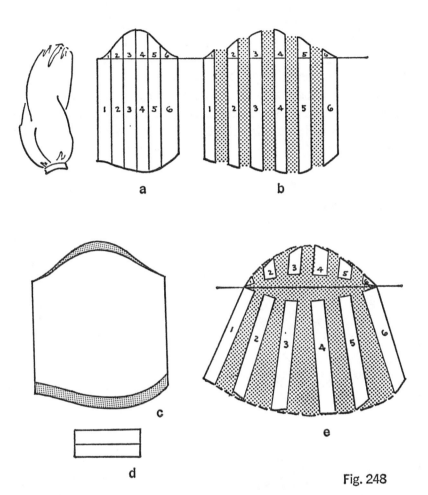

a

b

c

d

e

Fig. 248

THE BELL SLEEVE

The bell sleeve lends itself to the many exaggerated sleeve styles so endearing to today's young people. Hanging free without the constriction of a band the sleeve has the simplicity and innocence of an angel sleeve in an ancient frescoe—well, mostly. Consider the unangelic allure of the lacy bell sleeve of Fig. 249a.

Tied once, twice, many times, its puffs evoke the splendor of medieval costume (Figs. 249b and 249c). What matter a dip into history if the result is dramatically the present?

Fig. 249

HOW TO MAKE THE PATTERN FOR THE BELL SLEEVE

Fig. 250

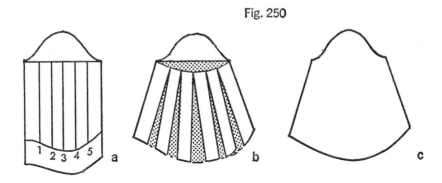

a   b   c

1. Trace the full-length sleeve sloper. (Fig. 250 shows the development of a pattern for a shortened bell sleeve.) Remove most of the ease from the cap. Extend the elbow dart across the entire sleeve and fold it out, thereby eliminating it from the sloper. Fasten to position with Scotch tape. Trace the sleeve. The sleeve will be so full that the dart will not be necessary. (Remember that the full, unfitted bodices and skirts did not need their darts, either?)

2. Draw a slash line across the cap of the sleeve (Fig. 250a).

3. Square a line from each cap end the length of the sloper. Draw the wrist line.

4. Draw slash lines from the cap line to the wrist line (Fig. 250a).

5. Cut away the cap. Slash all slash lines and spread for circularity to the desired fullness. The underarm tips of the cap and lower sleeve continue to touch. The center slash is spread a little more than the others (Fig. 250b).

6. Trace the pattern. Correct the wrist with a smooth, curved line (Fig. 250c).

7. Complete the pattern.

Have you noticed that the slashes in this pattern went only to the sleeve cap? This produces a smooth fit across the upper arm. Fullness is added below. The drop between the cap and the rest of the sleeve provides some extra length where needed when the arm is bent.

Should you want fullness from the armhole, slash and spread the entire sleeve from cap to wrist as in Fig. 245a.

A BELL BUT NO LIBERTY

It's a bell but there is no liberty at its edge.

It looks charming when its edge (elasticized) is pushed up on the arm (Fig. 251a). An elasticized casing can produce a lovely self-ruffle (Fig. 251b). A band and button is another way to coax the bell into a self-ruffle (Fig. 251c).

a

b

c

Fig. 251

Short-Sleeve Fullness

You can do with short sleeves anything you can do with long ones. Simply start with a short-sleeve sloper.

Short Sleeve With Fitted Armscye and Puffiness at the Hem

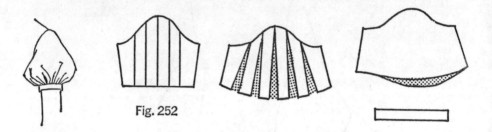

Fig. 252

Short Puffed Sleeve With Fullness at the Cap

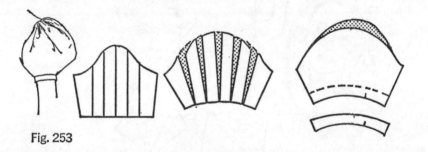

Fig. 253

Short Puffed Sleeve With Fullness at Both Cap and Hem

Fig. 254

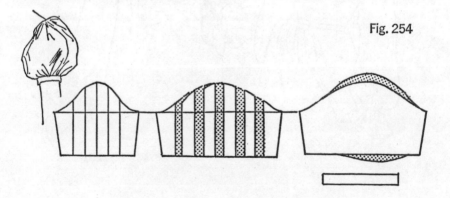

Short Pleated Sleeve

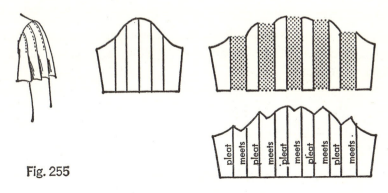

Fig. 255

The short sleeves may be as simple or as dramatic as you wish. They may be banded, cuffed, or worn free-hanging (Fig. 256).

Fig. 256

THE LEG-O-MUTTON SLEEVE

Another out-of-the-past sleeve that comes and goes in fashion—
the leg-o-mutton. It is slim and fitted below the elbow. Fullness is
added to its cap.

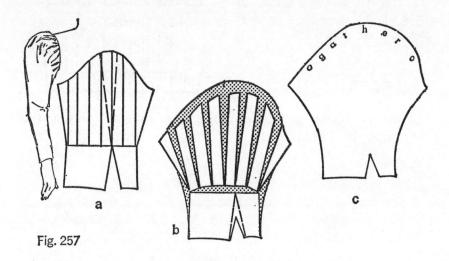

Fig. 257

Since this sleeve is quite fitted at the wrist, you will have to decide
what kind of closing you want before developing the pattern.

Part of the underarm seam may be zippered for a closing. Should
you choose to do this, start the pattern with a dartless sleeve sloper,
the same kind used for the bell sleeve.

Or, close the sleeve with a row of small loops and buttons. For this
type of closing, shift some of the elbow dart to the wrist at the little-
finger position to serve as the opening. Shift the rest of the dart
control as for gathers to the cap to be incorporated in the puff.

1. Trace the appropriate sleeve sloper. Draw a horizontal slash
line at the elbow (Fig. 257a).

2. Draw slash lines from cap to elbow (Fig. 257a).

3. Slash and spread the upper part of the sleeve to the desired
fullness (Fig. 257b).

4. Some additional length is added automatically by the separation of the upper and lower parts of the sleeve. More puffiness may

be added by drawing a freehand line that raises the cap (Fig. 257b). Shorten the wrist dart.

5. Trace the pattern, correcting the angularity of the underarm seams with curved lines (Fig. 257c).

6. Complete the pattern.

Obviously, the leg-o-mutton sleeve must be made of a fabric firm enough to sustain its shaped fullness. In addition, the puff should be bolstered by an underlining.

UP, OUT, AND AWAY

The leg-o-mutton sleeve is not the only sleeve that takes off in space. There are a host of others whose caps extend up, out, and away.

Here is a modification of the leg-o-mutton sleeve that has height and some fullness only in the upper part of the sleeve. The rest of the sleeve retains its slimness. Slash and spread a dartless sloper as illustrated below.

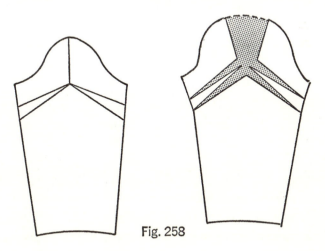

Fig. 258

By the use of *darts rather than gathers,* a square look is achieved.

Fig. 259

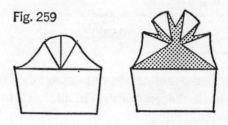

More darts require more fullness.

Fig. 260

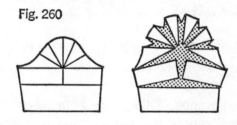

AN EXTENDED SLEEVE CAP

The sleeve consists of two parts—the extension and the original sleeve joined by a curved seam.

1. Trace two short-sleeve slopers without cap ease. Use one for the extension (Fig. 261a), the other for the sleeve (Fig. 261c).

2. On Fig. 261a, draw a style line across the sleeve cap as far down on the cap as you wish the sleeve to extend out from the armscye. Label A and B. Draw slash lines from style line to cap seam line. On Fig. 261c, locate the position of the style line on the cap seam line (A and B).

3. Cut away the yoke created by the style line. Slash and spread against a straight line, which becomes the new sleeve cap. This lemon-slice shape is the extension (Fig. 261b). The curved line becomes the seam line, which is stitched to the sleeve.

4. On Fig. 261c, draw slash lines from the center of the hem to the sleeve cap. The first and last slash lines extend to A and B.

5. Slash and spread so the seam line of the cap (AB) equals the seam line of the extension (AB) (Fig. 261d). Obviously, to be seamed the two lines must match in length. Correct the angularity of the hemline.

6. Trace the patterns and complete them.

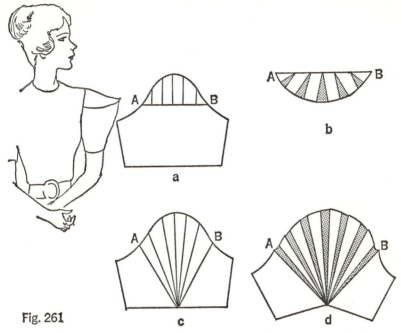

Fig. 261

Fig. 262 shows the construction pattern for an extended cap on a one-piece sleeve. Can you follow it?

Fig. 262a—the necessary slash lines

Fig. 262b—the cap spread

Fig. 262c—the lower sleeve spread and its restoration to the orignal sleeve height. Were it not for the latter there would be no extension—merely a sleeve yoke.

Fig. 262

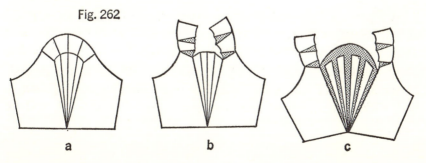

THE LANTERN SLEEVES

From a natural shoulder the lantern sleeves swell to rounded fullness at a style-line seam, then taper to a snug hem. The widest part of the sleeve may be at any length you choose. The width may be anything from just flare as in the melon sleeve (Fig. 263a) to a complete circle as in the barrel sleeve (Fig. 263b).

Fig. 263

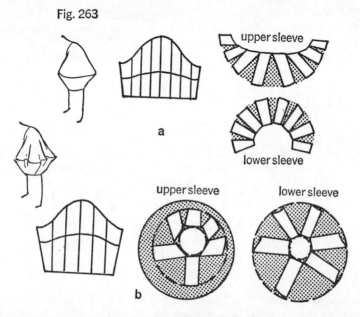

1. Trace the sleeve sloper with ease removed from the cap.
2. Shorten the sleeve to the desired length. Remove enough ease from the hem by the slash and overlap method so the sleeve fits snugly. In a below-elbow-length sleeve, eliminate the elbow dart.
3. Draw the style line that divides the sleeve into upper and lower parts.
4. Draw enough slash lines to provide an adequate guide for the seam lines of both upper and lower sleeves.
5. Cut the sleeve apart on the style line.
6. Slash and spread both upper and lower sleeves to the desired degree of fullness. Make the style-line seams match in length.
7. Trace the patterns and complete them.

The barrel sleeve is very popular for children's clothing. It is so easy to iron when the circles are pressed against each other.

Whenever there is a seam, there is an opportunity to insert some trimming—piping, cording, lace edging, braid. There is even a chance to modify the circular edges with interesting shapes (Fig. 264).

Fig. 264

CAPE SLEEVES FOR GRACE AND COMFORT

As you have discovered from the foregoing patterns, the cap of a sleeve may have any shape at all as long as it is the right length for the armscye. In the following cape sleeves the shape of the cap determines the slimness or fullness of the style line.

FIG. 265a. Hangs like a slim, little cape over the arms. It has an arched cap and a straight hem.

FIG. 265b. Adds fullness by reversing the pattern for Fig. 265a. The cap becomes the straight line while the style line is curved. Therefore, the cape is a little fuller.

FIG. 265c. Curves both cap and hem into a crescent shape. The deep curve of the cap means an even deeper (therefore longer) curve for the hem. This cape sleeve is more circular and more rippling than the previous ones.

FIG. 265d. Continues curving the cap until it becomes a full circle as does the hemline, too.

Each of the caps in Fig. 265 is exactly the same length—one that will fit the armscye without ease (none is necessary because of the fullness). Each has a different shape and therefore a different degree of fullness.

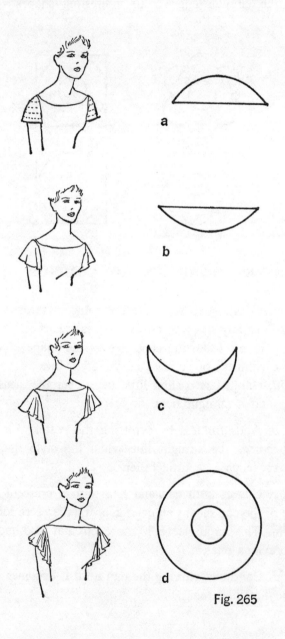

Fig. 265

CIRCLE SLEEVES

The circle sleeve of Fig. 265d, being the same depth and the same amount of fullness all the way around, falls in a cascade from shoulder to underarm when set into the armscye (Fig. 266a).

Should you wish to control the top-of-the-arm fullness and/or the underarm length (Fig. 266b), develop the pattern from the short-sleeve sloper. Slash and spread (Fig. 266c).

Several cape sleeves of varying lengths (perhaps of various colors) are a dramatic feature of an otherwise simple dress (Fig. 266d).

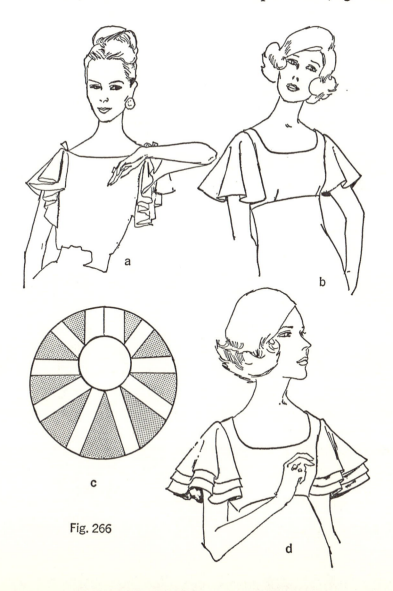

Fig. 266

DRAPES AND DRAPED EFFECTS

As with bodices and skirts, sleeve fullness need not always be vertical. It may be horizontal. Horizontal fullness may appear as pleats, tucks, gathers, or shirring. The shirring gives a draped effect. Needless to say, use soft materials that drape well. To hold the drapery in place use a lining or stay of sheer or lightweight material.

Here are a few construction patterns that show how to get draped effects (Fig. 267).

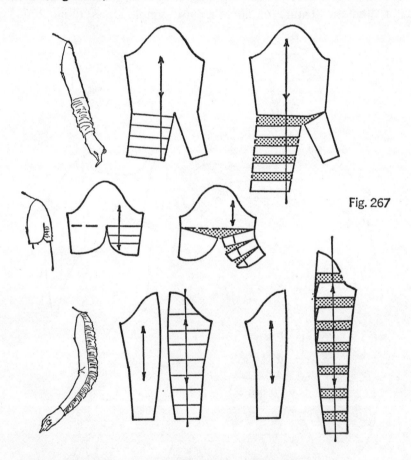

Fig. 267

SLEEVE DESIGNS VIA CONTROL SEAMS

Wherever there is a seam there is an opportunity for design.

Take the two-piece sleeve sloper developed in Fig. 81. Add an extension for buttoning (Fig. 268a) or leave it open as a vent (Fig. 268b). Add some shape to the opening (Fig. 268c).

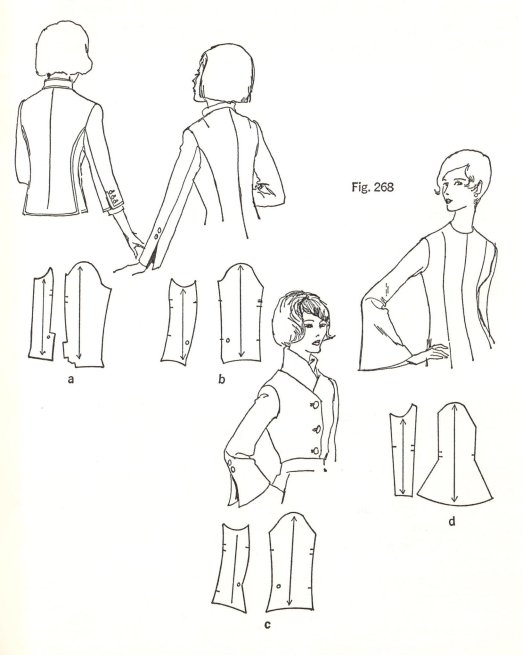

Fig. 268

An intricate sleeve pattern is easier to design on a two-piece rather than a one-piece sloper. It may even be that the style features are focused on one part of the sleeve. In Fig. 268d, the flare is confined to the lower sleeve.

Like all other control seams, those of the sleeve offer possibilities for design, too.

TWO-PIECE SLEEVE WITH VERTICAL CONTROL SEAM

1. Trace the long-sleeve sloper. Draw a slash line from shoulder to wrist, dividing the sleeve into two parts (Fig. 269a).

2. Extend the elbow dart to the slash line. Cut out the extended dart. Slash the dividing line from dart to wrist. Divide the control between wrist and elbow (Fig. 269b).

3. Extend the new (reduced) elbow dart clear across the sleeve, then eliminate it entirely by tucking or overlapping (Figs. 269b and 269c).

For a Shaped Control Seam

4. Correct the underarm seams so they are the same length and have the same degree of angle. Add a little width at the wrist (Fig. 269c).

5. Correct the position of the wrist dart so it is centered on the slash line (Fig. 269c).

6. Convert most of the ease in the cap to a dart (Fig. 269c). Notch the pattern as illustrated.

7. Cut out the darts at both cap and wrist. Cut the sleeve apart (Fig. 269d).

8. Correct the angularity of both sleeve sections with matching smoothly curved lines (Fig. 269e).

9. Complete the pattern.

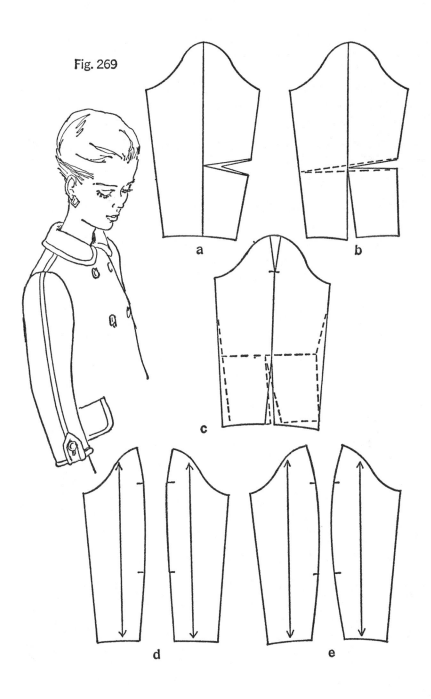

Fig. 269

a

b

c

d

e

For a Sleeve Seam Without Dart Control

1. Trace the corrected pattern of Fig. 269c as of Step 5. Use the wrist dart control as unstitched fullness (Fig. 270a).

2. Draw a slash line from shoulder to wrist, dividing the sleeve into two parts (Fig. 270a). Slash and separate the front and back patterns (Fig. 270b).

3. Complete the pattern.

With either two-piece sleeve pattern as a basis, add fullness or style lines to one or both parts of the sleeve.

If a sleeve is wide enough, it can be divided by style lines to match the control seam of the bodice whether it does or does not carry any of the control in its own seaming (Fig. 270c).

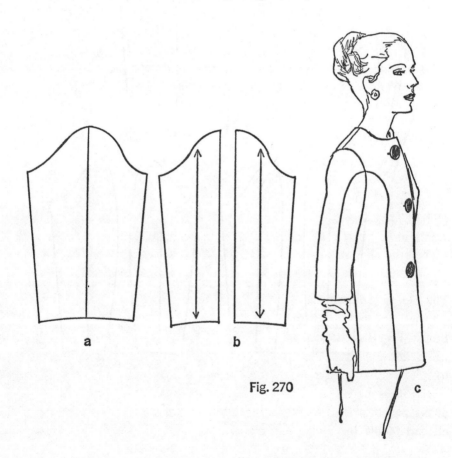

a   b

Fig. 270   c

SHOULDER-PAD ALLOWANCE

When a design calls for shoulder pads, an allowance for them must be made in the pattern.

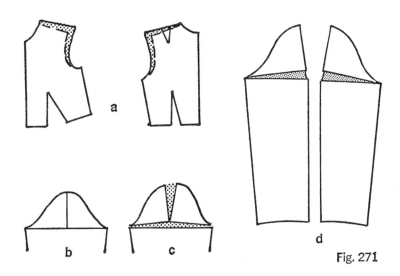

Fig. 271

The Bodice Adjustment

Raise and extend the shoulder half the thickness of the shoulder pad, both front and back. Draw a new armscye from the shoulder to underarm. The new shoulder line meets the old at the neckline (Fig. 271a).

For instance, if the shoulder pad is ½ inch thick, then raise and extend the shoulder ¼ inch in front and ¼ inch in back.

The Sleeve Adjustment

FOR A ONE-PIECE SLEEVE:

1. Draw a slash line across the cap. Draw a line at right angles to it extending to the top of the cap (Fig. 271b).

2. Slash these lines. Raise the cap to the amount of the thickness of the pad. For instance, the rise is ½ inch for a ½-inch pad. Keep all cap points together (Fig. 271c).

The spread at the top of the cap automatically opens to the right amount to accommodate the pad. Locate a new shoulder notch at the center of the opening.

FOR THE TWO-PIECE SLEEVE WITH A VERTICAL CONTROL SEAM
  1. Draw slash lines across the front and back caps.
  2. Slash and spread to the amount of the thickness of the pad (Fig. 271d).

A PATTERN FOR A SHOULDER PAD

There are many types of shoulder pads commercially available. If you can find just what you want, that's fine! So many times, however, the ready-made pads are not quite right for the lines of the garment. You fare better when you make the patterns for them.

The best pads are made from the garment pattern itself. This has the advantage of providing the exact shape that needs bolstering. Following are two standard patterns for set-in and kimono-type sleeves.

For a Set-in Sleeve

FIGS. *272a and 272b*
  1. On the bodice-front and bodice-back patterns, draw the shape of the shoulder pad (Fig. 272a). If the patterns for front and/or back are in two or more sections, join them to make complete front and back areas. The pad comes halfway down the armhole on both front and back. It may be triangular in shape at front and back. A squared-off front shape is preferable. It helps to fill out the hollow at the front armhole.
  2. Trace the front and back patterns. Join them at the shoulders for the complete shoulder-pad pattern (Fig. 272b).

3. Cut as many thicknesses and as many kinds of shoulder-pad material in this shape as will give the required height and firmness to the pad. Join with stitching.

Fig. *272c*

The pattern for a crescent pad to be stuffed and stiffened with rows of machine stitching.

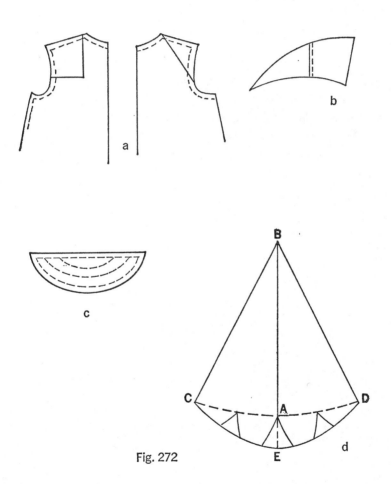

Fig. 272

FOR A KIMONO OR RAGLAN SLEEVE AND DROPPED-SHOULDER STYLES*

Your chances for getting away without shoulder pads are best in kimono or raglan sleeves and dropped-shoulder styles. The soft sloping lines are part of the charm of these designs. If padding is used to define the shoulder, it looks best when it is lightweight and when it cups the shoulder. Here is an easy-to-make pattern for this type of pad.

Fig. *272d*
>   AB equals the shoulder length
>   CA equals half the front armhole
>   DA equals half the back armhole
>   AE equals the desired depth of the pad
>   CADE is shaped by darts

---

* A complete discussion of these sleeves will be found in Chapter X. However, this seems a logical place to discuss shoulder pads for them.

CUFFS

What a collar is to a neckline, a cuff is to a sleeve.

A Band For a Separate Turnback Cuff

Fig. 273

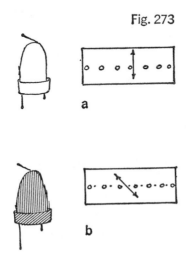

a

b

A straight band of fabric makes a fine turnback cuff. It may be cut on the straight of goods (Fig. 273a) or on the bias (Fig. 273b). To establish the straight grain, it is generally sufficient to fold the cuff in half and use the fold as the grain line. (Fig. 278 is an exception.) Use the 45-degree triangle to establish the bias from the straight grain.

The band is as wide as you would like it to be and as long as the sleeve edge plus ease. How much ease depends on the thickness of the material to be used. One-half inch is a safe amount to start with.

If you cut the band double, there will be no facing to cut or sew.

Cut underlining to the full length and width of the band. Cut interfacing to the fold and seam lines. Attach by hand stitching.

The Turnback Cuff All-in-one With the Sleeve

This cuff is an extension of the lower edge of the sleeve.

1. Trace the sleeve sloper. Make the wrist line a straight line instead of its usual curve. You cannot turn back a curved line (Fig. 274a).

2. Mark the width of the cuff on the sleeve (Fig. 274a).

3. Draw a line from the elbow dart to the little-finger position (Fig. 274a).

4. Fold the pattern on the wrist line. Trace the cuff and the little-finger dart line. Unfold the pattern and draw the cuff and the dart line (Fig. 274b).

5. Cut out the pattern. Cut out the elbow dart. Slash the little-finger dart line. Shift the elbow dart control to the wrist (Fig. 274c).

6. Add a shaped extension for design interest in the opening created by the wrist dart. Shorten the dart (Fig. 274c).

7. Locate the facing on the sleeve (the broken line in Fig. 274c). Make it deep enough beyond the wrist line so that the facing edge will not show when the cuff is turned back. Notch.

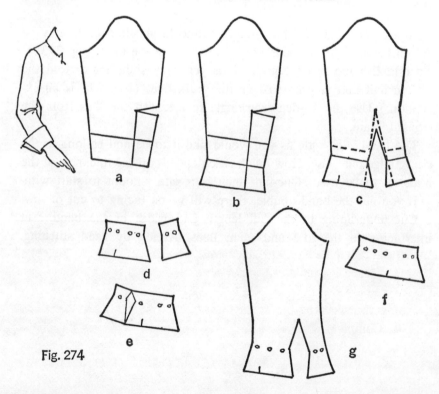

Fig. 274

8. Trace the two facing sections (Fig. 274d) and join them at the underarm seam (Fig. 274e). Since it is the facing which is the upper surface when the cuff is turned back add at least ⅛ inch to all outside seams as an allowance for rolling the seam to the underside.

9. Trace the complete facing, ignoring the shaped section at the underarm, which remains as ease for the turnback (Fig. 274f).

10. Trace the sleeve with its extended cuff. Trace the wrist line, which becomes the fold line for the turnback (Fig. 274g).

11. Complete the pattern.

A Fitted Cuff on a Fitted Sleeve

While this cuff lies fairly flat against the sleeve, it has just enough ease to make it stand away slightly.

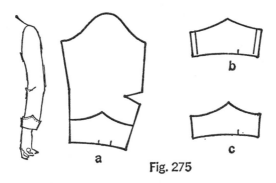

Fig. 275

1. On the sleeve sloper, draw the style line of the cuff (Fig. 275a).

2. Trace the cuff pattern. Add at least ¼-inch ease on each underarm seam—more if the fabric warrants it (Fig. 275b). When much more ease is needed it is preferable to add it by the slash-and-spread method. In this way, the shaping of the style line is preserved.

3. Trace the facing pattern (Fig. 275c). Trace the upper cuff from it and add at least ⅛ inch on all outside seams to allow for turning the seam to the underside.

4. Complete the pattern.

A Flared Turnback Cuff

1. On the sleeve sloper, draw the style line for the cuff (Fig. 276a). Notch the wrist line.

2. Trace the cuff and cut it out. Draw several slash lines on it (Fig. 276b).

3. Slash and spread to the desired fullness. Add some flare to each end of the cuff to balance the fullness (Fig. 276c).

4. Trace the flared cuff (Fig. 276d).

5. If a facing is necessary, trace it from the cuff. Since it will be the facing which will be the upper surface when the cuff is turned back, add ⅛ inch to all outside edges as an allowance for the seam roll.

6. Trace the patterns and complete them.

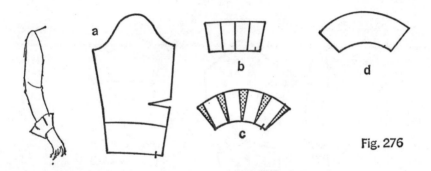

Fig. 276

A Flared Turndown Cuff

1. On the sleeve sloper, draw the style line of the cuff. Notch it. Draw slash lines on the cuff (Fig. 277a).

2. Cut the cuff away from the sleeve. Slash and spread at the hem edge to the desired fullness (Fig. 277b).

3. Trace the facing (Fig. 277c). Trace the cuff, making it ⅛ inch larger on all outside edges for a seam-roll allowance.

4. Complete the pattern.

Why not try a flared collar to match?

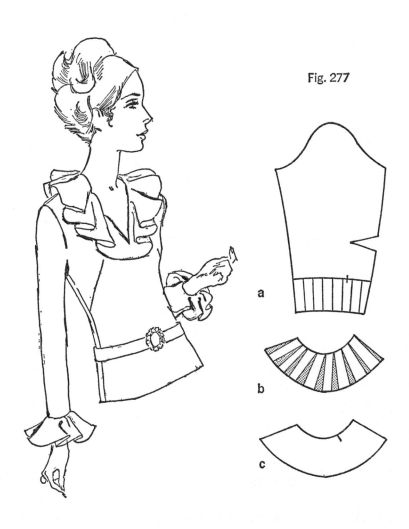

Fig. 277

A Fitted Cuff With a Closing Extension

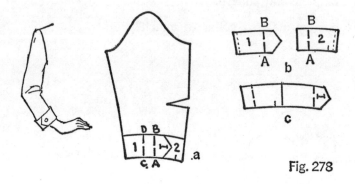

Fig. 278

1. On the sleeve sloper, draw the cuff just as you would like it to appear on the sleeve. Label AB, the closing line. Label CD, the underlap. Label section 1, which will include the extension. Label section 2, which will include the underlap (Fig. 278a).

2. Trace section 1. Trace line AB. Trace section 2. Trace line AB.

3. Add ¼-inch ease to each underseam. Even a fitted cuff must stand away slightly from the sleeve to look pretty.

4. Cut out sections 1 and 2 (Fig. 278b).

5. Join them on the underarm seam (Fig. 278c).

6. Trace the cuff facing in one piece (Fig. 278c). For the cuff add ⅛-inch allowance on all outside edges for the seam roll.

7. In a separate cuff the grain is usually centered over the top of the hand. In this case line AB of the extension meets that requirement so it becomes the straight grain.

8. Complete the pattern.

The French Cuff

When you think of a classic shirtwaist you visualize it with French cuffs. It is an elegant style.

The French cuff is a wide band that turns back to form a double cuff. There are four buttonholes on each cuff through which the cuff links (collected and treasured) are passed.

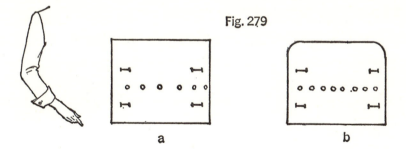

Fig. 279

a   b

1. Shorten the sleeve an amount equal to the width of the cuff.

2. Make the length of the cuff equal to the edge of the shortened sleeve. Double the width of the cuff. Add ½ inch to the turnback end of it in order to hide the seam which joins cuff to sleeve. The edges of the turnback may be square (Fig. 279a) or rounded (Fig. 279b).

3. Mark the buttonhole placement an equal distance from the fold line.

4. Trace the facing exactly the same as the cuff. (This cuff is an exception to the rule since all edges of the cuff are visible.)

5. Complete the pattern.

THE SLEEVELESS DRESS

A sleeveless dress is not just one with the sleeves left out. It is planned that way deliberately (Fig. 280).

A dress with sleeves must have an armscye deep enough and a bodice wide enough to provide ease for movement. Leave out the sleeves and you're left with a gaping hole too wide, too deep, and lacking in design. What's more, a part of your anatomy (never particularly noted for its beauty) is exposed.

In a sleeveless style, the underarm is generally built up however bare the shoulders and arms. The less there is of a dress, the more the amount of ease removed from the bodice.

In this fashion period of pleasant exposure, the designers have been the best barers of good views.

Fig. 280

Chapter X

MORE ABOUT SLEEVES
Sleeves Cut All in One with the Bodice

It is easy to understand the universal and timeless appeal of sleeves cut all in one with the garment. They are easy to cut, easy to sew, easy to wear. There is an ample grace to their appearance.

The Japanese kimono, the spiritual ancestor of our own, has given its name to a whole group of sleeves that resemble it more in style than in structure.

The Japanese kimono is a deep rectangle of cloth stitched at right angles to the main body of the garment (Fig. 281a). (Japanese fabric is loomed too narrow to cut the sleeve all in one with the garment.) It is a loose, comfortable, useful sleeve. An outer garment to be worn over it must have an even deeper matching sleeve to cover it. It is a style hardly suited to the pace of contemporary life—even for the Japanese.

Our kimono sleeve is usually a fitted one. Were it to be cut at right angles to the bodice of which it is a part, there would be considerable

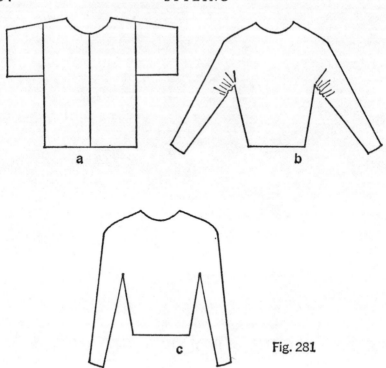

Fig. 281

wrinkling when the arms were brought into a normal position (Fig. 281b). As the kimono sleeve is cut at an angle that more nearly approximates the natural hang of the arms, it reduces the wrinkling but restricts the movement (Fig. 281c). With the insertion of a hinge (gusset), freedom of movement is restored.

Between the right-angle-sleeve placement of the Japanese kimono sleeve and the near-vertical hang of our fitted kimono sleeve are a whole group of kimono-raglan-dolman sleeves with varying degrees of fullness, depth, and angle (Fig. 282).

The angle at which the sleeve joins the shoulders is determined by the way in which the bodice front, bodice back, and sleeve slopers are positioned to produce the pattern.

Fig. 282

THE FITTED KIMONO SLEEVE

1. Trace the bodice-front sloper. Trace the bodice-back sloper and shift the shoulder dart to the neckline—out of the way of the kimono sleeve construction. Trace the sleeve sloper. Divide it into front and back with a line from shoulder notch to wrist. Cut out the slopers.

FIG *283a*

2. Place the bodice slopers in such a way that the shoulder seams touch at the neckline and are spread ½ inch apart at the armhole for ease.

3. Fold back the sleeve cap and place the sleeve sloper so that the underarm seams are an equal distance below the front and back armscyes on the side seams.

4. Trace all three slopers in this position.

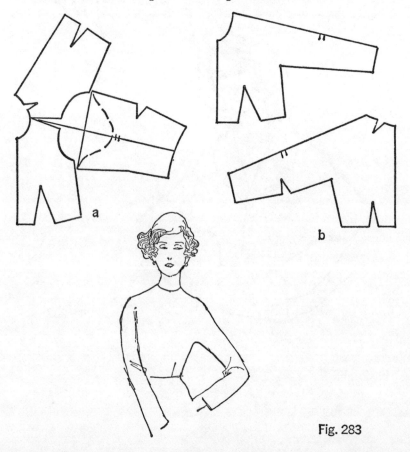

a

b

Fig. 283

5. Draw a line connecting the point at which the shoulders meet at the neckline with the dividing line of the sleeve.

Fig. *283b*

6. Cut out the pattern. Cut it apart on the dividing line.
7. Trace and complete the pattern.

A fitted kimono sleeve will need a gusset.

Fig. 284

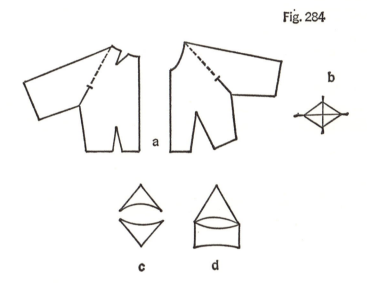

1. Draw a line from the underarm to the shoulder at the neckline (Fig. 284a).

2. On this line, measure up a distance equal to the length of one side of the gusset—small enough to keep it hidden on the underarm, say 3 to 4 inches. The pattern will be slashed to this point. Mark the end of the slash (Fig. 284a).

3. On separate paper, draw two lines perpendicular to each other. Draw a diamond-shaped gusset each side of which is equal to the length of the gusset slash line (Fig. 284b).

4. Complete the pattern for the gusset.

The diamond shape is the basic gusset shape. However, you know enough about designers now to know they are never satisfied with just basic shapes.

There are many variations of gusset shapes. Here are two frequently encountered; a two-piece gusset for more precise underarm
shaping (Fig. 284c) and one incorporated into the underarm section
of a short sleeve (Fig. 284d). Be as inventive with a gusset as with
any other part of a garment.

THE DEEPER THE SLEEVE, THE MORE DRAMATIC IT BECOMES

Draw identical curved lines from the side seams of the bodice to
the underarm seams of the sleeves both front and back. The drop
may be from just enough to provide movement without resorting to
a gusset (Fig. 285a) all the way to the waistline for the batwing
design (Fig. 285b).

Fig. 285

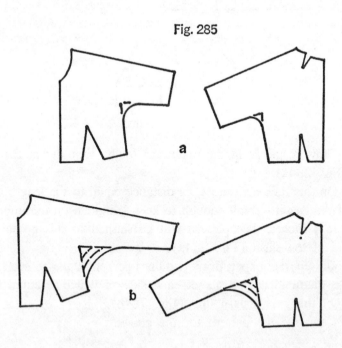

a

b

Don't be alarmed at the size of a long-sleeved kimono pattern—particularly that of the batwing sleeve. Remember that you now have not only the bodice pattern but the sleeve pattern, too.

Want to make the pattern even larger? Add balanced fullness for this enchanting draped kimono-sleeved dress (Fig. 286).

Fig. 286

NEW SLOPER PLACEMENT RESULTS IN NEW DESIGNS

By changing the basic arrangement of bodice-front, bodice-back, and sleeve slopers, the design of the kimono sleeve can be varied.

THE SHORT, WIDE KIMONO SLEEVE

1. Trace and cut out the sport-shirt slopers—bodice front, bodice back, and sleeve. Divide the sleeve into front and back by drawing a line from cap to hem.

2. Place the bodice slopers so that the shoulder seams overlap at the neckline and spread 1 inch at the armhole. Place the sleeve sloper as illustrated (Fig. 287a). Trace the slopers.

3. Draw a line from the point of overlapping to the dividing line of the sleeve (Fig. 287a).

4. Trace the front bodice with its original neck and shoulder line continuing into the sleeve line. Trace the back bodice and sleeve in the same way (Fig. 287b).

5. Correct the angularity of the shoulder line with a curved line.

6. Complete the pattern.

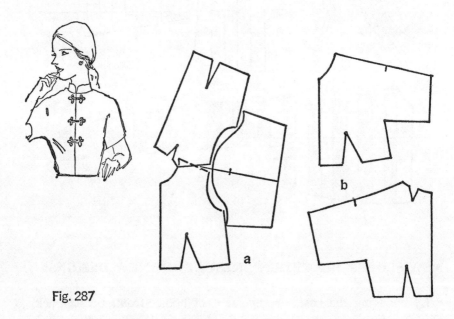

Fig. 287

To ADD FLARE: Steps 1 to 3: the same as for Fig. 287.

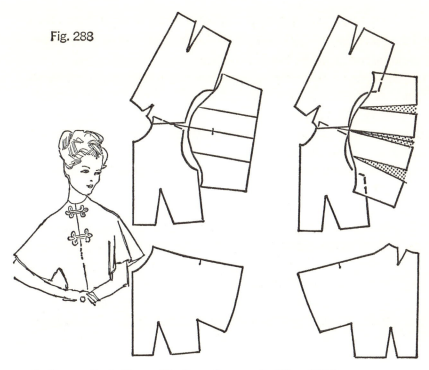

Fig. 288

4. Draw slash lines. Slash and spread (Fig. 288).
Continue as for Fig 287 from steps 4 to 6.

A KIMONO SLEEVE THAT FITS CLOSE TO THE BODY

1. Draw a right angle large enough to take the complete drawing.

2. Trace the bodice-front and bodice-back slopers so that the shoulders touch at the armhole and are spread open at the neckline. The center front is on the vertical line of the right angle. The center back is on the horizontal line (Fig. 289a).

3. Place the sleeve sloper so that it overlaps the bodices. The shoulder notch touches the bodice shoulders. The side seams of the bodice are equal in length. Trace the sloper in this position. Divide it into front and back with a line from cap to wrist (Fig. 289a).

4. Trace the pattern.

If the fabric to be used for this design is a plain linen weave, the pattern may be used as one piece (Fig. 289b). The center front is the lengthwise grain, the center back is on the crosswise grain, and the sleeve is on the bias. The shoulder shaping is accomplished by the dart that is formed by the placement of the slopers. It will fit better if the dart legs are curved. For the more usual front and back patterns, trace each separately (Fig. 289c). Correct the shoulder angularity with a curved line.

5. Locate the position for the gusset and construct it (Fig. 289c).

6. Complete the pattern.

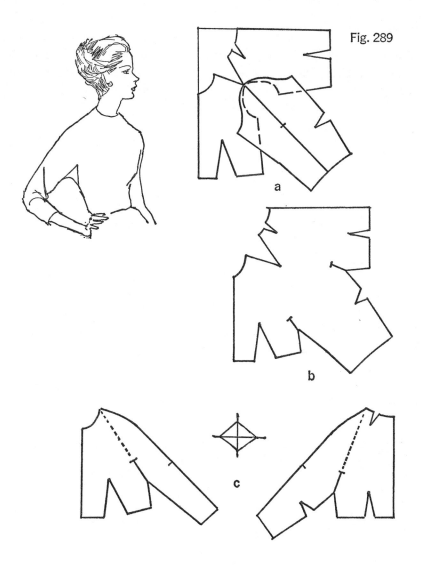

Fig. 289

a

b

c

THE BURNOOSE SLEEVE

There is a charming perversity to this sleeve. The underarm folds which we have been trying so hard to minimize emerge triumphantly and dramatically in this design as great drapes. In soft fabrics, the drapes fall in free folds (Fig. 290a). In stiffer fabrics, the folds can be arranged more formally (Fig. 290b).

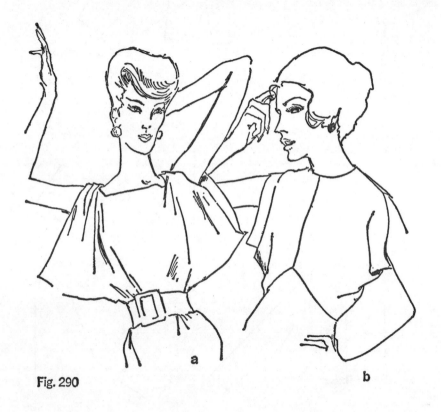

a

Fig. 290   b

HOW TO MAKE THE PATTERN FOR THE BURNOOSE SLEEVE

1. Place the bodice-front and bodice-back slopers so the shoulders touch. Trace them. Place the sleeve sloper so the shoulder notch touches the shoulders and the underarm drops below the bodice.

Make certain that the bodice side seams are equal. Trace. Divide the sleeve into front and back with a line that is a continuation of the shoulder line (Fig. 291a).

2. Shorten the sleeve (Fig. 291a).

3. Draw deep underarm curved style lines both front and back (Fig. 291a).

4. Trace the front pattern. Trace the back pattern. Mark the shoulder point (Fig. 291b). Only the front pattern is shown in this exercise. The back is developed in the same way.

5. Draw slash lines from the shoulder point to the underarm on both front and back patterns (Fig. 291b).

6. Cut out the pattern. Slash and spread (Fig. 291c).

7. Trace the new pattern, correcting the angularity of the shoulder with a curved line. Draw the underarm curve (Fig. 291d). You may cut away the sleeve on a new style line from shoulder to hem as in both designs in Fig. 290.

8. Complete the pattern.

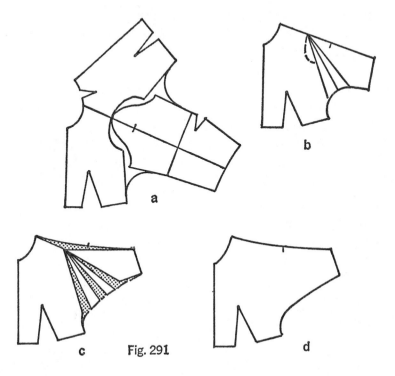

a

b

c   Fig. 291   d

THE DROPPED-SHOULDER DESIGN

The dropped-shoulder design is a kind of kimono sleeve. A great variety of designs are built upon it.

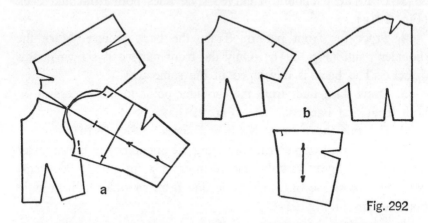

Fig. 292

Here is yet another way to arrange the bodice and sleeve slopers.

1. Place the bodice-front and bodice-back slopers so the shoulders touch at the armscye and spread open somewhat at the neckline. (Unlike Fig. 289 the center back is *not* placed at right angles to the center front.) Trace the slopers in this position (Fig. 292a).

2. Place the sleeve sloper so that the cap touches the shoulder and overlaps the bodice at front and back. Trace the sleeve in this position. Divide the sleeve into front and back (Fig. 292a).

3. Draw a line across the sleeve to shorten it (Fig. 292a).

4. Cut out the pattern. Cut off the lower portion of the sleeve. Cut the pattern apart on the shoulder seam (Fig. 292b).

5. Complete the pattern.

The short kimono sleeve of Fig. 292b is an interesting design of itself (Fig. 293a).

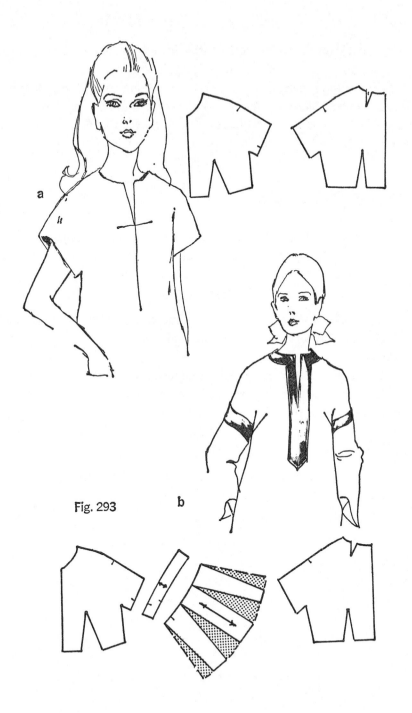

a

Fig. 293   b

If the sleeve is to be long there is not much point in cutting the pattern apart merely to join it again, unchanged, with a seam line. Make the separation meaningful by adding some design features to the lower sleeve: perhaps a band of trimming and some flare (Fig. 293b). Or added fullness—circular (Fig. 293c) or balanced (Fig. 293d).

JUGGLE THE PIECES

The variety of kimono sleeves in the foregoing designs are dependent on the relative placement of the bodice-front, bodice-back, and the sleeve slopers. Glance back over this chapter and note the effect created by the placement of front and back slopers with:

1. shoulders touching at the neckline and spread at the armhole.

2. shoulders overlapping at the neckline and spread at the armhole.

3. shoulders touching at the armhole and spread at the neckline.

4. shoulders touching at the neckline and armhole while the sleeve cap is dropped below the armscye.

5. shoulders open at the neckline and touching at the armscye while the sleeve cap overlaps the bodice.

It's like a game to juggle these three pattern pieces until one arrives at an interesting design.

c

d

Fig. 293

THE CAP SLEEVE

The cap sleeve is a very short version of the kimono sleeve. It is so simple a sleeve that the pattern can be made for it without juggling around of slopers.

1. Trace the bodice-front and bodice-back slopers.

2. Extend the shoulder lines to the desired length of the cap. The cap should be only deep enough to cover the shoulders. If it is any deeper, it must be drafted by the regulation kimono-sleeve method.

3. Lower the armhole 1 inch to 2 inches (Fig. 294a).

4. Connect the extended shoulder to the lowered armhole. You may use either a straight line (Fig. 294a) or a curved line (Fig. 294b).

On some figures such cap sleeves have a tendency to strain and tear at the armhole. Try this design: skip Step 3; substitute for Step 4 the following: connect the extended shoulder to the waistline (Fig. 294c). Stitch to normal drop for cap sleeve.

A modified cap sleeve is another solution for the problem of tearing at the armhole. This sleeve has the good features of both the cap

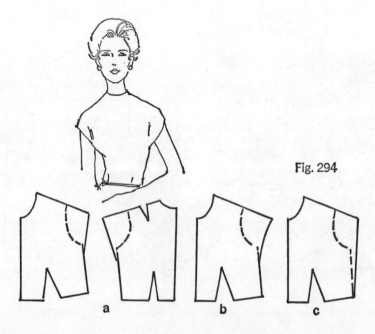

Fig. 294

a   b   c

sleeve and the sleeveless dress. The upper part looks like the cap sleeve, while the lower part retains the freedom of a sleeveless dress.

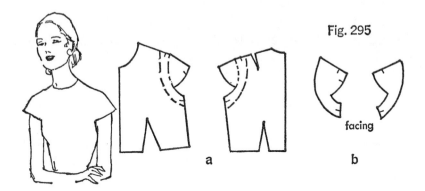

Fig. 295

a   b

facing

FIG. *295a*

1. Extend the shoulder line as for the cap sleeve.

2. Raise the underarm curve.

3. Draw the style line of the cap, bringing it to the raised underarm at or slightly below the usual notch position.

4. Designate the facing.

FIG. *295b*

5. Trace the facing.

6. Complete the pattern.

A CAP SLEEVE WITH A SHAPED STYLE LINE

The shoulder of this cap sleeve is stitched only to the shoulder point. The shaped cap requires a shaped facing to match.

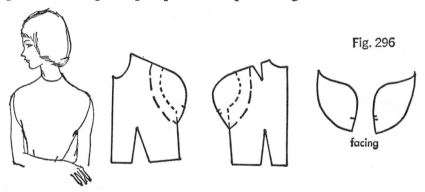

Fig. 296

facing

PART OF THE BODICE JOINED WITH THE SLEEVE

Sometimes only *part* of the bodice is joined with the sleeve. A whole new group of sleeves stems from this procedure—the dolman, the raglan, the saddle or strap, the dropped shoulder, and the yoke-and-sleeve.

THE DOLMAN SLEEVE

While the kimono sleeve was all bodice and part sleeve, the dolman sleeve is part bodice and all sleeve. Whereas front and back kimono sleeves are joined by a shoulder seam, bodice and dolman sleeve are joined by a bodice seam.

Use the bodice-back sloper with the shoulder dart. Hopefully, the dart can be incorporated in the style line.

1. Place the bodice-front and bodice-back slopers so the shoulders touch at the neckline and are ½ inch apart at the armhole. Fold back the sleeve cap and place the sleeve so that the ends of the cap extend an equal distance below the front and back armscyes on the side seams. Trace the slopers in this position (Fig. 297a).

2. Draw the style line for the dolman sleeve in a sweeping curve across the shoulders from the bodice-front side seam to the bodice-back side seam. Move the back-shoulder dart to the style line so that one dart leg becomes part of the line. (The style line, like all style lines, can be any shape you would like it to be.) Draw matching underarm curves from side seams to sleeves (Fig. 297a).

3. Cut the dolman sleeve away from the bodice at the style line. Cut out the bodice front and bodice back (Fig. 297b).

4. Correct the line of the remaining dart leg so it becomes continuous with the style line of the back bodice. Use the bodice dart control as gathers or unstitched control. An unfitted look is associated with this style. A stitched dart would greatly detract from the interest of the dolman-sleeve style line (Fig. 297b).

5. Divide the style line of the sleeve into quarters. Divide the underarm curve in half. Draw slash lines connecting the front and back quarter marks at the style line with the center point of each underarm curve (Fig. 297c).

6. Slash and spread about 1½ to 2 inches. This lengthens the underarm seam and provides more grace to the sleeve as well as more ease of movement (Fig. 297d). Trace the sleeve (Fig. 297e).

7. Complete the pattern.

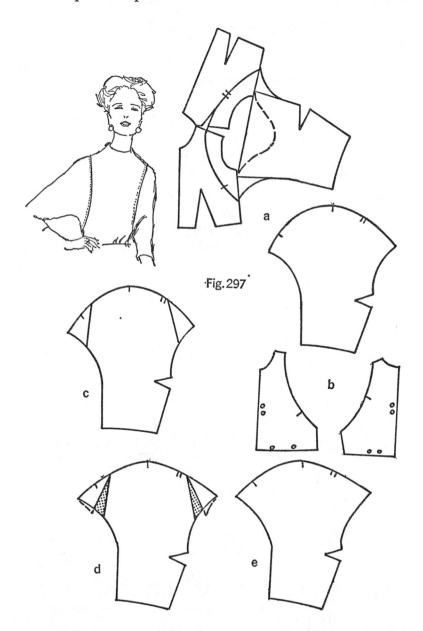

·Fig. 297

THE STRAP-SHOULDER (Sometimes called a saddle sleeve.)

Use the shirt-sleeve sloper for this sleeve. Normal cap ease is un-necessary (indeed it would be inaccurate) for this construction. Shift the back-shoulder dart to the back neckline out of the way of the strap.

1. Trace the appropriate bodice-front, bodice-back, and sleeve slopers.

2. Draw the style line of the strap, as you would a yoke, across the shoulder of front- and back-bodice slopers. The total width of the strap should not be more than 3 inches. If it is wider, it will not fit the cap of the sleeve very well. Notch the strap front and back. Notch the shoulder seam (Fig. 298a).

3. Cut the yokes away from the bodice (Fig. 298b).

4. On the sleeve sloper, draw a lengthwise guideline passing through the shoulder notch and extending the length of the strap above the sleeve cap (Fig. 298c).

5. Place the front and back yokes so the shoulder seams meet on the extended line and the armhole ends touch the sleeve cap (Fig. 298c). Fasten in this position. As you can see, the combined yokes form the strap, which is attached to the sleeve cap.

6. Trace the pattern (Fig. 298d) and complete it.

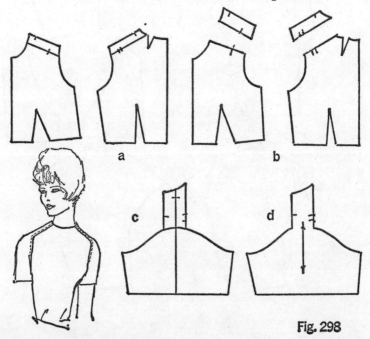

a   b

c   d

Fig. 298

THE RAGLAN SLEEVE

The raglan sleeve is constructed on the same general principle as the strap sleeve. Such differences as there are in the development of the patterns stem from the fact that a larger section of the front and back bodices are cut away on the diagonal to form the yokes. This is the characteristic shape of the raglan sleeve.

There are two types of raglan sleeves. Type A is made by the same method as the strap sleeve. Type B is made with a shoulder dart.

The pattern for the bodice is the same for both types. Use the shirt-sleeve slopers.

Part I—Bodice Pattern for Both Types of Sleeves

1. Trace the bodice-front and bodice-back slopers. Draw a diagonal style line—either straight or curved—from neck to armscye (Fig. 299a). Notch the style line and the shoulder line.

2. Cut the bodice yokes away from the rest of the bodice on the style lines (Fig. 299b).

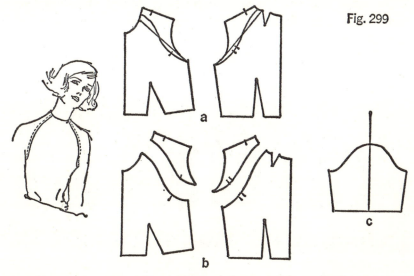

Fig. 299

3. Trace the sleeve sloper. Draw a lengthwise guideline passing through the shoulder notch and extending the length of the shoulder (Fig. 299c).

Part II—Type A Raglan Sleeve

1. Place the front and back yokes together so that shoulder seams meet. Fasten with Scotch tape (Fig. 300a). This forms the strap.

2. Because of the length and depth of its curves, the strap cannot accurately fit the cap of the sleeve. Since no adjustment is possible on the strap, an adjustment must be made on the sleeve cap. Draw curved slash lines on the sleeve cap from the shoulder point to the underarm tips (Fig. 300a). (The cap now looks like a handle-bar mustache.)

3. Place the sleeve strap on the sleeve cap so the shoulder line of the strap becomes an extension of the vertical sleeve line. The strap overlaps the cap about ½ inch at the shoulder (Fig. 300a).

4. Slash and spread the cap sections to meet the strap until the sleeve cap touches the armhole ends of the shoulder strap (Fig. 300b).

5. Connect the raised ends of the cap with the sleeve hemline. Correct the strap style line with a curved line to the underarm seam (Fig. 300b).

6. Trace the new sleeve pattern (Fig. 300c) and complete it. Note that the diagonal line of the raglan sleeve will have to be eased into the bodice.

Fig. 300

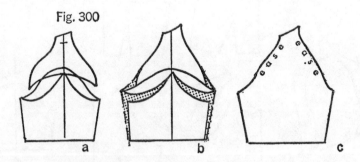

a   b   c

Part II—Type B Raglan Sleeve

1. Place the front and back yokes on the corresponding curves of the sleeve cap. A dart will form at the shoulder (Fig. 301a).

2. Draw several slash lines from the armhole edge of the shoulder yokes to the front and back style lines (Fig. 301a).

3. Slash and spread, slightly raising and extending the underarm ends of the sleeve cap (Fig. 301b).

4. Connect the extended yoke tips with the sleeve hemline. Correct the yoke style lines with smooth curves (Fig. 301b).

5. Trace the pattern (Fig. 301c) and complete it.

The raglan sleeve may be cut and used in one piece as shown in Figs. 300c and 301c. These can become two-piece raglan sleeves by slashing the Fig. 300c pattern from neckline to hemline (Fig. 301d) and the Fig. 301c pattern from the dart point to the hemline (Fig. 301e).

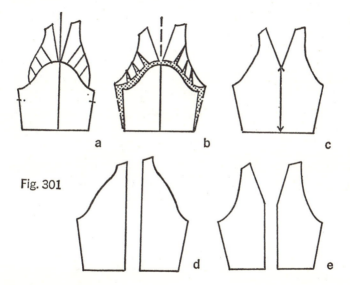

a   b   c

Fig. 301

d   e

Dart Control Variations

A dart is a dart is a dart. You may use this one (Fig. 301c) in any way a dart can be used. Here are a few suggestions.
Shift the dart control and use it for fullness.

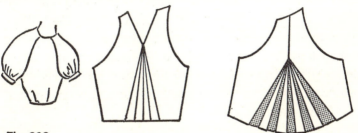

Fig. 302

Use the dart control in a seam.

Fig. 303

Convert the dart control into multiple darts.

Fig. 304

You see the same principles work in the same way wherever the same conditions prevail.

Raglan Round-up

There are just as many possibilities for designing with a raglan sleeve as with a set-in sleeve or no sleeve at all. Consider these: an unusual raglan style line (Fig. 305a), continuing into a standing neckline (Fig. 305b), below a dropped neckline (Fig. 305c), below a yoke or band (Fig. 305d), with circular fullness added for a bell-shaped raglan (Fig. 305e), or balanced fullness added for a puffed raglan (Fig. 305f). The list could go on and on for the fit and comfort of the raglan sleeve make it a great favorite in any of its design variations.

Fig. 305

MORE OF SLEEVE AND YOKE IN ONE PIECE

The strap-shoulder and raglan sleeves are examples of designs where sleeve and yoke are used as one piece. It is a frequent theme in design.

1. Trace the necessary slopers. Draw the yoke style line on bodice front and bodice back. Draw a lengthwise slash line on the sleeve, dividing it into front and back (Fig. 306a).

2. Cut out the patterns. Cut the yokes away from the rest of the bodice. Cut the sleeve apart on the dividing line.

3. Place the front yoke and front sleeve so they touch at the point of the yoke and are slightly spread at the shoulder. This positions the sleeve at a more comfortable angle for the arm (Fig. 306b). Do the same with the back yoke and sleeve, making sure that the angle of the back sleeve matches the angle of the front sleeve (Fig. 306b).

4. Trace the yoke-sleeve patterns, connecting them at the shoulder with a smooth, continuous, curved line. Trace the bodices (Fig. 306c).

5. Complete the pattern.

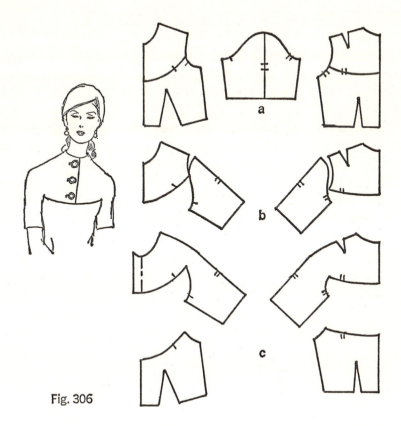

a

b

c

Fig. 306

SLEEVE IN ONE WITH A YOKE PANEL

Many current designs are based on this theme.

1. Trace the hip-length front and back slopers. Trace the short-sleeve sloper.

2. Draw the style line for the control seam and the yoke on the front sloper. Draw the style line for the control seam on the back sloper. Draw a line dividing the sleeve sloper into front and back (Fig. 307a).

3. Draw a right angle. Place the front and back slopers against the vertical and horizontal lines of the right angle. Place the sleeve sloper so it overlaps the front and back as illustrated (Fig. 307b). (This is the position for the slopers for Fig. 289.)

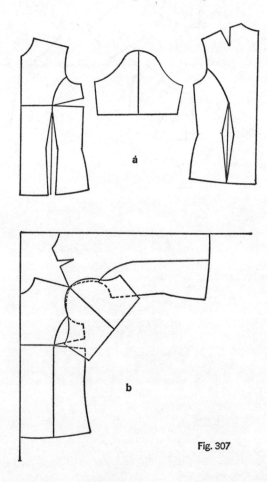

a

b

Fig. 307

4. Trace the front yoke panel and front sleeve all in one. Trace the side front. Trace the center back and back sleeve all in one. Trace the side back (Fig. 307c).

5. Cut out the patterns. Place the side front against the front yoke panel in position to divide the dart control between armscye and waistline. Establish the grain in the side front (Fig. 307d).

6. Cut apart the center-front pattern on the yoke line (Fig. 307d).

7. Trace all pattern sections, correcting the angularity. Complete the pattern.

To complete the pattern illustrated in the sketch, draft the neckline. Shape to suit. Add all necessary symbols and notations.

Fig. 307

THE DROPPED OR EXTENDED SHOULDER ON A YOKE

1. Trace the bodice-front and bodice-back slopers. Trace the sleeve sloper.

2. Draw yoke style lines on the bodice-front and back slopers. Draw a vertical line dividing the sleeve into front and back. Draw a horizontal slash line across the sleeve cap dividing it into upper and lower sections. Shoulder notch to slash line on the cap and shoulder to style line on the armscye are the same length (Fig. 308a).

3. Cut the sleeve apart into upper and lower sections (Fig. 308b).

4. Draw slash lines in each upper cap section (Fig. 308c). Slash to the cap but not through it.

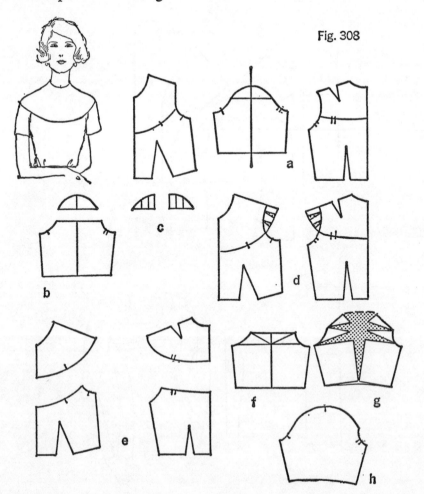

Fig. 308

5. Attach the front slashed cap section to the front armscye. Make the two touch from shoulder to yoke. This will automatically spread the cap to the right amount. Its style line should flow into the style line of the yoke. Fasten in this position (Fig. 308d). Do the same with the back.

6. Cut the yoke and cap away from the rest of the bodice. Trace the dropped-shoulder yoke. Trace the lower bodice (Fig. 308e).

> Actually this much of the pattern makes an interesting design all by itself. However, if this were all you wanted, it could be constructed much more easily by following the directions for the modified cap sleeve (Fig. 295). The style line of the yoke could be a continuation of the style line of the cap.
>
> To complete the pattern for this particular design you will need to adjust the lower sleeve cap to fit the spread of the upper sleeve cap now part of the yoke.

7. Draw a slash line across the sleeve from underarm to underarm. Draw two diagonal slash lines as illustrated (Fig. 308f).

8. Slash and spread until the new cap equals the combined lengths of the front and back yoke-caps (Fig. 308g).

9. Trace the sleeve pattern, correcting the angularity resulting from the spread (Fig. 308h).

10. Complete the pattern.

Wouldn't fullness added to the lower bodice and sleeves of this pattern make a glamorous blouse (Fig. 309)?

Fig. 309

ADD A PART

This business of cutting off a section of a pattern and adding it to another opens up all sorts of interesting possibilities in creating new designs. The following are but a few of the inexhaustible variations but they will serve to illustrate how ingenious one can be in combining parts.

The front shirtwaist yoke becomes an extension of the back.

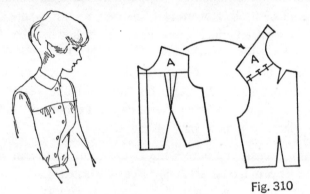

Fig. 310

A back bodice wraps around to the front.

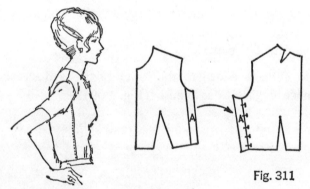

Fig. 311

A front skirt wraps to a back panel.

Fig. 312

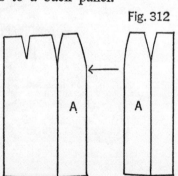

A raglan sleeve can be attached to a front—or back.

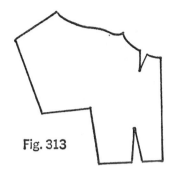

Fig. 313

THE END OF THE BEGINNING

The end of this chapter marks the end of your introduction to pattern making. You've come a long way—all the way from being frightened by a dart to making a complicated pattern. Now you must go on to study, investigate, experiment, perfect.

Even were you never to make a complete pattern of your own, as much learning as you have acquired in the course of this book would still be valuable. Thoughtful performance always deepens your understanding and appreciation of the problems involved in any skill. You understand painting a little better when you have tried to paint; or music a little better when you have tried to play an instrument; or farming a little better when you have struggled with a vegetable patch. Undoubtedly, in the future you will regard all patterns, both your own custom-made ones and the commercial ready-made ones, with a little more appreciation and respect for the time and know-how that go into their creation.

Chapter XI

REMNANTS

Everyone who sews knows all about remnants, those wonderful left-over bits and pieces of material too precious to discard, too small to make a whole big thing of.

Authors have remnants, too—important bits and pieces of information too diverse to lump under one heading, not quite large enough for each to merit a chapter of its own. That's a fair enough description of this last chapter.

SEW IT SEEMS

The grandest plans on paper may be totally unworkable in fabric! Many a dream dress has died a-borning on the drawing board. It is not enough to know the principles of designing and the techniques of pattern making. One must also know whether the design so artfully conceived and the pattern so painstakingly constructed can actually be put together. A knowledge of sewing is invaluable to the pattern maker.

One does not expect the designer or the pattern maker to be a skilled dressmaker or tailor. However, a reasonable background in the techniques by which design ideas are translated into finished garments will vastly improve the designs, the patterns, and the garments.

PATTERNS WITH A PURPOSE

Since all new patterns are variations of a basic pattern, it is a good idea to have a set of staples on hand for instant use. Here are some slopers it would be well to have ready:

Bodice Slopers

with darts shifted to favorite positions
with favorite control seams
with the ease removed for developing décolleté necklines, sleeveless dresses, and evening clothes
with favorite necklines or collars

Sleeve Slopers

with most of the ease removed from the cap
for a sport shirt with its adjusted bodice
for a shirtwaist sleeve
with varying lengths marked off on the long-sleeve sloper
for a two-piece dress sleeve

Skirt Slopers

with multiple darts or favorite control seams
for an A-line or four-gore skirt

Hip-Length Slopers

front and back

Full-Length Slopers

front and back

Slopers that will be used considerably should be on paper tough enough to stand frequent and long-time handling. Use either heavy wrapping paper or Manila tag. Both are easy enough to come by. The wrapping paper has the additional merit of being easy to roll up for storing.

Slopers for Jackets and Coats

In addition to the slopers already mentioned, you would probably enjoy having the slopers below for your tailoring projects. While this book has dealt with dress pattern design, the same pattern-making principles hold for tailoring.

The broken lines in Fig. 314 indicate the original dress sloper. The solid lines show the adjustments which must be made for tailored garments. Fig. 314 shows only the front slopers. Similar adjustments are made on the back hip-length slopers.

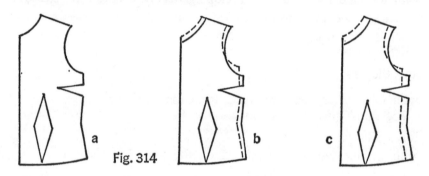

Fig. 314

HOW TO MAKE THE BASIC-FITTING JACKET SLOPER (Fig. 314b)

1. Start with the hip-length sloper (page 118) (Fig. 314a).
2. Drop the neckline ⅛ inch.
3. Add ¼-inch ease to the side seams.
4. Broaden the shoulders ½ inch.
5. Lower the armhole ½ inch.

HOW TO MAKE THE BASIC-FITTING COAT SLOPER (Fig. 314c)

1. Start with the hip-length dress sloper (page 118) (Fig. 314a).
2. Drop the neckline ¼ inch.
3. Add ½ inch to the side seams.

4. Broaden the shoulders ½ inch.

5. Lower the armhole 1 inch.

Note that in both the jacket and coat patterns, the neckline has been lowered, the shoulders widened, the armhole dropped, and width has been added across the chest, across the back, and at the side seams. Corresponding changes must be made in the jacket and coat sleeves. The sleeve cap is flattened and widened to fit the extended shoulder and the deepened armhole. The underarm seam is lengthened to compensate for the flattened cap. The wrist is widened.

SLEEVE SLOPERS FOR JACKETS AND COATS

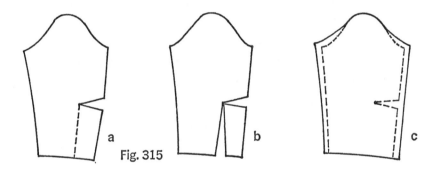

Fig. 315

HOW TO MAKE THE ONE-PIECE JACKET SLEEVE (Fig. 315)

1. Start with the one-piece dress-sleeve sloper (Fig. 315a).

2. Shift some of the elbow dart control to the wrist to widen it as unstitched dart control (Figs. 315a and 315b).

FIG. *315c*

3. Add ¼ inch to the side seams.

4. Raise the underarm curve ½ inch. (Use the same method as for the sport-shirt sleeve.)

5. Redraw the sleeve cap. Compare the length of the cap with the jacket armhole. Allow 1½ to 2 inches ease.

HOW TO MAKE THE ONE-PIECE COAT SLEEVE (Fig. 315)

Steps 1 and 2 are the same as for the jacket.

FIG. *315c*

3. Add ½ inch to the side seams.

4. Raise the underarm curve 1 inch. (Use the same method as for the sport-shirt sleeve.)

5. Redraw the sleeve cap. Compare the length of the new sleeve cap with the coat armhole. Allow 2 to 2½ inches ease.

All of the foregoing slopers—hip-length dress, jacket, and coat—are for fitted garments. More fullness is added in the usual way for semi-fitted or loose garments.

There is no shoulder-pad allowance in any of the above. Should you wish to use shoulder pads, make the same adjustments for a jacket or coat as for a dress. (See page 342.)

Two-piece jacket and coat-sleeve slopers are derived from the one-piece slopers by the method described for the dress sleeve. (See pages 112 and 338.)

TAILORED COLLARS

There are two collars traditionally associated with tailoring. In one (the shawl collar), the entire collar is part of the jacket front. It rolls back to position from the first button (Fig. 316a). In the other (the tailored notched collar), part of the jacket front rolls back to form lapels. A separate collar is set on the neckline and lapels (Fig. 316b).

Fig. 316

a

b

HOW TO DRAFT THE SHAWL COLLAR FOR A TAILORED GARMENT

FIG. *317a*

1. Trace the appropriate front sloper. Lower the neckline for style. Shift some of the front-waistline dart control to the center front. This lengthens the roll line from the break of the collar to the center back. It makes the collar fit with a little more ease. The amount of control that is shifted varies from about ¼ inch if the break is above the bustline, to ¾ inch at the bustline, to 1 inch or more if the break is at or close to the waistline.

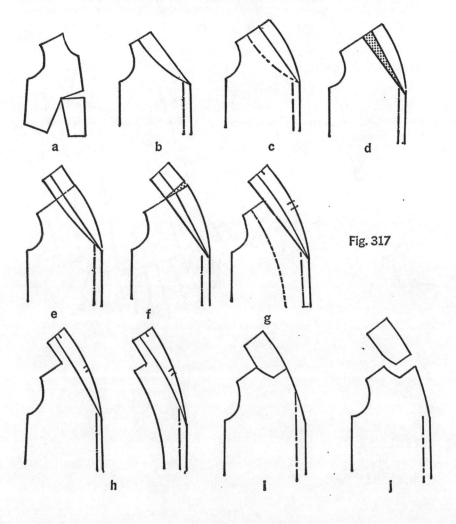

Fig. 317

FIG. *317b*

2. Draw the opening extension, the V-neckline to the break, and the collar style line just as you wish them to appear in the finished garment.

3. Cut out the pattern. Discard what's not needed.

4. Trace the pattern.

FIG. *317c*

5. Fold on the neckline and trace the collar. Unfold and draw the collar. (It will look as if the collar were flipped up on a cold day.)

FIG. *317d*

6. Slash the neckline from shoulder to break. Spread to the amount you plan for the stand of the collar. Trace the pattern. The upper line of the stand becomes the roll line.

FIG. *317e*

7. Extend the neckline and the roll line to half the back neck measurement less ¼ inch. (In the sewing, the collar is stretched to fit the neckline for a better roll.)

8. Connect the neckline and the roll line with a straight line; extend it to the amount of the fall of the collar plus at least ½-inch allowance for the turnover.

9. Draw the back style line to meet the front style line. Blend the lines.

FIG. *317f*

10. Extend the shoulder line through the collar. Slash and spread ½ inch so the angle formed by the collar and shoulders is less than a right angle.

FIG. *317g*

11. Locate the facing and trace it. Since it is the facing that will become the upper collar, add at least ¼ inch to the style line as an allowance for rolling the seam to the underside.

Fig. *317h*

12. Trace the jacket (or coat) pattern.

13. Complete the patterns.

Fig. *317i*

In many of the newer shawl collar designs, the under collar is applied as a separate collar in the same way in which the set-on notched collar is. It gives the tailor a little more control in fitting than the all-in-one shawl collar.

On Fig. 317i, draw a curved line from the shoulder to the roll line following the curve of the original neckline, then a straight line from the roll line to the style line.

The finished pattern will show the jacket (or coat pattern) with the undercollar cut away (Fig. 317j), the separate undercollar to be cut on the bias, and the facing cut all in one with the collar.

THE NOTCHED COLLAR

Steps 1 to 10 are exactly the same as for the shawl collar (Figs. 318a to f).

11. Connect the neckline of the back collar and the gorge (neck) line of the front collar with a curved line (Fig. 318g).

12. Cut the collar away from the rest of the pattern (Fig. 318h).

13. Correct the angularity of any lines.

14. Draw the facing (Fig. 318h) and trace it (Fig. 318i). Add ¼ inch on the outside edges of the facing lapel as an allowance for rolling the seam to the underside. Trace the jacket (or coat) pattern (Fig. 318i). Trace the collar and add ¼-inch allowance on all outside edges for rolling the seam to the underside. Trace the undercollar to be cut on the bias.

15. Complete the pattern.

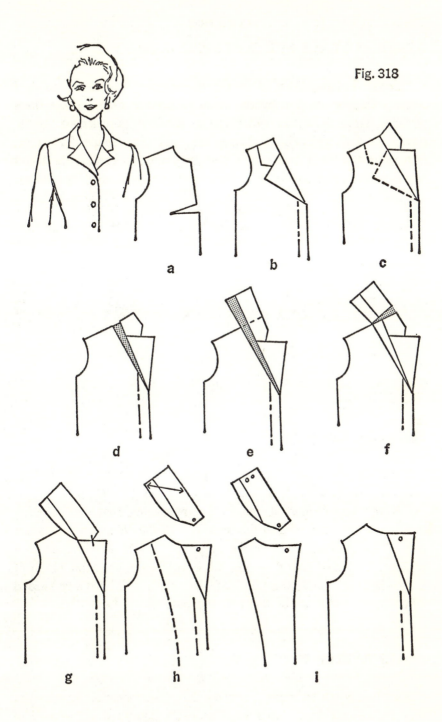

Fig. 318

a   b   c

d   e   f

g   h   i

OTHER COLLARS FOR TAILORED GARMENTS

Tailored collars, other than the shawl and the classic notched collars, may be drafted by the same procedure used for the dress patterns. Since the fabric will be heavier, allow more length for the turnovers and rollbacks. Because the bulk may make for excess fullness at the inner neckline, it may be necessary to dart the stand of the collar (Fig. 319a) or to make a separate stand (Fig. 319b).

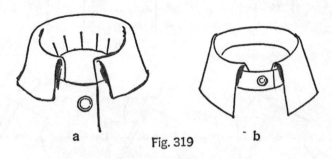

a   Fig. 319   b

TEST ALL COLLARS IN FABRIC

Even the finest paper can't tell you how a collar will fit. One needs the drapability of fabric to test the design.

Cut the undercollar of muslin or interfacing material. Overlap the center-back seams. *Lap* the seam line of the collar over the seam line of the neckline. This is the only way in which one can get a reasonable idea of how the collar fits and looks. Check the length of the collar, the stand, the fall, and the roll line. Make any needed adjustments and transfer them to the pattern.

PANTS PATTERN

Since pants are so much a part of the present fashion picture you may be tempted to try your hand at pants pattern design, too. Use all of the principles you learned for dress patterns. The problem with pants is in the fitting rather than in the designing.

To make a pants sloper follow the same procedure as for making a dress sloper. Buy a pattern for a very simple pair of pants. Adjust it to your measurements. Test it in muslin or cotton fabric. Transfer the adjusted muslin to wrapping paper or Manila tag for use as a sloper. (Complete directions for making and fitting the pants basic pattern will be found in *How to Make Clothes that Fit and Flatter* by this author, Doubleday & Company, Inc. or Mills & Boon Ltd., London.)

MAKING PATTERNS FOR CHILDREN'S CLOTHES

The techniques of pattern making are the same for children's clothes as for adults. The chief differences between the two are largely of styling and fitting. All you need is a sloper from which to derive your designs. Here again, the easiest way to get a sloper for a child's garments is to buy a very simple pattern and adjust it for fit. Vary the design according to all the pattern principles you have learned.

CHILDREN'S SLOPERS

A child's back is fairly straight with slight bulges. The back sloper resembles an adult's except that the darts are smaller (Fig. 320a).

Whereas the greatest bulge in misses' and women's clothing is at the bust, in a child's it is at the waistline. (Recall that adorable profile?) Therefore, the front control dart slides down to the waistline and flops over to the side seam (Fig. 320b).

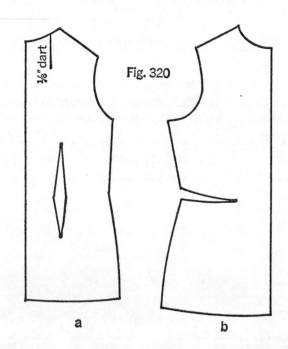

Fig. 320

As far as pattern making is concerned, the position of the control dart makes very little difference since it can be and is shifted to other positions for design purposes.

For instance: it is just as easy to move the control from the waistline to a yoke (Fig. 321a) or to shift it to a seam (Fig. 321b) as it is to move or shift the control from the bust.

.a

Fig. 321

b

All of the same rules apply for the shifting and division of dart control, adding fullness, styling necklines, collars, sleeves, etc.

While the measurements will be smaller, the proportionate amount of ease should be greater. For comfort, children's clothes must be roomy, particularly at the armscyes and the crotch. All-in-one garments such as snowsuits, creepers, or pajamas need a low crotch to provide ample room for sitting (particularly if there are diapers beneath). Necklines should have plenty of ease. Hems should be generous.

Even clothes for little children are designed à la mode. In addition to the aesthetics, however, there must be a degree of practicality. Keep in mind ease of laundering and dressing. (This advice is for others than mothers of little children, who hardly need to be told this.)

DRAPING

Draping is the oldest and longest continuous means of designing clothing. Understandably so. One can see the garment literally take shape in the hands.

Any art is limited by the character of its medium. There are things you can do with clay that you cannot do with wood, with water color that you cannot do with oil paints, with fabric that you cannot do with paper, even with one fabric that you cannot do with another. In draping one works directly with a fabric. This is an enormous advantage. It is so often difficult to visualize in a flat pattern the flow of a line in the cloth or to tell from a diagram whether the fit will be all one desires.

Inevitably all sewers as well as designers resort to some form of draping. If the design doesn't work out as you conceived of it, somehow, it seems very natural to take it in hand and make it do what you want it to do.

There are some great designers who develop their designs by draping directly in the fabric they plan to use for the garment. For them the color and texture of the fabric are the source of inspiration. Others work from sketches handed over to pattern makers and drapers for interpretation. Still others work out their own patterns.

There is no doubt that an understanding of pattern making is a great boon even to a draper. For the home sewer, often a combination of the two methods—drafting and draping—is an excellent way to work out a design. Every sewer who has done any fitting (and who has not?) has done some draping whether she was aware of it or not.

HERE'S WHAT YOU'LL NEED FOR DRAPING A NEW DESIGN

An eye for line, proportion, balance, detail.
Hands free to coax or caress the cloth into shape.
The courage to cut into cloth.
Fabric to inspire you.

A patient model or a dress form on which to do the draping.*

You'll also need: sharp scissors, lots of pins, some ½-inch cotton or twill tape, tailor's chalk, a yardstick or tape measure, a full-length mirror. (Somehow one can get a better perspective on the design in a mirror.)

LET THE FABRIC TELL YOU WHAT IT WANTS TO DO

A dress is only as exciting as the fabric that makes it. There is certainly no dearth of beautiful fabric, today. The only real problem in selection is what of the vast and gorgeous array to choose.

Once having chosen your fabric pay some attention to it. It has a mind and character of its own. It practically tells you what it wants to do. Don't fight it.

Fabric falls with the grain. No matter how you cut it or force it into other positions, in the end, it will fall with the grain. If you misuse the grain, you may end up with unexpected and perhaps unpleasant results.

Most fabrics hang best with the vertical grain. Pleats and soft folds should be on vertical grain. Horizontal grain can be used for trimming, for contrast, for areas that do not need to be closely fitted to the figure.

Bias grain has great elasticity. It can be molded to the body. Use it wherever roundness or curviness is sought without darts to do the shaping: collars, sleeves, belts, bodices with little shaping, skirts when easy movement is desired. Use it for decorative effect in drapery and soft folds.

The texture of a fabric may dictate the design. Obviously stiff fabrics cannot do what soft fabrics can and vice versa.

HAVE THE COURAGE TO CUT

To do any draping you must have the courage to cut. If you're apprehensive about cutting, then draping is not for you. Better

---

* For directions on making a dress form see Chapter VI—Fitting Aids, *How to Make Clothes that Fit and Flatter* by this author, Doubleday & Company, Inc.

stick to the pattern making. Of course, you're fearful you'll make a mistake. Cutting is so final! Just remember it's only fabric. If you ruin it, there are miles and miles more of the stuff. It's the release from fear of making a mistake you need most of all.

If your fear is based on the expense or the uniqueness of a particular fabric that cannot be replaced, then use an inexpensive fabric of a similar degree of drapability, unbleached muslin in a suitable weight, cotton, or voile.

LEARN TO USE YOUR HANDS

The eye dictates the line. The fabric tells you where it wants to go. The hand must follow these orders.

Learn to use your hands to smooth the material over the body (or form) until the fabric eases into position. Feel the design in your finger tips. Manipulate the fabric until the effect is what you want.

HALF A DESIGN IS OFTEN BETTER THAN THE WHOLE DESIGN

It is practically impossible to drape two sides identically. It is only a rare individual who has so sure an eye or so steady a hand. Only machines duplicate exactly. In handwork, there is always the element of human error.

Work out the design on one side of the figure. (An asymmetric design would be the exception to this rule. Even in such designs there are details that must be balanced on both sides.) Refine the design, perfect the fit, true up the pattern, and duplicate the second side.

SUGGESTED PROCEDURE FOR DRAPING

1. Experiment with the placement of any plaids, stripes, checks, design motifs. Decide how you wish to use the grain of the fabric.

2. Start with an approximate length and width of fabric for the design you have in mind. Allow sufficient material for any fullness, sleeves in one with the garment, turnback facings, hems, lapels, etc.

3. Anchor the fabric at strategic points: center back, center front, neckline, waistline, hips, or any special place in the design. Pin the fabric to the dress form, the underdress of your model, or to a length of tape placed as a base where needed.

4. Working around the figure, pin the fabric into darts, folds, fullness, or drapery. Cut the cloth into sections at control seams and style lines and pin them together. See that the front style lines flow naturally into the back.

5. Cut away any excess fabric at the neck, shoulders, armholes, side seams. Be sure to leave seam allowances. Clip all curves to the seam line (the line on which the garment will fit when stitched).

6. Check the grain, the shaping, the ease, the silhouette seams.

7. Remedy any wrinkles, bulges, gaping, or strain that need correction. Bulges at dart points mean that the dart is too large. Wrinkles (excess or drooping fabric or folds) may mean that more dart control is needed. "Hiking up" or "poking out" may mean that more dart control is necessary or that more length is needed or both. Don't throw the grain off by too much dart control in any one dart or seam. Keep the grain balanced on both sides of a seam or there will be pulling or puckering when stitched.

8. Mark the center front and center back with rows of pins or with tailor's chalk. In the same way, mark the shape of the neckline, the shoulder seam, the armscye, the side seams.

9. Determine and mark the waistline. Determine the approximate length of the garment, allow for a hem, then cut away the excess fabric.

10. Cut a length of material (on grain) to drape around the neck for a collar. Lap the collar neckline over the neckline of the garment, clipping as necessary to release the curve. Trim away excess material at the neckline. Mark the neckline of both collar and bodice. Check the stand, the roll line, and the fall of the collar. Cut the collar style line.

11. Cut a length of material for a sleeve. Placing the cloth on-grain, drape it around the arm. Pin the underarm seam from the armscye to a little above the elbow. Lap the cap over the armscye. Pin in small tucks or folds to represent the ease in the sleeve cap. Pin the cap into the armhole. Trim away any excess material. Clip as necessary. Check the grain and adjust as needed. Mark the seam line on the sleeve and the garment. On both sleeve and garment, mark the shoulder and front and back notches where arm and body meet. Now, pin in the elbow darts. Pin the rest of the underarm seam.

12. Decide the placement and size of buttons, pockets, and trimmings. Paper cutouts or scraps of cloth pinned to the garment will give some idea of the effect. Perhaps you would prefer to draw these directly on the muslin.

13. Be mindful of the fact that the garment is yet to get interfacing and/or underlining, facing, lining, perhaps an interlining. The lines of the garment will be sustained by all of these but they will make the garment fit a little more snugly when they are applied. Be sure to allow sufficient ease.

14. Experiment, pin, cut. Experiment, pin, cut. Experiment, pin, cut.

15. When the completed, draped garment is removed from the form or figure, mark in any way still necessary, unpin the garment, correct any jumpiness of the pins, true all lines with drafting instruments. Make certain that all corresponding seams match in length; that pairs of dart legs match in length. Do anything that will complete the pattern.

16. Transfer the design of each section to pattern paper. Cloth does not make for a trustworthy pattern. It is too easy to force into a layout without due regard for shape or grain.

Add all the pattern symbols that will make for accurate layout, cutting, and stitching.

GRADING

Grading is the process by which a pattern may be increased or decreased to the next size. The change is *gradual* rather than in one place (Fig. 322), hence the term "grading."

Grading is also *proportionate* rather than uniform. This is because, in growth, the bony structure of the body does not increase in the same amounts as the fleshy parts. Therefore, there is less differential in bony areas than in fleshy areas as patterns are graded from one size to another. Fig. 323 suggests a generally acceptable amount and placement of grades for misses' and women's sizes.

In industry, grading is now generally done by computers.*

For the occasional needs of the home sewer the following methods work well. There are two: one is to split or tuck the pattern to make the necessary changes (Fig. 325); the other is to shift the pattern pieces from one point to another (Fig. 326). Use whichever method seems easier for you.

The grading directions given below are for the five pattern pieces which make up the dress sloper—bodice front and back, skirt front and back, and sleeve. If you grade the sloper before you do your pattern designing, the changes will be easy enough. If you grade the pattern after the designing, it will be a little more complex. Decide how these over-all amounts can be allocated in the number of pieces that make your total pattern. Just remember that all pieces that join must have similar adjustments.

---

* Many manufacturers frown upon this since they insist (and rightly so) that some styling changes must be made when a pattern is increased or decreased in size. For instance, a blouson style size 10 if graded up mechanically to a size 18 would likely look monstrous. A degree of human judgment is still necessary for artistry.

Fig. 322

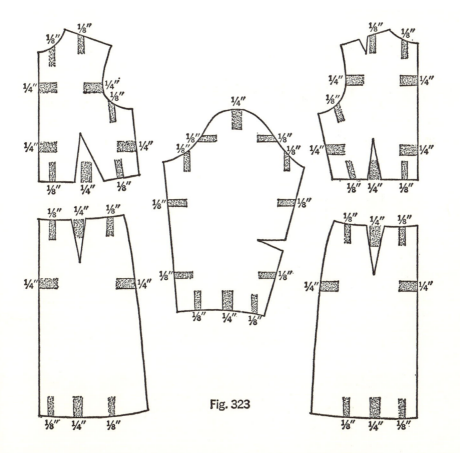

Fig. 323

PATTERN CHANGES ARE MADE IN THESE PLACES

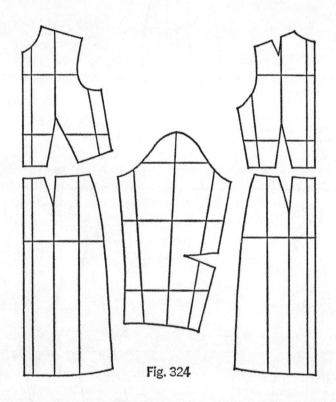

Fig. 324

THE METHOD FOR MAKING PATTERN CHANGES

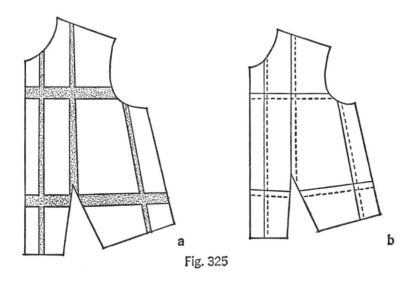

Fig. 325

To Make the Pattern Larger—slash and spread (Fig. 325a)

1. Draw slash lines where indicated in Fig. 324. Slash the pattern along these lines.

2. Spread the pattern to the amounts indicated in Fig. 323.

3. Fill in the open spaces with tissue (Fig. 325a).

To Make the Pattern Smaller—slash and overlap or tuck (Fig. 325b)

1. Draw slash lines where indicated in Fig. 324.

2. Either slash the pattern along these lines and overlap OR fold along the slash lines and tuck the pattern to the amount designated in Fig. 323.

3. Scotch tape to position (Fig. 325b).

THE SHIFTING METHOD

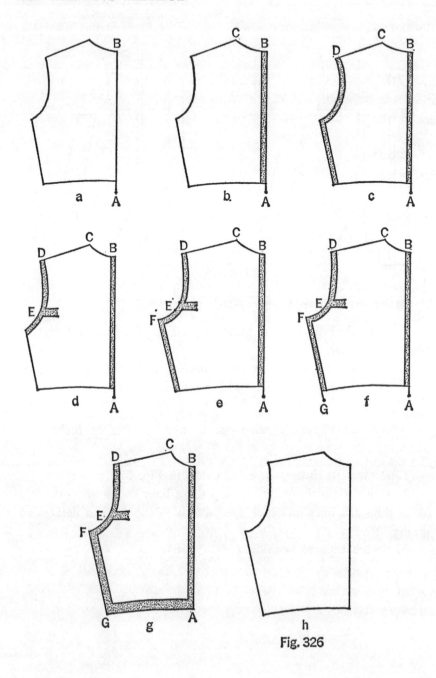

Fig. 326

FIG. *326a*. Draw a new center-back line. Place the center back of the pattern along this line then shift it up ¼ inch from A to B. Trace the B corner.

FIG. *326b*. Always keeping the center back of the pattern parallel to the new center-back line, shift the pattern out ⅛ inch. Trace the neckline to C.

FIG. *326c*. Once more, shift the pattern out ⅛ inch. Trace the shoulder to D.

FIG. *326d*. Shift the pattern down ¼ inch to E (notch). Trace from D to E.

FIG. *326e*. Shift the pattern out ⅛ inch. Trace the armhole from E to F.

FIG. *326f*. Shift the pattern down ¼ inch to G. Trace the corner at G.

FIG. *326g*. Shift the pattern down ½ inch and trace the waistline from G to A.

FIG. *326h*. This completes the grade

To make the pattern smaller by this method shift the pattern back rather than out in the same amount.

GRADE EACH OF THE PATTERN PIECES IN THE SAME WAY to the amounts suggested in Fig. 323. This is a faster method (once you get on to it) than the slash-and-spread or the slash-and-overlap or tuck methods though the latter may be a littler easier and more accurate for inexperienced graders.

LET'S MAKE THE PATTERN!

Comes a time when one is anxious to put together in one great, beautiful dress pattern all the separate learnings and skills acquired during the study of this book. How to go about it?

Here is a suggested procedure.

1. Design the dress.
2. Select the appropriate slopers (see page 417).
3. Collect all the materials you will need to draft the pattern—paper, instruments, sketch, and any pertinent information.
4. Draw the style lines.
5. Decide the shaping. Deal with the dart control accordingly.
6. Add fullness where necessary.
7. Work out each part of the pattern as directed in this book. You may use this book as you would a cookbook. Open to the proper page for the recipe.
8. Cut and fit a trial muslin (see page 422). Make any needed changes. Transfer any changes to the pattern.
9. Line up the pattern and complete it.
10. Work out an economical layout for cutting (see page 424).

Often it is helpful to develop the pattern in a smaller scale until you have solved all the pattern problems. Then tackle the full-scale pattern. It is quite a thrill to see this complete full-scale pattern materialize.

WHERE DO DESIGN IDEAS COME FROM?

Designing a dress, like any other creative activity, deals with the expression of an idea—not just any idea, but *your* idea. That is not to say that if you want to design a pattern for a dress you must invent something absolutely brand new, something never seen before. All of us, even as great designers do, build on what has gone before.

Actually, for the few famed giants of design—those who lead the way—there are countless others who, with less acclaim, make very significant contributions to fashion. And there are literally millions of women who have worthwhile and original ideas.

The same sources of inspiration are there for all. Some are more able by talent, by training, and by the very habit of creating to view, to select, to interpret, to adapt, to organize, to present as much of the past, as much of the present, and as much of themselves as will give their work their own unmistakable imprint.

You've heard it said that there is nothing really new. There are only new ways of looking at old ideas. Creative as Dior was, even his most widely heralded contribution was only a "New Look." It is this "new look" that any of us can take from past styles or existing trends. When filtered through our own individuality, this gives us the right to say, "This is my idea." This is as true of creating a design for a dress as of creating a poem or a song or a picture.

Well then, where do the design ideas come from? Anywhere, everywhere. A picture in a magazine and a painting in a museum. A glimpse in a window and a glance at a book. A candid camera shot of a celebrity or an unknown girl hurriedly crossing the street. Some yardage of irresistible fabric and a piece of jewelry that needs a proper setting. A fashion report in the newspaper and an overheard description on the bus. A memory out of the past of a dress that made you feel beautiful and a dream of "taking a flyer" at that daring new thing from Paris.

A WORKING SKETCH

Clip pictures of designs that appeal to you for color, line, and detail. Make a sketch of something you've seen that you particularly like. You don't have to be an artist to do this. You need only a kind of pictorial shorthand that shows style line, proportion, seams, darts, and decorative details. For you, a work of art is not important; a working sketch is. Note the silhouette, the proportion and relationship of its various parts, the important style lines, or any special features that attract you to the design.

INFORMATION, PLEASE

Now go back and analyze the design for details. In drafting a pattern a general observation is not enough. Every aspect must be specifically and carefully considered.

1. Where is the shaping? How is the dart control used? Is there one dart or several darts? Are the darts straight or curved? What direction do they follow? Do any of the style lines conceal the dart control? Which are the decorative seams and which the control seams? Do any of the darts enter a control seam? Do any of the darts enter other darts? How much dart control for a "relaxed look"? What is the best place for additional dart control for a very fitted garment? Does the dart control appear as a dart, a tuck, a dart tuck, a pleat, gathers, shirring, smocking?

2. Is there fullness in addition to the dart control? Where is the fullness? How much fullness is there? In what form does the fullness appear? Where should the pattern be slashed? How much shall the slashes be spread?

3. Which are the important style lines? Where do they start and where do they end? How much above the waistline? How far from the center line? How much in from the side seam? How much below the neckline? How far above the knee, below the knee? Where in relation to the hip? Where in relation to the armscye? Where on the shoulder seam? Does the style line of the bodice continue into the skirt? Does it include any part of the sleeve? Are the style lines curved or straight? Are they simple lines or complex lines? What direction to the line? Is it repeated in any way?

4. Where is the straight grain? (If you are copying a picture or dress, the grain line is an important clue to its construction, especially if there are several sections to the pattern.) Where is the straight grain on each piece? Where is the straight grain on the sleeve? Is the sleeve on the bias? Where is the straight grain on the collar and cuffs, the pockets, the peplum, the panel, the decorative band?

5. Are there any decorative features of special interest? Are there buttons or bows? Where are they placed? How large are they? Is there any trimming? How much trimming? What kind of trimming? How is it applied?

6. What kind of neckline does the garment have? Is it raised or lowered? Is it asymmetric or formally balanced? What neckline for front, what for back? Is there a collar? What type of collar? How large is the collar? How much stand? What is the style line of the collar? Is it made of contrasting material or self-fabric?

7. What kind of sleeves, if any? Are they short, long, or in between? Are they set-in, kimono, raglan, dolman? Are they fitted, puffed, bell, full, rippled, cape?

These features are by no means all that could be noted, but they will serve to give you some idea of the kind of detailed observation that is required to determine the type of construction for each part of your pattern. As you train yourself to see these many necessary things, you will have the happy experience of discovering just how much there is to see when you look at a design.

You will find that by the time you have completed gathering the information you need for your pattern (as nearly in your judgment as you can at this stage; more questions will pop up as you work along), you will have a pretty good idea of how to proceed.

SELECT THE APPROPRIATE SLOPERS

By now, you undoubtedly have a set of suitable slopers. The selection of the right one for the design requires a little consideration. For instance:

There is *the one-piece dress that really isn't one piece* at all (Fig. 327a). It may have many pieces joined by seaming. However, since it is slipped over the head or stepped into in one motion, that seems to qualify it as one piece.

Such a dress can be fitted, semi-fitted, or unfitted. Its fullness may be "cinched" in by a belt or sash.

Use the hip-length slopers to develop the design, then extend them to full length. If there is design detail below the hips, use the full-length slopers.

Then there is *the one-piece dress with a waistline seam* (Fig. 327b). Easy enough. We've been doing exercises like this throughout the book.

Fig. 327

Use the bodice and skirt slopers for developing the pattern.

What of the one-piece dress with a "waistline" where you would not expect to find it: *below the normal waistline* for a long torso design (Fig. 327c), *above the normal waistline* for the Empire design (Fig. 327d)?

Use the hip-length slopers and extend them or use the full-length slopers.

d

e

Fig. 327

Dressing in parts is the secret of many a successful wardrobe. The parts may be "separates"—that is, unrelated, designed and made separately (Fig. 327e) or two parts of the same design (Fig. 327f).

Use the skirt and hip-length slopers for these designs.

Dresses with control seams (Fig. 327g) are designed on the hip-length slopers. The princess-style dress is an example of such a design.

Fig. 327

f

g

If the *dress is décolleté* (Fig. 327h) use the bodice sloper without ease.

Fig. 327

TRIAL RUN: THE MUSLIN MODEL

In industry every new model gets a trial run. This is essential in order to get all the "bugs" out of the design. You, too, will need to give your pattern a trial run. Your test is a muslin model (or batiste, if your design involves drapery) made from your completed pattern.

The muslin will give you a good idea of how your dress will look when made up. It will reveal whether your pattern produces the effect you have in mind and whether that particular style is flattering for you.

Drape the muslin on your dress form or on yourself. Usually half a muslin garment is sufficient for testing. Sometimes, however, you cannot judge the effect unless you have a complete muslin—a collar, for instance, a double-breasted, or asymmetric garment, fullness for any special effect.

You may be tempted to skip this step, but don't, particularly at the beginning of your pattern-making experience. You may find that you want to make changes in your design as well as in your pattern. Perhaps the pattern is too wide or too skimpy. Maybe the sections don't match. It could be that the darts or seams don't line up. Perhaps the fit would be improved if parts were cut on the bias rather than the straight grain. You may find the proportions are not pleasing. Or that a style line needs shifting. You may sadly discover that while the original was perfectly enchanting the style looks dreadful on you.

Try, Try, Again

Don't be discouraged. Practically no one hits it right the first time. Some correction is almost always necessary. This is the stage in which your pattern is perfected. Pattern companies and manufacturers spend a great deal of time on this muslin sample. If they're lucky, they perfect it after a second or third time. Sometimes it takes even a fourth and fifth try.

All of this entails many consultations among the stylist, the fashion artist, the draper, the pattern maker, and the sample maker. An error could be very costly for these people. It could be for you, too. A test muslin may save you an expensive or favorite length of fabric or many hours of finished sewing on a garment that turns out to be a dud.

It's a Pattern!

Make the corrections on your pattern which the muslin fitting indicates. Make certain that you have a pattern for every part of your design from the tiniest to the largest piece (Fig. 328). Trace the perfected and completed pattern. Add the seam allowance and all the necessary symbols. Make any notations on the pattern that will help in assembling the garment. You may want to jot down some sewing directions for any particularly difficult or tricky part.

Fig. 328

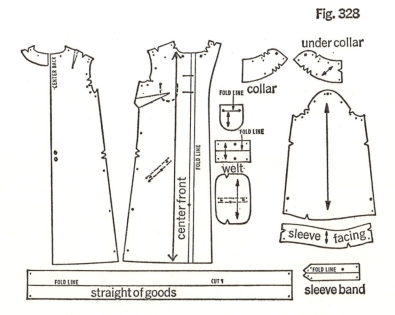

A JIGSAW PUZZLE

Commercial patterns give you a layout chart and the yardage requirements, in addition to the pattern and the sewing directions. When you make your own patterns, you will have to work these out for yourself. A study of commercial patterns can be quite helpful in this matter.

Possible Pattern Layouts

Laying out the pattern pieces is like playing with a big jigsaw puzzle. All of the pattern pieces must be so placed that the various shapes fit (reasonably) against each other, with a proper respect for the grain. All this must be accomplished with the least amount of material, for economy's sake.

On a Fold When Possible

It is always easier if you can cut two of any pattern pieces at the same time. This makes for more accurate cutting and marking. It also saves time. Whenever possible lay out the pattern on a fold (Fig. 329a, b, and c) or a double thickness (Fig. 330).

Folding the Material

A *lengthwise fold* (Fig. 329a) is the one most frequently used.

A *crosswise fold* (Fig. 329b) is for fabrics without nap or directional design and for pattern pieces too wide to fit half the width of the fabric.

A *double fold* (Fig. 329c) is used when several pieces need to be cut on a fold, for instance, both the center front *and* the center back of a skirt. Measure the widest part of the pattern. Mark the required depth in a sufficient number of places to provide a fold line on grain. Fold along the marked line.

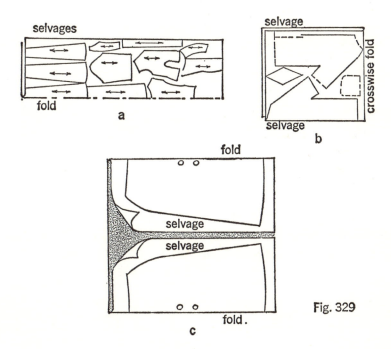

Fig. 329

selvages

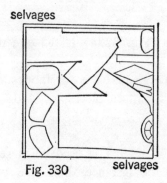

Fig. 330   selvages

Open double layout—(two thicknesses of full-width fabric (Fig. 330)—is for fabric with nap, pile, or directional design and for patterns too wide to fit half the width of the fabric.

selvage

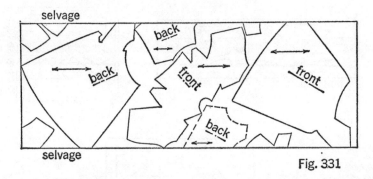

selvage

Fig. 331

The patterns for asymmetric and bias designs are usually complete patterns and must be cut individually. The layout is on a single thickness of fabric opened right side up to *full width*.

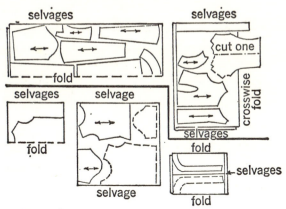

Fig. 332

Combinations (Fig. 332)—there are all sorts of combinations of layouts possible. Part of the garment may be placed on one type of layout, a second on another.

Fig. 333

When the layout chart shows a complete pattern piece, half of which is drawn in a solid line and the other half in a dotted line, it means the pattern is cut on a fold in that space. A complete pattern indicated by dotted lines means it is to be used a second time (Fig. 333).

You can save a lot of confusion in layout if you cut a complete pattern when that is necessary or cut two patterns when they are to be used twice.

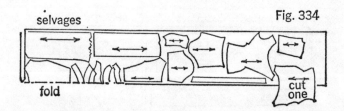

Fig. 334

If a pattern piece is shown extending beyond a folded edge (Fig. 334), it means that this piece must be cut in that space after all the other pieces have been cut and the remainder of the cloth is opened out.

How Much Yardage?

It is a good idea to keep on hand several lengths of wrapping paper cut to the standard widths of fabric—35 inches, 39 inches, 44 inches, 54 inches. Have them long enough to test the yardage necessary for your design. Mark the edge which corresponds to the selvage. Fold the paper in the appropriate manner. Lay out the pattern pieces with the grain parallel to the selvage. First place the largest pieces and/or those that must lie along a fold of fabric. Arrange the smaller pieces around the larger ones in the spaces left.

When the fabric has a nap, pile, or directional weave or print, arrange all the pattern pieces so they go in the same direction —that is, from neck to hem.

They've Got to Fit!

You may have to do a bit of juggling to fit all the pieces in economically, with due regard for the grain, nap, pile, direction of fabric design—all this within the confines of the standard fabric widths. If the pattern doesn't quite fit the fabric width or length, several changes may be made in the pattern.

1. Piece the pattern. Make sure the grain of the "piece" is the same as the grain of the section from which it was cut. Whenever possible try to piece in some place where the joining seam will be inconspicuous or where it will be lost in a fold of the material.

2. Remove some of the fullness until the pattern fits the width of the fabric.

3. Shorten the pattern where and if possible.

4. Eliminate any expendable detail.

5. Change the grain on certain pattern sections. Facings, yokes, pockets, collar, cuffs, sleeves—all are possibilities.

6. Combine the fabric with other fabric for contrast of color or texture. This may be done for facings, insets, yokes, panels, or wherever consistent or effective in your design.

These changes involve a certain amount of restyling. Sometimes interesting ideas emerge because of limitations. Often the result is an improvement over the original. (At least you can try to persuade yourself that this is so.)

When your pattern and layout chart are completed, fold them neatly or roll them up. Store them in any manner convenient for you. It is well to attach a picture or sketch of the design so you will know just what that precious bundle of paper represents when you finally do get around to using it.

"I MADE THE PATTERN FOR THIS MYSELF!"

Now your pattern is really complete. Between you and your astonished public remain only those comparatively slight details involved in assembling your materials (fabric and findings) and assembling your dress (the sewing-fitting-ripping-sewing). Just think how proud you will be when you announce, "I designed and made this myself." And while your friends are clucking admiringly, you can further stagger them with a certain ostentatious modesty when you say quietly, "I made the pattern for this myself, too." You are sure to be the center of attention from that moment on whenever you make an appearance.

Bargain Patterns

The experience of making your own patterns will unquestionably affect your attitude toward commercial patterns. While freeing you from your dependence upon them, your new knowledge also serves to make you more appreciative of what they have to offer.

You get in each pattern envelope a style created by a talented and sometimes big-name designer. It is the fruit of much experimentation, much consultation, much perfecting by a staff of experienced technicians. It includes a listing of all the materials necessary for production, step-by-step directions for sewing, suggestions for suitable fabrics, and even, in some cases, a label to add prestige. You certainly must agree that you are getting a bargain.

FREEDOM OF CHOICE

Will what this book offers you make you abandon the use of commercial patterns? Of course not. Make your own patterns when you wish. Use commercial patterns when the designs appeal to you. You now have the freedom that comes with choice.

Often you can start with a pattern that basically has the features you want. That can be a timesaver. Then change any features which will bring the design closer to your own ideas or which will make the design more becoming to you. The knowledge of pattern construction will provide you with new confidence in handling commercial patterns. You will find that you are no longer fearful of changing the position of a dart or the line of a seam or of eliminating a detail or adding or removing some fullness. Your knowledge of patterns will even help in the actual sewing. You will understand why and how pattern pieces are joined in a particular way. You will be emancipated from that little sheet of printed instructions.

There is a great deal you can learn from a commercial pattern. Study the shapes of the pattern pieces and try to analyze how they were arrived at. Note any particularly ingenious use of pattern principles. Examine the layout charts carefully for hints on the best use of space. Build up a library of commercial patterns that have interesting design details you may want to incorporate with your own ideas. Handle the commercial pattern as you would any other piece of research material. It has important information that you can use creatively.

YOU'LL NEVER BE THE SAME!

The experience of making your own patterns will inevitably result in your seeing fashion with a new eye. It will be difficult for you to be merely a passive observer. No longer will you just sit quietly daydreaming on bus or subway. You will be trying to figure out how to make the pattern for dress after dress that you see and admire on others. A new fashion book will send you flying to your paper, pencil, and scale models. Watching a movie or a television show will become a mental exercise as you trace the lines and solve the problems of pattern construction of the heroine's dress long before she solves her own problems. You will enjoy a wonderful new sense of power that comes with discovering that you can produce just what you want in clothes!

Pattern making, fascinating as it is in itself, is merely a means to an end. The larger end is the creation of works of beauty. In this instance, happily, that beauty may adorn you.

Measurement Charts

Approved by the Measurement Standard Committee of the Pattern Fashion Industry—Butterick, McCall's, Simplicity, Vogue

MISSES'

Misses' patterns are designed for a well-proportioned and developed figure; about 5'5" to 5'6" without shoes.

Size	6	8	10	12	14	16	18
Bust	30½	31½	32½	34	36	38	40
Waist	22	23	24	25½	27	29	31
Hip	32½	33½	34½	36	38	40	42
Back Waist Length	15½	15¾	16	16¼	16½	16¾	17

MISS PETITE

This new size range is designed for the shorter Miss figure; about 5'2" to 5'3" without shoes.   (NEW SIZE Range)

Size	6mp	8mp	10mp	12mp	14mp	16mp
Bust	30½	31½	32½	34	36	38
Waist	22½	23½	24½	26	27½	29½
Hip	32½	33½	34½	36	38	40
Back Waist Length	14½	14¾	15	15¼	15½	15¾

JUNIOR

Junior patterns are designed for a well-proportioned, shorter-waisted figure; about 5'4" to 5'5" without shoes.

Size	5	7	9	11	13	15
Bust	30	31	32	33½	35	37
Waist	21½	22½	23½	24½	26	28
Hip	32	33	34	35½	37	39
Back Waist Length	15	15¼	15½	15¾	16	16¼

JUNIOR PETITE

Junior Petite patterns are designed for a well-proportioned, petite figure; about 5' to 5'1" without shoes.

Size	3jp	5jp	7jp	9jp	11jp	13jp
Bust	30½	31	32	33	34	35
Waist	22	22½	23½	24½	25½	26½
Hip	31½	32	33	34	35	36
Back Waist Length	14	14¼	14½	14¾	15	15¼

WOMEN'S

Women's patterns are designed for the larger, more fully mature figure; about 5'5" to 5'6" without shoes.

Size	38	40	42	44	46	48	50
Bust	42	44	46	48	50	52	54
Waist	34	36	38	40½	43	45½	48
Hip	44	46	48	50	52	54	56
Back Waist Length	17¼	17⅜	17½	17⅝	17¾	17⅞	18

HALF-SIZE

Half-size patterns are for a fully developed figure with a short back-waist length. Waist and hip are larger in proportion to bust than other figure types; about 5'2" to 5'3" without shoes.

Size	10½	12½	14½	16½	18½	20½	22½	24½
Bust	33	35	37	39	41	43	45	47
Waist	26	28	30	32	34	36½	39	41½
Hip	35	37	39	41	43	45½	48	50½
Back Waist Length	15	15¼	15½	15¾	15⅞	16	16⅛	16¼

YOUNG JUNIOR/TEEN

This new size range is designed for the developing pre-teen and teen figures; about 5'1" to 5'3" without shoes.

Size	5/6	7/8	9/10	11/12	13/14	15/16
Bust	28	29	30½	32	33½	35
Waist	22	23	24	25	26	27
Hip	31	32	33½	35	36½	38
Back Waist Length	13½	14	14½	15	15⅜	15¾

SKIRTS, SLACKS & SHORTS:

Select by waist measurement or if hips are much larger in proportion to waist, select size by hip measurement.

MISSES'

Waist	22	23	24	25½	27	29	31
Hip	32½	33½	34½	36	38	40	42

MISS PETITE

Waist	22½	23½	24½	26	27½	29½
Hip	32½	33½	34½	36	38	40

JUNIOR

Waist	21½	22½	23½	24½	26	28
Hip	32	33	34	35½	37	39

JUNIOR PETITE

Waist	22	22½	23½	24½	25½	26½
Hip	31½	32	33	34	35	36

WOMEN'S

Waist	34	36	38	40½	43	45½	48
Hip	44	46	48	50	52	54	56

YOUNG JUNIOR/TEEN

	22	23	24	25	26	27
	31	32	33½	35	36½	38

GIRLS'

Girls' patterns are designed for the girl who has not yet begun to mature.

Size	7	8	10	12	14
Breast	26	27	28½	30	32
Waist	23	23½	24½	25½	26½
Hip	27	28	30	32	34
Back Waist Length	11½	12	12¾	13½	14¼
Approx. Heights	50″	52″	56″	58½″	61″

CHUBBIE

Chubbie patterns are designed for the growing girl who is over the average weight for her age and height.

Size	8½C	10½C	12½C	14½C
Breast	30	31½	33	34½
Waist	28	29	30	31
Hip	33	34½	36	37½
Back Waist Length	12	12¾	13½	14¼
Approx. Heights	52″	56″	58½″	61″

CHILDREN'S MEASUREMENTS

Measure around the breast, but not too snugly. Toddler patterns are designed for a figure between that of a baby and child.

Dress Lengths from Back Neck Base to Lower Edge

Size	½	1	2	3	4	5	6	6X
Toddler	14″	15″	16″	17″	18″			
Child		18″	19″	20″	21″	23″	25″	26″

TODDLERS'

Size	½	1	2	3	4
Breast	19	20	21	22	23
Waist	19	19½	20	20½	21

CHILDREN'S

Size	1	2	3	4	5	6	6X
Breast	20	21	22	23	24	25	25½
Waist	19½	20	20½	21	21½	22	22½
Hip				24	25	26	26½
Back Waist Length	8¼	8½	9	9½	10	10½	10¾
Approx. Heights	31″	34″	37″	40″	43″	46″	48″

Spadea's Ready-to-wear Size Charts

Regular sizing

Sizes	6	8	10	12	14	16	18	20
Bust	32	33	34	35	36½	38	40	42
Waist	22	23	24	25	26½	28	30	32
Hip (5″ below waistline)	33	34	35	36	37½	39	41	43
Length (nape of neck to waist)	16	16¼	16½	16¾	17	17¼	17½	17¾

For mature figures

Sizes	14	16	18	20	40	42	44
Bust	36½	38	40	42	44	46	48
Waist	27½	29	31	33	35	37	38
Hip (5″ below waistline)	37½	39	41	43	45	47	49
Length (nape of neck to waist)	17	17¼	17½	17¾	18	18¼	18½

For diminutives (short figures, 5'5″ and under)

Sizes	8	10	12	14	16	18	20
Bust	33	34	35	36½	38	40	42
Waist	24	25	26	27½	29	31	33
Hip (5″ below waistline)	34	35	36	37½	39	41	43
Length (nape of neck to waist)	15¾	16	16¼	16½	16¾	17	17¼

For tall girls

Sizes	8	10	12	14	16	18	20
Bust	33	34	35	36½	38	40	42
Waist	23	24	25	26½	28	30	32
Hip (5″ below waistline)	34	35	36	37½	39	41	43
Length (nape of neck to waist)	17	17¼	17½	17¾	18	18¼	18½

For half-sizes

Sizes	12½	14½	16½	18½	20½	22½
Bust	35½	37½	39½	41½	43½	45½
Waist	27½	29½	31½	33½	35½	37½
Hip (5″ below waistline)	35½	37½	39½	41½	43½	45½
Length (nape of neck to waist)	15¾	16	16¼	16½	16¾	17

For junior sizes

Sizes	5	7	9	11	13	15	17
Bust	31½	32½	33½	34½	36	37½	39
Waist	21½	22½	23½	24½	26	27½	29
Hip (5″ below waistline)	32½	33½	34½	35½	37	38½	40
Length (nape of neck to waist)	15½	15¾	16	16¼	16½	16¾	17

Coats (*capes, stoles, aprons*)

Sizes	Small	Medium	Large
Bust	33–34	35–36½	38–40
Waist (used if garment has waistline)	23–24	25–26½	28–30
Hip (5″ below waistline)	34–35	36–37½	39–41

INDEX

A

Abdomen. *See also* Skirts; Waistlines
  and dart control, 3
Accordion pleats, 153, 154
Armhole darts, 16–17
  and division of dart control, 66, 67
Armhole facing, with neck facing, 92
Armscyes, 10. *See also* Sleeves
Asymmetry,
  in closings, 238–42
  in collars, 298–99
  in control seams, 117
  in dart design, 23–25
  and draping, 405
  in necklines, 189–90
  and pattern layout, 426

B

Bands and bandings, 107
  buttoned closings on, 232–33
  collars, 269–72
  on sleeves (*see* Sleeves)
  for zippers, 224, 225
Barrel sleeves, 333
Basic patterns. *See* Slopers
Bateau necklines, 206–7
Batwing sleeves, 358–59
Bell skirts, 128, 129

Bell sleeves, 322–24
Belts, 107
  contour, 105 (*see also* Hip yokes)
Bertha collars, 280
Bias-fold collars, 271–72
Bias grain, 52, 54, 55
  and draping, 404
  and pattern layout, 426
Bishop sleeves, 319
Block patterns. *See* Slopers
Blouses. *See also* Bodices
  pattern markings for hems, 60
Boat necklines, 206–7
Bodices. *See also* Closings; Necklines;
    Sleeves
  dart control for (*see also* Bodices,
    darts)
    division of, 62–72, 74–81, 83–87
    pattern whys, 3, 4, 5–6
    pleats, gathering, smocking for,
      31, 32–34
    refining pattern after changing,
      42ff.
    with seams, 83–97, 100ff.
    yokes for, 91ff.
  darts, 7–8
    asymmetric design of, 23–25
    curved, 22–23